Starting a Business
FRANCE

CADOGANguides

Contents

Introduction 1

01
The Big Picture 3
Why France? 4
How Many People Are Setting Up Businesses in France? 6
Who is Doing What, and Where? 7
Opportunities and Gaps in the Market 7
General Scope for New Businesses 7
Inspiration 8
The Right Experience 9
Eureka! 9

02
Getting to Know France 11
Geography 14
Climate 14
Culture 14
National Culture 15
Business Culture 16
Language and Dialects 18
The Economy 18
Government 23
Political Divisions 23
The Law 24
The Constitution and Code Civil 24
The Legal Profession 24
The Courts 27
Legal Aid 28

03
Business Ideas 29
Experience and Qualifications 30
Research 31
Basic Strategy 31
Common Ideas: Pros and Cons 35
Property 36
Tourism 56
Catering 60
Translating 63
Secretarial Work 64
E-Commerce 64
Art 66
Gardening 66
Farming 66
Medicine 70
Continuing What You Did at Home 74
Other Small Business Ideas 75

04
Setting Up a Business in France 77
First Steps 78
Taking Advice 78
Choosing a Structure 79
Licences and Registration 86
Planning 87
The Business Plan 87
Your 'Life Plan' 95
Working from Home 96
Relating to a 'Parent' Business 96
Setting Up Your Own Business or Buying Into an Existing Business 102
Raising Finance 106
Ways of Delaying Full Financial Commitment 106
Grants and Aid 110
French Banks and Loans 116
Acquiring Business Premises 116
Employing Staff 118
Summary: A Step by Step Guide to Setting Up Your Business 121

05
Red Tape 123
Registering Your Business 124
Social Security 125
Taxes 127
Should You Pay Corporate or Personal Tax? 127
Corporate Taxes 128
Personal Taxes 142
Immigration and Work Permits 153
EU Citizens 153
Non-EU Citizens 154
Citizenship 156
Professional and Other Qualifications 157
Provision of Services 157

Establishment 158
Getting Your Qualifications
   Recognised 159

06

Working in France 161
Business Practices 162
Finding a Job 164
Job-hunting 165
The Curriculum Vitae and
   Covering Letter 169
Interviews 169
Terms and Conditions
   of Employment 170
Employment
   Contracts 170
Terms of Employment 171
Dismissal and
   Redundancy 172
Benefits 172
Pensions and
   Retirement 174

07

Living in France 175
Learning French 176
Finding a Home 178

Buying a Property 179
Renting a Property 209
Home Utilities 210
Mobile Phones 214
The Internet 215
Television and
   Satellite 216
Postal Services 216
Money and Banking 217
Shopping 218
Transport 220
Crime and the Police 226
Taking Your Pet 227
Health and
   Emergencies 228
Social Services and
   Welfare Benefits 230
Retirement, Pensions
   and Death 232
Education 233

08

References 237
France at a Glance 238
Useful Contacts 239
British Consular Services
   in France 242

Maps
France *inside front cover*
Touring maps 259–74

French Telephone
   Codes 243
Regional Climate 243
Départements 244
Largest Cities 245
National and Local
   Holidays 246
Further Reading 247
Dictionary of Useful and
   Technical Terms 249
Internet Vocabulary 258

09

Appendices 275
Sample CV in French
   Format 276
Sample Job Application
   Letter 277
Helpful Words and
   Phrases 278

Index 279

About the author

John Howell established John Howell & Co in Sheffield in 1979 and by 1997 it had become one of the largest and most respected law firms in the north of England, employing over 100 lawyers. On moving to London in 1995, John Howell has gone on to specialise in providing legal advice to clients buying a property in France, Spain, Italy and Portugal and more recently Turkey and Croatia.

Cadogan Guides
2nd Floor
233 High Holborn
London WC1V 7DN
info@cadoganguides.co.uk
www.cadoganguides.com

The Globe Pequot Press
246 Goose Lane, PO Box 480, Guilford,
Connecticut 06437–0480

Copyright © John Howell 2005

Cover photographs: Front: © Foodfolio/Alamy, Images-of-France, Medioimages, Graham Light/Alamy, Images Etc Ltd/Alamy. Back: © Banana Stock/Alamy
Maps © Cadogan Guides, drawn by Maidenhead Cartographic Services Ltd
Cover design: Sarah Rianhard-Gardner
Editor: Rhonda Carrier
Proofreader: Susannah Wight
Indexing: Isobel McLean

Produced by **Navigator Guides**
www.navigatorguides.com

Printed in Finland by WS Bookwell
A catalogue record for this book is available from the British Library
ISBN 10: 1-86011-209-9
ISBN 13: 978-1-86011-209-4

The author and publishers have made every effort to ensure the accuracy of the information in this book at the time of going to press. However, they cannot accept any responsibility for any loss, injury or inconvenience resulting from the use of information contained in this guide.

Please help us to keep this guide up to date. We have done our best to ensure that the information in it is correct at the time of going to press. But places are constantly changing, and rules and regulations fluctuate. We would be delighted to receive any comments concerning existing entries or omissions. Authors of the best letters will receive a copy of the Cadogan Guide of their choice.

All rights reserved. No part of this publication may be reproduced, stored in a retrieval system, or transmitted, in any form or by any means, electronic or mechanical, including photocopying and recording, or by any information storage and retrieval system except as may be expressly permitted by the UK 1988 Copyright Design & Patents Act and the USA 1976 Copyright Act or in writing from the publisher. Requests for permission should be addressed to Cadogan Guides, 2nd Floor, 233 High Holborn, London, WC1V 7DN, in the UK, or The Globe Pequot Press, 246 Goose Lane, PO Box 480, Guilford, Connecticut 06437–0480, in the USA.

Introduction

Many thousands of British, Irish and American people move to France every year, attracted by a gentler pace of life, a more healthy work–life balance, better pay in many spheres, a lower cost of living, cheap property, a good climate, a rich culture, and wonderful food and wine. Add to this the world's best medical system, the superb (if rather old-fashioned) education system, the excellent and inexpensive public transport network, the sense of regional diversity (*le terroir*), the way the diversity of the French rural economy has been protected, and its advanced science and technology industries (and the business opportunities they represent), and it becomes clear why very few come back. Presumably they find that these factors outweigh the negatives (high taxes, a bureaucracy that makes the USSR look like amateurs, a less than squeaky-clean political system) and the xenophobic attitude of some French people.

This book assumes that you want to live wholly or mainly in France and run your own business, though it also contains a section on finding work in France for those with partners who want an independent source of income or those who need an income while that business gets under way. It is written primarily for British and Irish readers, but almost all of what is said will also apply to those from other EU countries. Much will also apply to non-EU residents, though the latter have the additional obstacle of dealing with the French immigration system – at certain points I have made special reference to them.

Many people who set up a business in a foreign country do so not out of a passionate desire to be their own master but as a result of realising that it will be difficult to find a regular job, and that it's a question of self-employment or starvation. This is not the best reason to start a business; if you're going to set one up *faute de mieux*, it's particularly important to take advice and check (and check again) that your plan stands a good job of working. This is especially so if you have no previous experience of running a business.

Don't let my words of caution put you off, however: setting up a business in France is no more difficult than setting up a business in the UK, provided you recognise the problem areas and take steps to deal with them. Most important of all is to take much more professional advice than you might take if starting a business in your own country. This book is intended as a starting point to enable people thinking of setting up a business to understand some of the issues involved and to ask the necessary questions of their professional advisers.

Bonne chance!

The Big Picture

Why France? 4
How Many People Are Setting Up Businesses in France? 6
Who is Doing What, and Where? **7**
Opportunities and Gaps in the Market 7
General Scope for New Businesses 7
Inspiration 8
The Right Experience 9
Eureka! 9

> ### The Linguistic Minefield
>
> Throughout this book, whenever possible (or sensible), I use the English term, often followed by the French equivalent in brackets and italics. At the back is a simple glossary including the English and French terms for various legal and financial terms. However, always bear in mind that there is often no true translation of legal and financial terms because they can relate to institutions, systems or procedures that do not have an equivalent in the other country. Beware, too, that words can mean radically different things in different contexts (think about 'My brother has an interest in a house in France. Mr Smith is interested in buying it from him. He is concerned about future interest rates.') Don't let translations give you a false sense of security.
>
> Note also that I've often drawn comparison with English law as applicable at the time of writing; Scottish law is somewhat different, although where the points also apply to Scottish law I've tried, depending on the context, to refer to either UK or British law.

British people starting a business in France face the same problems as they do in starting a business in the UK, plus a number of other hurdles.

The first is that they seldom speak French as fluently as their own language, especially business or legal French, or government jargon. Secondly, however well they know France, they won't be as familiar with French culture as their own – the practical consequences of this fact will only come to light the more involved they become in French working life. Lastly, they are starting a new life, often without a job, a credit history, savings or the network of contacts they enjoyed at home, where they could ask friends to recommend an accountant or lawyer. All of this makes careful planning and preparation much more important.

This book should not be taken as a substitute for professional advice, because, although we have done our best to cover most topics of interest to those wanting to set up a business in France, we cannot take into account every individual's circumstances. Also, the size of the book means our advice cannot be comprehensive (for example, a detailed description of one small exemption from French company tax, here covered in 50 words, takes 11 pages in the leading practitioners' textbook).

Why France?

Apart from the lifestyle benefits that draw many people to start a new life in France, those planning to set up in business will be encouraged by the fact that the the World Bank's survey *Doing Business: Removing Obstacles to Growth* of September 2004 ranked France first in Europe in terms of the time and cost involved in starting a new business. In August 2003 the French government had adopted a series of measures, the **Loi Dutreil** or *loi pour l'initiative économique* ('law for economic initiative'), intended to ease the process of setting up businesses and creating companies. These supplemented much-needed measures of 1999 and 2000: simplifying the VAT declaration requirements for smaller companies, plus social security declarations and payments; harmonising and unifying social security and tax returns; and reducing taxes imposed by the state on the creation of a business. A new law of July 2005, the **Loi PME**, took this all further by providing grant aid for various purposes, including training, easing restrictions on certain types of investment, and allowing for new forms of working together, such as the contract of collaboration between the liberal professions. The resulting increase in activity is something the French government is keen to maintain.

Unless the business you are thinking of pursuing falls within one of the regulated professions or it is illegal, there are no specific restrictions on any category of business in France, and a citizen of any EU member state is free to move to France and set up such a business on exactly the same terms as a French person. A person from outside the EU member state would have to obtain the necessary immigration paperwork (*see* pp.154–6), but the paperwork needed to establish a business is generally easier to obtain than that required to work in a salaried capacity.

This said, France remains a bastion of bureaucracy, and though the total time it takes to create a company there has been reduced to one day (according to a study by the clerk's office of the Parisian Commercial Court), there is miles of red tape waiting to frustrate the effort of the would-be entrepreneur – a fact

Facts on File

According to a 2002 study by the Centre for Economics and Business Research (CEBR) for MarketPlace at Bradford & Bingley, people in the UK may earn more than people in France but they are missing out in terms of 'quality of life'.

- Cost of living: the cost of living is 13% lower in France than in the UK.
- Disposable income per household: in the UK: £24,407; in France: £22,668.
- Percentage of disposable income put into savings: in the UK: 5%; in France: 15.8%.
- Paying taxes: it takes a UK household from 1 Jan to 15 April to pay their gross income tax bill; in France, households fulfil their tax obligation almost 3 weeks earlier, on 22 March.
- Working hours: the average working day in the UK is 8.7hrs; in France it's an hour less.
- Holidays: in the UK, a worker can expect 28 days off (holidays and bank holidays); in France, workers get 47 days off per year on average.

that partly explains France's very low rate of entrepreneurship. Learning how to deal with that bureaucracy quickly and cost-effectively, learning which bits you must comply with and which bits you can safely ignore, and becoming comfortable with the French system, should be high on the list of anyone wanting to set up a business in France. See **Red Tape**, pp.123–60.

The government's moves to encourage small businesses are vital in a country with such a high rate of unemployment (more than 10% at the time of writing), but the fact that they are still few and far between by British standards means there is quite a lot of scope for those moving to France and wanting to start a business. See 'Opportunities and Gaps in the Market', opposite.

How Many People Are Setting Up Businesses in France?

From an international perspective, very few people run their own business in France; according to the EIM (a government-funded Dutch organisation focusing on small businesses round the world), in 2001 (the last year for which figures are available) the figure was 1,817,000, as opposed to 3,002,000 in the UK. Both countries have roughly 60 million inhabitants. Many commentators claim that the control of the economy by a strong élite group, often referred to as a meritocracy, over the last three decades has inhibited the development of small to medium-sized enterprises (SMEs). At the summit of the European Union in Lisbon in March 2000, France was dubbed Europe's laggard: too stubborn to abandon its old ways, reluctant to pursue market reforms, and too proud to admit to the merits of American liberal economics.

In 2002, the last year for which INSEE, the French National Institute for Statistics, has figures, 178,000 new businesses were set up. These included 152,000 SMEs. The Agence pour la Création d'Entreprises (APCE) states that 199,399 new businesses were set up in 2003, in a 12% increase on 2002; 82% of them were 'one-man bands', and the majority were in trade, business services or construction. According to other sources, the implementation of the 2003 Loi Dutreil (see p.5) increased the number of new businesses to 230,000 per year.

This apparent rise is still way down on the average number of start-ups from 1987 to 1999, which was about 280,000 a year. However, this number practically equalled the average annual number of closures, either voluntary or due to insolvency, in the same period. I will deal this fact at some length in the sections on taxation (see pp.127–50) and social security (see p.125), both major triggers for the closure of new businesses.

Since the 1970s, there has been a large increase in the number of non-French entrepreneurs in the country: in 1982 they accounted for approximately 7% of the total number of business-owners there, whereas now the figure is more like 10%.

Who is Doing What, and Where?

According to the INSEE study of 2002, 26% of businesses created in 2002 were set up by women, 12% were by university graduates, and 35% were by unemployed people/jobseekers. Most new entrepreneurs were in their 30s. The businesses they set up are classified into three categories: artisans, regulated services and unregulated services. Artisans are skilled manual workers or craftspeople, and 70% of those setting up in business do so in a field similar to the one they had while employed. 'Regulated services' refers to the professions (lawyers, doctors, etc.) and to 'intermediate professionals' requiring administrative authorisation, including workers in many trades, in transport, in financial activities, in education, in health and social work, in estate agency, and in many other areas of interest to foreigners thinking of setting up in business. 'Unregulated services' is a category comprising shopkeepers, the hotel industry and any type of activity that does not require either formal professional training or administrative authorisation. These areas of activity diminish each year. People (whether French or foreign) setting up business in this field have little or no previous experience, and the start-up enterprise represents a brand new occupation for them.

The regional breakdown of small businesses by the Agence pour la Création d'Entreprises (APCE) demonstrates the extremely centralised nature of French society and the fact that the vast majority of activity takes place in the Ile de France (centred on Paris) and the Côte d'Azur. The resulting differences in wealth between these areas and less advantaged regions such as Languedoc-Roussillon are worth bearing in mind when thinking about opening a business. It is also worth looking at the figures for previous years. For an annual breakdown, see **www.acpe.com**.

Opportunities and Gaps in the Market

General Scope for New Businesses

Since 1985 people have proven that just about anything is possible if you set your mind to it, creating businesses, among others, in the following sectors: property sales, rental, development or maintenance; retail; restaurants; bakeries; launderettes; bars; nightclubs; hotels; B&Bs; saunas; pool maintenance; package holidays; jet ski hire; ski schools; windsurfing hire or tuition; flying schools; yacht chandleries or brokerages; transport companies; truck or bus driving; car hire or repair; taxis; PR and advertising; law; accountancy; financial advice; IT consultancy; computer training or maintenance; teaching; painting; sculpture; pottery; design consultancy; solar energy supply; bricklaying; shoemaking; dentistry; import–export; warehouses; cleaning; and ice-cream sales.

At present, however, there is growing demand in the areas of culture, sports, education, tourism and the environment, and in services providing better living conditions in general, so these niche activities are well worth considering. Many people are inspired to start up a business, such as a hotel, B&B, restaurant or bar, when they go on holiday to France and perceive a gap in the market. Indeed, one's own experience of a shortfall in local facilities can be very good basis for a new enterprise, but it is vital to do your research to make sure that that what you want to do is viable and legal.

Alternatively, new types of businesses, such as IT consultancies, have been made possible by developments in technology. These have the benefit of not being as strictly regulated by the French administration as traditional artisan activities or regulated services (though the government is trying to reduce the barriers to entry for certain professions – restricted intake, permits, etc. – in order to revive small towns). You will also be much in demand if you have specialist knowledge of overseas markets and marketing techniques.

This said, it's worth pointing out that the truly successful business – the real moneymaker – is the one that comes from nowhere to create a new product or the demand for a new service. Think Microsoft, Google or the cash machine. If you come up with one of those, congratulations.

Inspiration

Though many people have a very clear idea what sphere of activity they wish to engage in, others have little idea except that they want to live to France, or have a few vague ideas but none that are going to produce enough income. If you fall into the latter category, it's helpful to keep a finger on the pulse of French life by reading French newspapers (these can be obtained from most newsagents) and specialist French business magazines, and reading the websites of the French **National Institute for Statistics** (**www.insee.fr**), the French **Chambre de Commerce et d'Industrie** (**www.cci.fr**) and the French **Chambre de Métiers et de l'Artisanat** (**www.apcm.com**).

It's also worth reading some of the specialist UK-based magazines dealing with life in France. Titles such as *French Property News*, *France Magazine*, *French Magazine* and *Living France* contain lots of useful articles about people who have already set up in business abroad. There are also a number of specialist websites and discussion groups within them from which you can glean a good idea of what other people have been doing or are thinking of doing, which are worth looking at if only to ensure that you don't end up doing the same as everybody else. See, for instance, **www.escapeartist.com**, **www.expatica.com**, **www.frenchentree.com**, **www.angloinfo.com** and **www.totalfrance.com**.

It's worth stressing that it is almost impossible to do too much research. Although we very occasionally see people who are undertaking so much they are in danger of never getting round to starting their business, most people do not do anything like enough. See p.31 for more on researching your idea, but bear in mind that the fruits of such research need to be balanced by your intuition and considered within the context of your previous career history.

The Right Experience

For the majority of French people, the trigger to create a new small business is a pre-existing network of clients and suppliers, and a good working relationship with their previous employer. For foreigners who are newly arrived in France, this is less likely to apply. It can still be worth considering getting some experience as an employee before launching your own business, in order to learn the ropes, familiarise yourself with the culture, acquire fluency in the French language, make contacts and – just maybe – save yourself from making a major mistake. For many, however, this will not be practicable, if only because of their lack of language and other relevant skills (see **Working in France**, pp.164–5).

On principle, if you're qualified to exercise a profession in your home country, you're qualified to exercise it in any other EU country. In practice, there can be significant differences between the training provided and the diplomas awarded in the various countries, with the result that it can sometimes be difficult to have your training and skills fully recognised abroad.

The current EU position is that if your profession is not regulated in the country in which you wish to work, no recognition of your qualifications is necessary and you can't legally be prevented from working there on the grounds of training or qualifications. If your profession is regulated, there are two possibilities. In the case of many medical professions (see pp.70–73) and architects, the qualifications have been co-ordinated at EU level and you need only validate them, and, usually, prove you have the necessary language skills. For the other regulated professions (lawyer, engineer, psychologist and so on), you must apply for recognition of your qualifications in the country in question. The authorities have four months in which to reply. If your training is significantly different, in duration or content, from that given in the host country, they may require evidence of additional professional experience, an adaptation period or an aptitude test.

For more on the recognition of qualifications, see pp.157–9.

Eureka!

For our clients starting a small business, the starting point has almost always been a 'Eureka!' moment. Larger enterprises tend to have committees analysing various options – this isn't as much fun but generally works rather better. The problem with 'Eureka!' is that the person in the bath can get so carried away with the idea they've generated, they lose all sense of objectivity. That is not to say that there aren't some truly great 'Eureka!' ideas that have resulted in massively successful businesses: I'm thinking of the client who started importing British crisps and Branston pickle into southern Spain, the one who set up an OAP dating agency, the one who became a surveyor in France...

For me, as for many, it really did start in the bath, my 'think tank'. For weeks I'd been pondering about ways of developing my legal practice, which at that time (1984) was a large but specialist practice dealing with criminal, matrimonial, immigration and civil liberties work in the north of England. We were heavily dependent on the legal aid fund, and, as the writing was on the wall for publicly funded legal work, were looking to diversify. We had adopted computerised legal systems (essential to make a profit when doing low-paid legal aid work) very early on, and wanted to use our expertise in that field in another context. I also wanted to use my language skills and continue to travel – I'd already been doing immigration work in India, Pakistan and Bangladesh.

And there it was – we would help people buy houses in France and Spain. This would involve travel, languages, computers (to reduce drafting problems when preparing documents in a foreign language) and, above all, provide interesting and challenging legal work opportunities in a new field. I discussed the idea with colleagues, subjected it to a 'reality check', undertook a lot of market research (in the UK, France and Spain), did financial projections, made a preliminary business plan, and then did further research to make sure that that plan would work. We then launched the product, slowly and quietly at first so that we could make our mistakes in (relative) private.

It didn't turn out exactly as planned – things never do – but we got the general direction right and foresaw some of the problems, and the business eventually worked, growing into a multi-million-pound concern over the last 20 years. Since then we've dealt with many clients who've had their own 'Eureka!' moment and started businesses abroad. This book charts the progress of many of them, whom I thank for allowing us to pass on their stories (I've changed some names and personal details) in the hope that their experiences and the solutions they found to their problems will help you.

The key to 'Eureka!' is letting your imagination run wild and then being ruthless in testing whether the idea will work. That usually involves running the idea past people who know the market and industry concerned. If you find someone to do that for free, great – provided they don't steal your idea. If you don't know anyone with the knowledge to help, seek professional assistance – it won't cost much, and could save you from wasting a lot of time and money.

Getting to Know France

Geography 14
Climate 14
Culture 14
National Culture 15
Business Culture 16
Language and Dialects 18
The Economy 18
Government 23
Political Divisions 23
The Law 24
The Constitution and Code Civil 24
The Legal Profession 24
The Courts 27
Legal Aid 28

There are many emotions that come with moving abroad, but the one that overrides them all is excitement. It is probably a safe bet to assume you have a working knowledge of French culture, history, art and food. Familiarity with France is a part of every person's basic intellectual scope. Moving to France to work means you will soon know it better than most. You will embark on a new learning process, and if things go according to plan you will broaden your horizons, change your outlook, find new stimuli and be provoked by unexpected situations. You will become a little less British and a little more French. More exciting is the realisation you will undoubtedly have – as all integrated expatriates eventually do – that, no matter how well you think you know your new country, there is more to learn.

Useful Websites

French
- **www.all-about.france.com**: general information about France.
- **www.all4france.com**: info about living, working and buying property.
- **www.alliancefr.org**: the site of the Alliance Française.
- **www.culture.fr**: the Ministry of Culture and Communications site.
- **www.finances.gouv.fr**: economic information.
- **www.francealacarte.org.uk**: the site of the French Embassy in the UK.
- **www.franceguide.com**: the French Tourist Board site.
- **www.legifrance.gouv.fr**: legal information.
- **www.leprogres.fr**: the site of a daily newspaper covering central France.
- **www.letudiant.fr**: information for students.
- **www.parisnotes.com**: information about Paris (published in California).
- **www.paris-touristoffice.com**: Paris tourist information.
- **www.pratique.fr**: practical information.
- **www.seniorplanete.com**: information for older people.
- **www.service-public.fr**: the official French government portal, with links to all ministries and other sites.

General
- **http://aaro-intl.org**: information about US citizens' rights abroad
- **www.aca.ch**: information for Americans living abroad.
- **www.australia.shop.com**: expat shopping for Australians.
- **www.britishexpat.com**: a site keeping British expats in touch with events. and information back home.
- **www.disabilityworld.com**: a comprehensive site for disabled people.
- **www.escapeartist.com**: an outstanding expat site.
- **www.expatexchange.com**: a magazine-style expat site.
- **www.expatforum.com**: more than 20 country-specific forums, plus cost of living comparisons.

The aim of this chapter is to paint a general picture of the country's geography, climate and language. France's population is around 60 million, and more than half those people live in towns of 50,000 inhabitants and up. Some 10 million people live in the metropolitan Paris area, and Lille, Lyon and Marseille each count about 1.2 million inhabitants. One per cent of the world's population is French, and France is the world's biggest tourist destination – each year it welcomes an astonishing 65 million tourists, of whom 15 million are British and Eire residents. Almost one million Britons spend more than three months each year living outside their country, and more than half a million have purchased property in France. And the British expat community is growing faster now than ever before.

- **www.expatshopping.com**: a site selling your favourite foods from home.
- **www.expatworld.net**: info for US and British expat.
- **www.expatica.com**: a great general site with a growing section on France.
- **www.expatexpert.com**: advice and support.
- **www.expatnetwork.com**: the UK's leading expat site, essentially an employment network with a few extras.
- **www.europelaw.com**: information about legal issues in France.
- **www.frenchpropertyinsider.com**: information about real estate.
- **www.fusac.fr**: a useful source for US expats.
- **www.peoplegoingglobal.com**: country-specific information, with the emphasis on social and political issues.
- **www.livingabroad.com**: country profiles.
- **www.outpostexpat.nl**: extensive country-specific information and links provided by Shell for its expat workers but available to all.
- **www.parlerparis.com**: a US-run site about living in Paris.
- **www.realpostreports.com**: relocation services, recommended reading lists and 'real-life' stories written by expats around the world.
- **www.savewealth.com/travel/warning**: travel information and advice.
- **www.tradepartners.gov.uk**: a UK-government-sponsored site providing trade and investment (and general) information about most countries.
- **www.tmvc.com.au**: a country-by-country vaccination guide, which gives further medical advice.
- **http://travel.state.gov**: travel warnings and US consular information sheets.
- **www.travelfinder.com**: travel information with links to government sites.
- **www.who.int**: World Health Organization health information.
- **www.theworldpress.com**: links to media sites worldwide.
- **www.ukworldwide.com**: a British expat resource.
- **www.wtgonline.com**: a general site for world travellers and expats.
- **www.yankeedoodleiow.com**: a firm importing US products.

Geography

Protected by mountains to the northeast and flanked by two bodies of water, France occupies one of the most beautiful and fertile corners of the European continent. The so-called Hexagon spans 543,965 sq km, making it the largest country in western Europe, accounting for one-fifth of the European Union. There are 3,427km of coastline, including 644km of Corsican coast, and the territory is criss-crossed by an elaborate network of rivers – the Rhône, the Seine, the Loire, the Gironde, the Garonne and the Rhine – and hundreds of smaller tributaries. The basins left by these rivers support the agriculture that fuelled much of the prosperity and influence that France enjoys today.

At well over twice the size of the UK, with roughly the same number of inhabitants (60 million), France is largely empty, with arable land accounting for a third of its space. For a person setting up in business, this very size raises various issues: do you attempt to cater to the whole country, or just your region or town? How do you deal with distribution if you wish to provide a nationwide service, despite France's excellent transport system and irrespective of whether you are providing a service or goods? How do you apply a conventional British business model to very scantily inhabited rural areas? The problems inherent in distribution may account, at least in part, for France's well-preserved regional and local identity.

If you are moving to France for lifestyle reasons, as most people do, you will probably already have decided where you want to live, and it is unlikely to be in one of the major cities, unless it is Paris or Nice. So the first question you will confront is: is there enough business in the area to support your enterprise? Look at the figures very carefully if you are thinking of setting up in a very rural area. Are you prepared to compromise on where you would love to live in order to produce a more favourable business market? If so, by how much?

Climate

France has one of the most moderate climates in the world but, because of its size and its varying altitudes, this can vary considerably from one region to the next. Mountain areas such as the Alps and Jura mountains have heavy snows in winter months, the north enjoys a temperate climate, and northeastern areas have a continental climate, with wider temperature extremes between summer and winter. The Atlantic gives the coastal and inland areas from the Loire to the Basque region their hot and sunny summers. The Riviera, Provence and Roussillon have a Mediterranean climate with mild weather most of the year and beach-perfect summers. Yet inland from here, in Auvergne, Burgundy and the Rhône Valley, strong winds force the thermometer down.

> ### Average Temperature and Rainfall: Comparisons
>
> | City | Jan min | July max | Jan rain | July rain |
> |---|---|---|---|---|
> | London | 2°C | 22°C | 15 days (54mm) | 12 days (57mm) |
> | Dublin | 1°C | 20°C | 13 days (67mm) | 13 days (70mm) |
> | New York | −4°C | 28°C | 12 days (94mm) | 12 days (107mm) |
> | Los Angeles | 8°C | 27°C | 6 days (79mm) | 0 days (0mm) |
> | Cherbourg | 4°C | 19°C | 19 days (109mm) | 12 days (55mm) |
> | Paris | 2°C | 25°C | 17 days (56mm) | 12 days (59mm) |
> | Bordeaux | 2°C | 25°C | 16 days (90mm) | 11 days (56mm) |
> | Marseille | 4°C | 29°C | 8 days (43mm) | 2 days (11mm) |
>
> If you think in °F, multiply by 9, divide by 5, then add 32. If you think in inches, divide by 25.

France is generally subject to maritime influences, particularly low fronts from the Atlantic. Much of the nation experiences heavy thunderstorms at the end of August, marking the beginning of autumn. More rain comes during October, November, March and April. The seasons are distinct everywhere in the country.

These dramatic climatic variations affect not only where people moving to France choose to settle, but also the many businesses that are linked with agriculture or with tourism. *See* the temperature and rainfall box above for a few examples, or check out www.bbc.co.uk/weather/world/city_guides or www.usatoday.com/weather/resources/climate/worldcli.htm.

Culture

National Culture

When we think about France, we're lulled into a false sense of security. It is, for the British and Irish at least, a fellow western European nation sharing the same Judaeo-Christian values. Its language is full of the same images and metaphors, much of the food and wine is familiar (except that the French do it rather better), and many of the same sports are played and the same music listened to. But underlying all of these apparent similarities are an even greater number of differences, the existence and importance of which you will appreciate the more you get to know French society. (Read *Au Contraire* by Gilles Asselin and Ruth Mastron for a full look at this subject, albeit one from an American perspective.)

France is distinguished by its culture of personal independence and social solidarity, by its reverence for debate and for aesthetics, and by its intellectual rigour, reflected in the exacting standards demanded in ordinary schools. Then there is the respect for manners – not just on the level of form but also in terms of consideration for other people. Contrasting with the quest for personal independence, however, is the acceptance of a rigid centralisation of government and society. There is also a willing acceptance of double standards: everything is considered first *en principe* and then *en réalité*.

In short, France is much more than Britain with a warmer climate and better food, and an awareness of the need to acclimatise is crucial to all Brits, Irish and Americans, especially those who want to do business there.

Business Culture

An appreciation of the cultural differences between the UK, Ireland or the USA and France can determine the success or failure of a new enterprise – a business that is planned to run in a way that flies in the face of French culture is highly unlikely to succeed.

Differences in Attitudes towards Work

Brits and Americans tend to live to work, and when we meet socially we tell people our job at a very early stage in the conversation; this is far less likely to happen in France, where people have never bought into the Protestant idea that hard work is good for the soul, and where work is balanced with quality of life. All employees have a minimum of five weeks' paid holiday per year, three of which must be taken together, and then there is the famous 35-hour week. Many businesses away from the coast close for the whole of August as the French take their holidays.

Differences in Attitudes towards Entrepreneurship

As already pointed out, the idea of starting up your own business is far less attractive to French people than it is to those from the USA, Britain or Ireland. Even if they do decide to become self-employed, most French people prefer to take over an existing business rather than start from scratch.

Differences in Attitudes towards Workers and Employers

The French, even today and particularly in rural areas, view employment as a long-term commitment, and French businesses have a much more paternalistic attitude towards their workers than their UK or US counterparts. At the same time, and although French workers enjoy many more social benefits arising from their work, they tend to view their employer as a natural enemy, somebody always seeking to outmanoeuvre them and secure more of their labour for no more reward. Somehow the concept of the exploited worker coexists with the expectation of treatment with respect and dignity.

When McDonald's opened in France, for instance, it encountered major opposition from its staff not because of the quality of its fast food but because of its very prescriptive regulations as to how that food was to be made, how the staff would address customers, and so on. Disney had similar problems when it opened its European theme park near Paris. In both cases, the problems were only solved when the foreign employer made some adjustments to the French way of doing business. Though this difference *is* diminishing, relationships between employer and employee remain very different from those 'back home'.

These same differences are reflected by the attitude of workers to demands made of them – the French propensity for strikes, particularly in the public sector, is legendary. And when the French strike, they strike. In the UK and USA, a strike can be a gentlemanly affair with the odd picket protesting their case at the factory gate, whereas in France a strike can be little short of insurrection, with barricades, burning vehicles and the complete paralysis of major sectors of industry or commerce.

So you have the paradox of a workforce that is treated exceptionally well by international standards, and subject to enormous protection, but that, in order to show that it has not been subdued, insists on flexing its muscles from time to time and positively enjoys a bit of anarchy to liven up the day.

Differences in Attitudes towards Planning

The French, in general, are far more inclined to plan a project in detail before starting work; the British-American tendency to (more or less) make it up as they go along, redefining the plan as problems arise, is alien to them. On a practical level, this means that French banks and other potential investors expect a great deal more in the way of paperwork and planning then you might have to produce in Britain when setting up a relatively modest business.

Differences in Attitudes towards Regulation

The French accept regulations as an irritant and a minor obstacle to doing what they want to, and sometimes even obey them; the British, Irish and Americans are driven to distraction by extensive regulation yet can't find it within themselves to ignore the rules completely.

Differences in Attitudes towards the State

The French readily accept the central role the state plays in many aspects of their life; it gives them a sense of security. And there is often something to be said for central planning, as anyone who has moved a child from a school in one part of Britain to one in another and discovered that not a single subject in the second school was following the same curriculum, or even being examined by the same examining authority, will agree.

But the question arises: is it this feeling of security that allows the French the luxury of their anarchic attitude towards life, or does this attitude demand that the state be more heavy-handed?

Language and Dialects

French, spoken by more than 200 million people around the world, is the language not only of France but also of Belgium, Luxembourg, Switzerland, Canada and a long list of African countries. Though English is the dominant language of the Internet, French holds its own as the international language of diplomacy along with English in the European Union and at the United Nations.

The country's regional linguistic differences were officially wiped out in 1539 with the Edict of Villars-Cotterêts, yet France is by no means a monolinguistic and monocultural society, no matter how hard linguistic fundamentalists with the Académie Française, the celebrated institution charged with safeguarding French from contamination by foreign – namely English – words, will have you believe. In fact, the issue of France's linguistic minorities, many of which are on the expressway to extinction, has been the focus of renewed debate.

The seven recognised minority languages of France are Provençal, Breton, Alsatian, Corsican, Catalan, Basque and Flemish. Corsican is an Italo-Roman language thanks to the long time the island was ruled by Genoa. In Brittany, a version of Celtic is spoken, as is Flemish in northern spots. Alsace is heavily influenced by German, and the mysterious language of the Basque region is pre-Indo-European. Catalan and Provençal both form part of the Occitan languages, which are a mix of Gallo-Roman and Ibero-Roman. According to UNESCO's *Atlas of Endangered World Languages*, all of these except Corsican are among the 3,000 languages spoken on our planet that are in danger of disappearing. Although some Occitan/Provençal languages are making a comeback, the French government is being blamed for not doing enough to protect them. A few programmes are in place to teach them as electives in state-run schools, although textbooks and dictionaries simply don't exist in many cases.

It's extremely unlikely that anyone will ever address you in one of these minority languages, because they're only spoken within their communities. More of a problem are geographical variations in accent – if you learnt French in Brittany, for instance, you may have trouble understanding someone from Marseille, especially if they use a lot of colloquial expressions or slang. There's not much to be done in such cases except to ask them to speak more slowly and to repeat themselves if necessary (and take heart in the fact that a native speaker may not even understand all of what they are saying).

The Economy

The French economy has been roughly the same size as the British economy for many years, but this similarity disguises many significant differences between the two, some of which go to the very heart of what it is to be French. A knowledge of the state of the economy is central to the process of planning

Vital Statistics (2005)

	France	UK	USA
Population	60,656,178	60,441,457	295,734,134
Population/km^2	111.88	246.88	30.70
% Pop. over 65	16.4%	15.8%	12.4%
Internet Users	21.9 million	25 million	159 million
Median Age	38.85	38.99	36.27
Pop Growth Rate	0.33%	0.28%	0.92%
Birth Rate	12.15/1,000	10.78/1,000	14.14/1,000
Death Rate	9.08/1,000	10.18/1,000	8.26/1,000
Migration Rate	0.65/1,000	2.18/1,000	3.31/1,000
GDP (PP Parity)	$1.737 trillion	$1.782 trillion	$11.750 trillion
GDP Growth	2.1%	3.2%	4.4%
GDP Per Capita	$28,700	$29,600	$40,100
GDP per Sector			
Agriculture	2.7%	1%	0.9%
Industry	24.3%	26.3%	19.7%
Services	73%	82.7%	79.4%
Invest % GDP	19.2%	17%	15.7%
Household Spend			
Lowest	10%	2.8%	1.8%
Highest 10%	25.1%	28.5%	30.5%
Inflation Rate	2.3%	1.4%	2.5%
Labour Force			
Agriculture	4.1%	1.5%	not available
Industry	24.4%	19.1%	not available
Services	71.5%	79.5%	not available
Unemployment	10.1%	4.8%	5.5%
Budget			
Income	$1.005 trillion	$834.9 billion	$1.862 trillion
Expenditure	$1.008 trillion	$896.7 billion	$2.338 trillion
Debt as % GDP	67.7%	39.6%	65%
Industrial Growth	1.7%	0.9%	4.4%
Oil Imports	2.281 million b/d	1.498 million b/d	not available
Oil Consumption	2.026 million b/d	1.498 million b/d	19.65 million b/d
Oil Reserves	144 million B	25.41 billion B	22.45 billion B
Current A/C Bal	–$305 million	–$33.46 billion	–$646.5 billion
Exports	$419 billion	$347.2 billion	$795 billion
Imports	$419.3 billion	$439.4 billion	$1,476 billion
FX/Gold Reserve	$70.76 billion	$48.73 billion	$85.94 billion
Military Expenses	2.6% GDP	2.4% GDP	3.3% GDP

Source: CIA World Fact Book (www.cia.gov/cia/publications/factbook).

your business, and the comparision chart on p.19 will repay careful study, as does the following overview from the same source:

France is in the midst of transition, from a well-to-do modern economy, that has featured extensive government ownership and intervention, to one that relies more on market mechanisms. The Socialist-led government partially or fully privatized many large companies, banks, and insurers, but the government retains controlling stakes in several leading firms, including Air France, France Telecom, Renault, and Thales, and is dominant in some sectors, particularly power, public transport, and defence industries. The telecommunications sector is gradually being opened to competition. France's leaders remain committed to a capitalism in which they maintain social equity by means of laws, tax policies, and social spending that reduce income disparity and the impact of free markets on public health and welfare. The current government has lowered income taxes and introduced measures to boost employment. The government is focusing on the problems of the high cost of labour and labour market inflexibility resulting from the 35-hour work-week and restrictions on lay-offs. The government is also pushing for pension reforms and simplification of administrative procedures. The tax burden remains one of the highest in Europe (43.8% of GDP in 2003). The current economic slow-down and inflexible budget items have pushed the 2003 deficit to 4% of GDP, above the EU's 3% debt limit.

Analysis of Statistics

Birth Rate

The fact that France has a significantly higher birth rate than the UK gives rise to a number of obvious business opportunities regarding children and, extrapolating these figures forward, to several more.

Migration Rate

Well over three times as many foreigners come to live in the UK every year as come to live in France, and the relative homogeneity of the French population is a significant factor for anyone wanting to set up in business. Most notably, there are fewer of your countrymen or -women wanting to consume the products of your native land, so if you are trying to import items from your own country (see pp.62–3) you will usually have to penetrate the local market.

Agriculture

France derives almost three times the percentage of its GDP from agriculture as the UK, and agriculture employs more than three times as many people as a percentage of the population. The many political and cultural reasons for this include the Common Agricultural Policy, which allows French farmers to subsist on farms far smaller than would be economically possible in the UK. This presents a number of business opportunities for those wishing to turn their hand to smallholding or farming, and for those who want to supply goods and services to the farming community. But don't be deluded into thinking that the fields of France are planted with gold – French farmers, by and large, remain relatively poor, and they work extremely hard. The European Union and subventions from the Common Agricultural Policy merely convert businesses that would be unsustainable into ones that are marginal. Similarly, those selling products to them tend to spend long hours travelling great distances between customers through the vastness of rural France. One area, however, where we have seen a good deal of activity among foreigners moving to France is speciality agricultural products. The market for these is much stronger in France, and the subsidies available from the government can make their production profitable, if far from a goldmine.

Egalité

The percentage of household consumption by the lowest 10% of the population is significantly higher in France than it is in the UK, Ireland or the United States, and the percentage by the highest 10% is significantly lower. This creates a somewhat different business market and, with thought, certain opportunities and certain challenges for the person coming from one of those countries.

Unemployment

At more than double the prevailing level in the UK, unemployment is one of France's biggest social problems. It's spread unevenly through the country and through society, so anybody thinking of setting up business should look carefully at the detailed unemployment statistics for the area where they are thinking of establishing their base.

Unemployment is a two-edged sword. Though high levels would seem likely to reduce the market for your services or product in a given area, they often trigger substantial EU, French, regional and local subventions in the form of grant aid and other assistance. These are dealt with in the section on grants and subventions on pp.110–15.

The Budget

The French spend a lot more money than the British, Irish or Americans, and also raise a great deal more by way of taxation. Though they have a similar size population and economy, the French spend 25% more than the British and raise 25% more by way of miscellaneous taxes. This higher level of public spending is a major factor for anybody contemplating setting up a business in France.

Firstly, if your business seeks to provide goods or services to the public sector, you might feel that this higher level of expenditure is a good thing, even when you receive your tax and social security bills. But there is an important paradox within the French business culture: although the government is strenuously seeking to improve entrepreneurship, a huge majority of government expenditure is channelled through preferred (usually large government) contractors. Breaking into this pot of gold as a small business is not easy: you have to have a very persuasive product and the means of bringing its attention to the mandarins and decision-makers.

Balance of Payments

Despite France's vast level of national debt, this is a country that understands the term 'balance of payments' – its exports almost precisely balance imports. It's a long time since we could say that of either the UK or the USA.

This balance has enjoyed a much higher priority in the French set of political priorities, but it's also a result of the fact that France produces a wide range of innovative and sought-after products for export – not only its internationally renowned agricultural goods, but also a huge range of hi-tech products, from trains and aeroplanes to modern pharmaceuticals. Added to these factors is the lower French demand for imports – the country remains proudly self-sufficient in many areas where the British renounced the need years ago, from food to car tyres. The French ethic is towards buying French, especially in times of high unemployment.

The Service Sector

Financial services and banking, insurance and tourism are the three brightest stars of the service sector. The market capitalisation of shares listed on the Paris stock exchange equal 50% of GDP, ranking Paris as the seventh largest *bourse* in the world. Major banks include Crédit Agricole, Société Générale and Banque Nationale de Paris (BNP). The insurance sector is the world's fourth largest and has been consolidated to include a handful of major firms.

But tourism is the major cash cow for the French economy. More tourists come to France than any other country in the world, and the income it derives from tourism is the third largest following that of the United States and Italy.

Foreign Trade

France is a force to be reckoned with in this area as well. The country is the second largest exporter of services and farm products and the fourth biggest exporter of goods. Fellow EU countries account for 65% of its trade and its main customers are the UK, Germany, Italy, Luxembourg, Spain, Belgium and the United States.

Government

France's president and head of state – who enjoys considerable power under the constitution and more still in practice – is Jacques Chirac, who was first elected in May 1995. Presidents are elected for a five-year term. The prime minister is nominated by the National Assembly and appointed by the president; Dominique de Villepin has filled the role since May 2005. The main body of government is the Council of Ministers, which is appointed by the president on the suggestion of the prime minister.

The Parliament (Parlement) consists of the Senate (Senat) and the National Assembly (Assemblée Nationale). The Senate has 321 seats – 296 for metropolitan France, 13 for overseas *départements* and territories, and 12 for French nationals abroad. Members are indirectly elected by an electoral college to serve nine-year terms (one third is elected every three years). Between 2005 and 2010, 25 new seats will be added to the Senate to increase the total to 346 seats – 326 for metropolitan France and overseas departments, two for New Caledonia, two for Mayotte, one for Saint-Pierre and Miquelon, three for overseas territories, and 12 for French nationals abroad. Members will be indirectly elected by an electoral college to serve six-year terms, with half of the seats being elected every three years.

The National Assembly has 577 seats. Members are elected by popular vote under a single-member majority system to serve five-year terms. The next elections will be held not later than June 2007.

There are more than 500,000 politicians in France and many more 'serious' political parties than those in the UK, Ireland or the USA are used to, including the Parti Socialiste (PS; Socialist Party), Parti Communiste Français (PCF; French Communist Party), the Union pour la Démocratie Française (UDF; Union for French Democracy), Les Verts (Greens), Rassemblement pour la France (RPF; Rally for France) and the Front National (FN; National Front).

Political Divisions

France is divided into 22 *régions* and a collection of smaller (though still large) administrative divisions in the form of 95 *départements* (see p.244). These divisions are very real in France – the French identify much more closely with their *région* and even *département* than the English with their region or county, for a number of reasons that range from the historic through the trivial to the purely practical. These *régions* and *départements* have significant powers and can thus be a source of significant financial aid for new businesses, so where you choose to base your new business can have immediate financial consequences.

Alongside the regions and departments there are the *pays* ('lands'), which often correspond with older, pre-Revolution political entities but have been recognised by the government as useful marketing tools and, therefore, may also influence your choice of where to establish your business.

Below the level of the *département* lies the *commune*. Part of French heritage and culture, it is usually small and its mayor carries substantial local power – far higher than one would expect in the UK.

The Law

A rudimentary knowledge of outlines of the French legal system is essential for anyone thinking of doing business in France. It will also help you understand some of the later chapters of this book.

The Constitution and *Code Civil*

The foundation stone on which the entire law is based, the constitution incorporates by reference the *Declaration of the Rights of Man and the Citizen* of 1789, and the preamble to the constitution of 1948. Article 1 provides that France shall be a single lay, democratic and social republic, shall assure all its citizens equality under the law without distinction on the basis of origin, race or religion, and shall respect all beliefs.

The civil code is a much more detailed document dealing with most aspects of what is known as civil law (*droit civil*), which covers, for example, family and inheritance issues. This is supplemented by a large number of other codes that govern various aspects of French life and are the backbone of French law. The five basic codes are the *code civil*, the civil procedure code (*nouveau code de la procedure civile*), the business code (*code de commerce*), the criminal code (*code pénal*) and the criminal pocedure code (*code de pocédure pénal*).

The Legal Profession

The main problem for the British person dealing with French lawyers is that the service they provide is somewhat different from the service they would expect from their solicitor back home. Most lawyers operate as sole practitioners or in small firms of two or three, so there is much less specialisation than is now common in the UK. This is reflected in the difficulty in getting a clear initial opinion about the three essentials in every case: what is the best way forward? How much will it cost? And how long will it take?

Most lawyers do not have a culture of keeping their client informed about matters such as costs or the progress of the case. They are not required to do it, and their offices are not geared up to do so (often there will be one secretary/receptionist shared by all the lawyers). French people, in general, don't expect this level of service.

Then there is the language barrier: an English client will seldom speak French, or French of a sufficient standard, while the French lawyer may not speak English well enough to communicate complex technical issues accurately. There are law firms providing a northern European style of service to corporate or private clients from the UK or Germany, but they are relatively scarce.

Avocat

The primary role of the *avocat* is to advise and defend the interests of the public. They generally see themselves as independent professionals more akin to English barristers than solicitors, though taking direct instructions from the public. *Avocats* have traditionally played very little part in the conveyancing process or in managing wills or inheritances, all of which have been dealt with by the notary public. With the recent advent of many foreign buyers to France, this has changed. *Avocats* act as legal and tax advisers and represent clients before the courts. Avocats are required to keep client accounts and have professional indemnity insurance, but although it is possible to get compensation if an *avocat* makes a negligent mistake, it is in practice much rarer to do so in France than in England. Most *avocats* operate in small practices or as one-man bands, but they are also permitted to group together and to practise in a group with accountants and auditors.

Avocat au Conseil d'Etat et à la Cour de Cassation

This specialist lawyer, of a status similar to an English QC, alone has the right to appear before the two most senior courts. He or she is a public official (*officier ministeriel*) combining the traditional (and now defunct) separate roles of solicitor (*avoué*) and barrister (*avocat*). The office is taken over from its previous holder by a duly qualified person, usually by way of purchase. Numbers are very limited.

Avoué à la Cour

Often translated as 'solicitor', this is a lawyer who acts as a manager of the paperwork and liaises with the court in, above all, court of appeal cases. The profession was, for most other purposes, merged with that of the *avocat* in the 1970s.

Huissier de Justice (Bailiff)

Huissiers de justice, in many ways similar in role to an English bailiff, are specialised professionals who serve process, give official notice of documents, conduct the execution of judgments and seizure orders by courts, and record facts for subsequent use in legal proceedings.

Greffe (Clerk to the Court)

As well as dealing with the court's administration and paperwork, the clerk to the court maintains certain public registers such as the register of the civil state, where births, marriages and deaths are registered.

Expert

These are local people, usually but not always professionally qualified, called in to produce reports to assist the court. For example, an *expert* may be appointed to examine the wreckage of a car or the disputed boundaries of a house.

Juge (Judge)

There are various categories of judge, variously called *juges* or *magistrates*. Do not confuse the words with their English equivalents: some judges are professional, others are lay. They comprise not only sitting judges (*juges de siège*), who sit in court and make decisions, but also floor judges (*juges du parquet*), whose role depends on the type of case they are dealing with – in a criminal case the *juge d'instruction* (who decides whether to launch a criminal case) is a floor judge, whereas in a civil case, floor judges have roles alien to our system (they can, in certain cases, initiate or defend proceedings; they appear on behalf of persons who are incapable; or they can intervene in important cases).

Judges in France are selected from law graduates – not necessarily practising lawyers – by examination. They are then trained at the College of Judges for about three years. Junior judges, while intellectually very able, usually have no practical experience, which is no doubt one of the factors leading to a very high level of appeals from first-instance decisions. Senior judges are as awesome as their British counterparts.

Juges-commissaires and *Administrateurs Judiciaires*

These are individuals appointed by a court to manage businesses on a temporary basis, when they are in judicial receivership.

Notaire (Notary)

The notary is a relic from an illiterate society where there was a need for somebody of substance and integrity to confirm that various transactions had taken place. Little used in England, in France *notaires* have adapted with the times and can provide comprehensive assistance to the client in much the same way as a solicitor does in England. All title deeds and many other documents *must* be prepared by and signed in front of a notary, and most wills are made in front of one. There are other documents which, by law, must be in the form of a deed (*acte authentique*) that is drafted, verified and legalised by a *notaire*. Often the final stage before litigation will be a formal demand sent via a notary.

Notaries are private practitioners authorised by the state but also public officers, appointed and regulated by the state. Their main roles are to confer probative force, which renders a document final and binding in the absence of a successful challenge through the courts; to ensure that the parties understand what they are signing; and to act as witness and 'gatekeeper', ensuring good-quality input into the land and mercantile registries. Especially in property transactions, they commonly act for both parties, though each can insist on appointing their own (in which case they will share the same, statutory fee).

French notaries keep a 'protocol' or archive containing the originals of all documents signed in front of them. The person who signs is given an official copy and can obtain further copies should the need arise in the future.

The Courts

In the parts of France in which foreigners tend to congregate – undeveloped parts of the coast and rural areas – the judicial system is grossly overloaded. New rules have improved matters, but the old adage about a poor agreement being better than a good court case remains as true in France as in the UK.

France has a complicated court system. Traditionally, the jurisdiction of French courts has been divided (with a few exceptions) between administrative courts (*l'ordre administratif*) and normal courts (*l'ordre judiciaire*). In 1958 the Constitutional Council (Conseil Constitutionnel) was created, with the power to review the constitutionality of legislation.

The *ordre administrative* deals only with cases involving the public administration. From the **administrative court** (*tribunal administratif*) and the other special administrative tribunals (relating to pensions or the military, for example) there is an appeal to the administrative appeal court (*cour administrative d'appel*). The ultimate appeal lies to the Council of State (Conseil d'Etat).

Ordre judiciaire courts deal with both **civil and criminal cases** that do not involve the public administration. For civil cases, there are higher courts (*tribunaux de grande instance*) and lower courts (*tribunaux d'instance*). Each has set areas of competence. For example, the *tribunal de grand instance* deals with all claims involving more than €3,800, divorce, adoption, family law, succession, commercial disputes, patents, and so on. Another court (*tribunal des affaires de sécurité social*) deals with social security matters.

Industrial conciliation tribunals (*conseils des prud'hommes*) deal with labour disputes. Again, they have are no professional judges; they comprise a board of an equal numbers of employers' and employees' representatives. In addition, there are specialised courts: the *tribunal de commerce*, or **commercial court**, is presided over by a panel of judges elected from and by the business community. It has exclusive jurisdiction over litigation between merchants and in matters involving commercial acts. It is also responsible for the commercial register (*registre du commerce et des sociétés*), which oversees the creation of companies. There is also a rent tribunal dealing with rentals of rural properties, which is presided over by a judge of the *tribunaux d'instance* but comprises equal numbers of the landlord's and tenant's representatives.

Certain serious **criminal cases** (*crimes*) are tried by assize courts (*cour d'assises*). Of the rest, middle-ranking offences (*délits*) are dealt with in courts of correction (*tribunaux correctionnels*) and minor offences (*contraventions*) by the police courts (*tribunaux de police*). These criminal courts are often known collectively as *tribunaux répressifs*.

There is also a special **family judge** (*juge aux affaires familiales*) who brings together the bits of jurisdiction attributed to various courts so that all aspects of a family problem can be dealt with under one roof. He will deal with contested and non-contested divorces, separations, financial provision, visiting rights, and so on. There are also other specialist judges dealing with children.

Except for decisions of the assize court and small cases in the lower civil court, the decisions of all of these civil and criminal courts can, with limited exceptions, be referred to one of 35 **courts of appeal** (*cour d'appel*), which deal with the case by a rehearing, examining both the facts and the law. From the court of appeal there is, in most cases, a further appeal to the **supreme court** (*cour de cassation*), which only determines whether the law was properly applied by the inferior courts.

In addition to the courts, it is worth mentioning the French equivalent of the Criminal Injuries Compensation Board (Commission d'Indemnisation des Victimes d'Infractions).

Rights of Audience

Unless it is otherwise specified by law, a person appearing before the lower civil courts, the commercial court, the police court, the social security court or the industrial relations court need not be represented. In a criminal case the parties have the right to be represented at each stage in the criminal process but can renounce that right.

In certain cases, no *avocat* is needed for an appearance before the *juge aux affaires familials*; these include financial provision, residence and visiting rights. In other cases, a lawyer is required, including for divorce and separation.

Subject to exceptions, for an appearance before the higher civil court, the courts of correction and the assize court, an *avocat* is required.

For appearances before the court of appeal, you need both an *avocat* to address the court and an *avoué* (often translated as a solicitor, *see* p.25), who deals with the paperwork and relationship with the court.

For an appearance before the supreme court or the Council of State, you need to use a specialist *avocat au Conseil d'Etat et à la cour de cassation* (*see* p.25).

Legal Aid

At present, full *aide jurisdictionelle* is limited to people whose monthly income is less than about €800 (£550), and partial aid is available for people whose income is less than about €1,200 (about £800). In serious criminal cases there is an automatic right to free representation.

Legal aid is available in almost all situations where the citizen comes into contact with the law, including cases where the intervention of a lawyer is not formally required.

Business Ideas

Experience and Qualifications 30
Research 31
Basic Strategy 31
Common Ideas: Pros and Cons 35
Property 36
Tourism 56
Catering 60
Translating 63
Secretarial Work 64
E-Commerce 64
Art 66
Gardening 66
Farming 66
Medicine 70
Continuing What You Did at Home 74
Other Small Business Ideas 75

The vast majority of business ideas can work in France. Even those that don't seem like obvious choices may produce excellent results provided you have the the skill and energy. But the old adage about fools rushing in counts here as in most spheres of life, so take time to get it right from the outset and save yourself a lot of time, money and heartache. Above all, talk to your lawyer and other professionals from the outset. And don't assume it will work: two out of five new businesses in France disappear within five years, for much the same reasons as those that fail in the UK – poor planning and control, cash-flow problems, loss of clients, and lack of support from banks.

By and large, all similar businesses and most types of business have the capacity to earn, very roughly, the same levels of returns for your investment of cash and effort, and these returns depend, essentially, on the overall state of the economy in question. Hard work and luck are very important, but a good car hire company will make about the same as a good pool maintenance firm or organic cheese-producer. Which means that you might as well choose a type of business that you will enjoy spending your time engaged in.

Beware of business propositions that appear to offer exceptionally high returns. There must be reasons for this, be they high risk, a heavy workload, or unpleasant working conditions – or all three. Or the activity might be illegal and you could end up in prison. Schemes that seem to offer rewards that are too good to be true usually are.

Experience and Qualifications

The survival of an independent business has much to do with whether you have worked in the same sector and in a similar job, and can therefore build on existing skills rather than learning from scratch.

There are jobs that require qualifications in France for which none was needed in the UK; however absurd it may seem to you to have to obtain these after carrying out your work in Britain without them, you have to follow the rules – the penalties for not doing so can be substantial. Remember that the more successful you are, the more likely it is that disgruntled competitors will rat on you to the authorities.

The need for qualifications depends on the field in which you intend to set up. For instance, artisans in France are part of a well-organised system dating back to the Middle Ages; the professional bodies, which often act like medieval corporations, often require artisans to undergo specific training assessed by the regulatory bodies before being allowed to work. In a few professions, entry into the profession is not only a result of many years of study after school, but also one of *numerus clausus*: a newly qualified *notaire* cannot just open an office, for instance, but must buy a firm (*étude*) from another *notaire* or enter into partnership with him.

I have outlined the qualifications required for some of the most common spheres of business entered into by foreigners moving to France later in this chapter; see 'Common Ideas: Pros and Cons', pp.35–75.

Research

Serious research is needed when setting up any business in France; identify the areas that require investigation at your preliminary meeting with your lawyer/adviser if you haven't already got cracking off your own bat. These are generally areas that you need to know about in order to prepare your business plan (see pp.87–95).

The **Internet** has revolutionised the process of finding out about practices and procedures in France, as well as about specific business opportunities, although it is important to look at the dates when web pages were written to make sure your information is up to date. Be wary of believing everything you read there, too – double check, if possible, all facts. There are also some **specialist books** worth reading, including *Setting up a Business in France* (French Chamber of Commerce in Britain, 2003, £20; call **t** (020) 7304 4040) and *Comment Créer sa SARL* by Marie-Odile Lagrifa (DeVecchi, 2002, €14), and some French **magazines** geared at entrepreneurs, including *Défis* (***www.defis.com***). Reading the latter is a good way of increasing your business vocabulary and of improving your French.

This said, the most important step is **talking to people** who have done it – the experience they have gained in setting up a similar enterprise to what you have in mind will save you hundreds of hours of wasted time and, probably, lots of money by way of legal expenses and so on. Perversely, people who have jumped through the hoops are usually only too delighted to share their experience with fellow Francophiles, rather than seeing you as competitors from whom they should withhold commercially sensitive information. Finding such people is often a case of personal recommendation; otherwise look for business ads and trawl the Internet, then send a polite letter of request for advice (it helps to invite them to dinner!).

Basic Strategy

Who is Your Target Market?

It's very tempting to set up a business to cater to the requirements of your compatriots who are resident in or visiting France, or to the needs of English-speaking tourists or residents from other countries. This has several advantages, not least that you speak your clients' language and so if you don't speak French, or speak it badly, it won't matter so much. Additionally, you'll be familiar with the levels of service that are required by your customers, and you may be familiar with the manner in which such services are delivered in their home market, which gives you a head start in providing customer satisfaction.

A classic example of this approach are surveyors who set up businesses inspecting property on behalf of British buyers. There's a gap in the market for this because the form of survey in France is very different from the form of survey customary in the UK (*see* pp.186–8), as well as being written in French. A surveyor who is prepared to grasp the technical differences between British and French construction and to prepare intelligible documents written in good English in a format that the customer is expecting might make a lot of money.

However, there are a number of problems inherent in going down this route. First, the market in any one locality may not be big enough to sustain your business, meaning that you might have to travel large distances to create a sustainable business. Secondly, if your business is based solely on tourism, fluctuations in demand can hurt you badly: many businesses catering to American tourists foundered when the number of tourists fell by two-thirds for several months after the World Trade Center attacks, for instance. And lastly, you are not really integrating into French life.

Remember that, whoever your clients are, success or failure will depend on the quality of the goods or services you provide. Don't think that British clients will treat a British-run business with greater charity than a French-run one.

Where are You Going to Base the Business?

If the decision as to where you are going to base your business is to be made entirely on where such an enterprise stands a good chance of flourishing, things are relatively straightforward: you examine the statistics, study your potential market, and define the nature of your business, then choose a place that gives you the best business opportunities (and, possibly, the best chance of getting grant aid). I deal with this process further in the section on producing your business plan (*see* pp.87–95).

If you've already decided where you want to live and are looking to run a business from that location, your key decision is whether you are prepared to compromise on where you would like to live in order to operate in a place that may have more commercial potential. If you're not, then you need to pay particular attention to the nature of the business, and, most importantly, to how you are going to deliver your products or services to your customers. The Internet has made life a lot simpler in this respect, and some people have set up successful businesses in the most unlikely of destinations.

If you are prepared to compromise on where you live, choose a business base and then decide on the maximum travel time you would find acceptable, which you can then use as a basis for finding a pleasant place to live within a reasonable distance. This is often not feasible in rural areas, and you may have to sacrifice desirability of location for business viability.

Are You Going to Take Over an Existing Business or Start a New One?

Comparatively few of our clients who have set up business internationally have taken over an existing business. This, in part, reflects the British inclination to start from scratch (the French prefer to take over a going concern), but it also reflects the additional complexity involved in buying an existing business – you have to establish its worth, negotiate with the seller, who may not speak English, deal with existing staff and their embedded rights, and perhaps set about remodelling the business according to your own ideas.

Still, there are advantages in taking over an existing business. If it's been there for a number of years and the seller is retiring or moving away (rather than giving up on it), it suggests that there is a local demand for the goods or services. There may be accurate records of the financial performance of the business that help you decide whether you are going to be able to turn sufficient profits to meet your income requirements. And all the necessary licences and permits to run the business will be in place and will just need transferring into your name.

Ultimately, it's a case of personal preference or context (there may not be an existing business to take over in your particular field or area).

The Façade: Frogs' Legs or Chez Paul?

Should you be open about the fact that your business is run by foreigners, or should you pretend that it's French? There are many businesses and, more importantly, government departments that have a strong preference for dealing with the natives, and may even be markedly reluctant to deal with a non-French business. Approaching them as an openly foreign business makes

Case Study: The Restaurant

Henry ran a restaurant. Well, actually it was his son, Paul, who ran the place. Henry had a bit of a problem: he had served just a teeny bit of time at Her Majesty's pleasure and was bankrupt, after an unfortunate misunderstanding about £400,000 in VAT that went astray between his accounting system and the Inland Revenue. Prison changes people. Many of them find God. Henry found cooking, and after several years practising his skills in prisons around Britain he was released back into the world and decided to set up a restaurant, via his son Paul and his French girlfriend. Frogs' Legs, a restaurant serving French food in a small tourist town in the south of France, was a complete flop. Paul's girlfriend told him why – the French found the name insulting and the fact that he was foreign a turn-off, while the tourists thought they might have to eat frogs' legs and went elsewhere. They changed the name to Chez Paul, and both the French and the British came to try it.

It was still a complete flop: the food was terrible.

the hill much steeper. This attitude is not entirely illogical – dealing with foreign-run businesses requires an understanding of their culture and subtext, as well as opening up issues of reliability, longevity and whether their product will, when pressed to its limit, fully match the needs of the native market. This is true in any country. While writing this book, for example, I looked at some French-written business software that had been translated and repackaged for the UK market. It seemed fine at first, but when you tried to do something complicated, it proved almost unusable.

Some businesses get round all this by concealing their true identity behind a French corporate structure and name; others remain stubbornly foreign. The right approach may depend on the nature of your business. If you perform a backroom role and employ French people to meet the public, deal with correspondence and so on, then hiding can work (though if the truth is discovered some customers may lose faith), but this won't work if you have face-to-face contact with your clients, particularly if your French is not perfect.

Going Solo or Working with Local 'Partners'?

Many people setting up businesses abroad have no desire to work with anyone else, or perhaps only with immediate family. Many have just left big business after 20 years of grinding away and don't want anything to do with it.

But closing your eyes to the possibility of working with other people can be a mistake. There are many cases where a mutually beneficial arrangement can be made whereby you keep control of your business while providing another local business with the facilities, expertise or language skills they lack. In return, the French business has the contacts and local market, cultural and legal knowledge you lack. The businesses may remain independent, operating on a 'best friends' basis, or, after a period of courtship, they may form a closer relationship.

Alternatively, you can set up a joint venture at the outset, or even invest directly in a local person's business. These are more risky approaches, and you should take the most careful legal and tax advice before heading down this route. If done well, however, such approaches can be very successful, particularly if you have skills that are sought after by your local partner and lacking in the area. They're generally less successful if you are simply the banker to the local partner's business.

> ### Case Study: The Jeweller
> Many years ago I had a client who was a specialist jeweller. He went to live close to a commercial French jeweller who was trying to appeal to a more upmarket clientele. My client became a consultant to the larger jeweller, who was his main and then his only customer. The arrangement allowed him to change his product range easily and inexpensively. After three or four years the businesses merged, and after another five or six years, my client retired and made a tidy sum by selling his interest in the new business.

Those who have research and development skills may be able to interest large corporations in subcontracting specialist work. This attractive proposition is made even more so by the grants and tax breaks that are available for new businesses in many fields (see pp.110–15).

How Much Money Do You Want/Need to Make?

This may seem like a stupid question – surely the answer is 'as much as possible'? In fact, many people who move to France to set up a business are middle-aged and have some independent income, others move shortly before retirement and want to continue working to supplement their pension, and then there are those who have worked hard in a commercial environment in the UK and want to set up in business in such as way as to give them a better quality of life, even though they will earn much less than in, say, London.

If you aren't motivated by earning as much as possible, you need to decide how much money you will actually need. Prior to moving, you will have little idea of your likely living expenses in a given region, and little idea about the extent to which, in practice, you will be prepared to lower your lifestyle expectations. It's worth talking to your lawyer at this point: he or she should be familiar with people setting up business in France and in this region, and should be able to give you some indication of the likely cost of living there, either personally or via contacts. Estate agents can also be helpful in this regard. Your own research should involve making a record of what you typically consume 'at home' and checking the price of similar items at the local hypermarket or market. You should also study your annual budget and work out what you think is indispensable and what you would be happy to do without (making sure your spouse or partner agrees with you).

If your aim, on the other hand, is to earn as much as possible, you still need to decide the minimum you require to keep you and your family alive. You should also decide the amount that you want to turn over to make the venture worthwhile from a personal perspective.

Common Ideas: Pros and Cons

In this section I discuss some of the most popular fields of activity for new businesses that are set up by foreigners moving to France, together with the advantages and disadvantages of each where applicable. However, there is almost no limit to what someone wanting to set up in business in France can turn their hand to, given sufficient time and enthusiasm. The worst-case scenario is that they have to obtain a qualification in France if they have no suitable one from their own country and there's no means of exempting themselves. In most cases, people can use their existing qualifications and/or experience to at least speed up the often rather arduous process of getting permission to work (which is, however, getting easier, especially if you come from an EU country; see **Red Tape**, pp.153–6).

The most important point to make is that, if you are thinking of undertaking any business activity in France, you must seek professional advice at the earliest opportunity to establish what barriers lie in your path, what shortcuts there might be through the jungle of bureaucracy, the tax and legal consequences of starting the business, and, most importantly, whether your business idea is likely to work in France.

Property

Real estate ventures in one form or another constitute the single largest sector of activity among our clients. One of the cardinal rules of setting up in business in fields involving property – not just development, restoration, letting houses and *gîtes*, and so on, but also in service sectors such as bars, restaurants and campsites – is that you must buy the right property in the right place at the right price, or your business will never work.

Property Development

This is a huge subject that could fill a book all on its own. Strategies, legal and tax structures and the required documentation vary enormously according to the nature and location of the development and the nature and legal status of the developer. Probably more than with most other business activities, it is absolutely vital to have a clearly worked-out business plan (*see* pp.87–95), including financial projections. The returns, while not in the same league as in emerging market countries such as Bulgaria or Turkey, can still be attractive, especially since you can get good loans as part-finance.

Property development in France is in full swing, and there are opportunities at all levels, from large commercial developments to small residential units. This sphere of activity attracts both full-time professional developers and people with other business interests. There is no legal restriction on foreigners, even non-EU members, engaging in property development in France, but the actual building project will involve a number of regulated professions, including architects, builders, electricians and plumbers. If you're doing the work as a business or profession, you need to be registered as a business and pay the appropriate taxes and social security. If you are tax resident in France (*see* pp.144–5), you have no excuse for not complying with any of these requirements.

Property Restoration

In a country where most foreign buyers want older properties either in the countryside or in historic *quartiers* of cities such as Paris and St Malo, there is a substantial market for renovated properties, particularly since many of the people who desire such a property are those who have the least time on their hands to do the job themselves. The French, historically, have not been much interested in the renovation of rural properties (though that has begun to change) – the love of the derelict and the desire to create a silk purse out of a sow's ear seems to them something quintessentially British. Unsurprisingly, a good number of British specialists have emerged in this field, many of them doing magnificent jobs (though some seem to specialise in pastiches of traditional French rural cottages).

Property restoration in France does not require a professional qualification but, as with property development, the execution of the project will involve a

Employing Building Workers

Though there are some master builders and building contractors in France, you will generally deal with a multitude of individual artisans or, sometimes, small trade-specific businesses. Each is independently regulated.

The artisan or business must be registered at the Chambre de Métiers, and each business (including sole traders) must have a French SIRET number (*see p.124*), which specifies the areas of activity within which they are qualified to practise as well as the geographical area within which the business is registered. Someone running two businesses will have two numbers; someone running the same business in several geographic areas will have several. This number must be printed on all advertisements, flyers, *devis* (quotes) and bills. The words *SIRET en cours* means the number is being processed. Horror stories abound about people trying to operate without the SIRET number, especially foreigners, many of whom feel they can bypass the French system, while many French businesses operate beyond the scope of what is permitted by their registration. There are several consequences of these illegal practices. First, any work that is done will not be insured. Secondly, you are unlikely to be able to recover the cost of the work as a tax-deductible expense for your business or against any capital gains tax liability arising on the sale of the property. Lastly, there are penalties for those who are caught.

In short, those engaging a business in France to provide building services are advised to check that it has been properly registered, however reputable it appears, by going to **www.infobilan.fr** and typing in the SIRET number; the site will show you the name of the person holding the number and the areas of activity it covers. You should also either ask to see the *carte d'identification* (issued by the local Chambre de Métiers), a white card with green writing listing the trades, contact the Chambre de Métiers and ask them directly, or ask to see insurance documents for *responsabilité civile* (responsibility for third-party losses or claims made against them as a result of the work undertaken) and *décennial* (guaranteeing the work), which are obligatory and list the items or trades the artisan is insured to undertake.

variety of professions, including architects and builders. Again, if you are doing the work as a business or profession, you need to be registered as a business and pay the appropriate taxes and social security, especially if you are tax resident in France.

When restoring old property it is vital to remember the character and preferences of your customer – the requirements of British buyers differ, often in surprising ways, from those of Danish, German or Scandinavia buyers. One problem that often arises is the difficulty in gaining planning consent for the work desired – particularly, in some areas, the construction of swimming pools. It can also be hard to find contractors of the right quality who are prepared to work to an agreed timetable – there are lots of good French workers, but they are overworked in popular areas. Lastly, most projects run over budget, usually because of unexpected problems discovered during the demolition phase.

Building Trades

To set up in any of the building trades, you must obtain all the documents mentioned in the box on p.37. However, before even contemplating registration of the business, you need to confront the burning issue of qualifications.

Building standards in France are very different from those in the UK, particularly when it comes to plumbing and electrical work – an electrician who rewired a French house to British standards would not only find that the work did not pass examination in France but that it would cause grave danger to his or her colleagues and customers. The question of qualifications, however, is currently one of considerable confusion, due to the proposals in the new EU Services Directive, which would permit any company or individual licensed to perform an activity in any EU country to work in the same category in another. The French are concerned not only that artisans from countries such as Greece and Poland will come and underprice French workers, driving up the already high level of unemployment, but also that, say, a Greek plumbing company might operate to much lower standards than are required in France, that the paperwork in ensuring compliance with standards might not be as robust, and that the foreign workers will not know enough about the technical aspects of French plumbing to do the job properly.

This is going to be a major battleground, with two possible outcomes: the continuation of the existing system, which requires you to undertake training if your qualification does not match French standards, or what boils down to a free-for-all in the area of services generally. Watch this space.

Property Maintenance and Repair

Many foreigners living in France do this on an informal basis, mainly in relation to holiday homes belonging to their compatriots. Though it's not a regulated activity and does not have a separate classification, individual aspects of it are regulated – electrical and plumbing work, for instance; *see above* – and it is imperative that you check that any workers you hire are registered and insured (*see* box, p.37).

Estate Agency

Being an estate agent in France is a regulated activity; the two national bodies are the **FNAIM** (Federation Nationale des Agents Immobiliers et Mandataires; *www.fnaim.fr*) and the **SNPI** (Syndicat National des Professionnels Immobiliers; *www.snpi.fr*), both of which operate strict codes of conduct. Professionally qualified estate agents should hold a licence to practise (*carte professionnelle*). In most cases they will also have indemnity insurance and a bond (*pièce de garantie*), which means that if they run off with your deposit you should be able to get your money back.

Obtaining a licence to work as an estate agent in France involves complying with the Loi Hoquet of 2 January 1970 and the requirements of Article 2 of the *Décret du 20 juillet 1972*. Application can be made by either individuals or companies to the Préfecture. You can apply either to deal only with real estate, or with real estate and the sale of businesses.

For the foreigner wishing to set up as an estate agent in France the position is still, perhaps not accidentally, a little unclear, though the new EU directive on the mutual recognition of qualifications that was imminent as this book went to press (*see* p.157) should clarify matters.

In the meantime, applicants need to provide proof of the following:

- **Their professional qualification.**

- **The existence of a bank guarantee/bond. As far as the bond is concerned, you have to elect either not to receive clients' money (all funds payable in respect of a transaction must be paid to the notary involved) or to receive client funds into your bank account. In the first case you need a guarantee from an approved insurer for a sum in excess of €30,000. In the second case you require a larger guarantee, which is normally fixed at a minimum of €30,000 for the first two years of practice but then rises to at least €110,000. These amounts have been fixed for nearly 10 years and are woefully inadequate to protect clients in today's property markets, particularly in Paris and the south of France.**

- **Insurance against civil claims in respect of your professional activity (professional indemnity insurance). Both of the main professional bodies insist on a minimum of €175,000, which is, again, tiny compared with the value of property transactions today and compares unfavourably with the English Law Society's insistence on a minimum figure of £4 million.**

- **Registration of the business with the Chamber of Commerce.**

- **Details of your client bank account if you are to receive client funds.**

- That there is no bar on your practising or incapacity to practise, as stipulated in the law of 2 January 1970.

If you are also applying to deal with the transfer of ownership of businesses, further documentation will be required.

Letting Your House or Apartment

Technically, most property rentals are handled by estate agencies, but there are many unlicensed and unregulated property rental companies in France. There are also rental companies handling property located in France but based outside France; these are beyond the scope of this book. As a foreigner, however, it is most likely your own property that you will be letting – 70% of outsiders who buy houses in France let them when they are not occupying them. About half of those do so 'seriously' – that is to say, as a way of making money. The other half let casually to family, friends and friends of friends, usually as a way of defraying some or all of the costs of ownership. The latter group need make few concessions to their tenants; changes to accommodate visitors can be limited to a space where they can lock away their valuables when not in residence, extras sets of bedding, and a 'house book' with details of local attractions and emergency contact numbers in case of illness or plumbing problems.

The following considerations are aimed mainly at the first group, who need to put themselves inside the heads of the people they want to rent their property, which should be equipped solely with the prospective tenants in mind. Which part of the market are they trying to capture? A single person or childless couple wanting to enjoy French culture and cuisine will have very different requirements from a family wanting a cheap, quiet holiday in the countryside. What type of property would tenants prefer? What features do they require? You also need to be prepared to make your property available from July to early September and at Easter if you want to maximise your income from it, rather than occupy it yourself.

If you're thinking about letting your property, it is absolutely essential that you get advice from a lawyer who understands both the French and English law and tax systems. A few properties in France cannot be let on a professional basis, and all letting has far reaching tax consequences in both countries.

The Right Area

Your choice of area in which to buy a rental property is far and away the most important decision you will make. There are many parts of France where it is fairly easy to let your property sufficiently regularly to make it a commercially viable proposition, but there are others where it is almost impossible. Beware, too, that there are areas with restrictions on the ability to let property as a commercial landlord, so you need to make sure there will be no **restrictions** where you are buying, though your activities are unlikely to cause you to be classed as a commercial landlord in any case. Restrictions are normally only in

Case Study: The B&B

A few years ago I had a client who set up a *table d'hôte* in France. Though she was very professional (she had experience of running a small hotel in the UK) and seemed to be doing everything right, the business just wasn't working as well as expected. One day I was in the area and decided to stay at the B&B. When I phoned to book and get directions, my client told me to go up the N999 to Inconnue, then the D444 to Soandso, then on the minor road to End-of-the-earth. You get the picture. I spent more than an hour on my mobile phone.

'I've just got to a T-junction – which way do I turn? Aren't there any signposts?'

'Yes, the one by the milk churns.'

When I arrived, the place was fabulous, with a glorious pool and spectacular food. But nobody could find it, since my client hadn't thought of providing either a detailed location map or some little unofficial signs.

place in a very small number of apartments or condominiums (*copropriétés*) where the community imposes rules. If you are a professional landlord (that is, if your rental income exceeds €23,000 a year or makes up more than half your income), letting in an area with less than 10,000 inhabitants requires you to apply for the normal prohibition on such lettings to be waived.

The factors to take into consideration when deciding upon an area depend on your **target clientele** and your preferred way of administering the property. Strangely, the decision as to how you are the going to let your property is one of the first that you are going to have to take – if you decide to use a professional management or letting agency (*see* pp.48–9), this will have a bearing on your target market and therefore the area in which you ought to be buying. Contact such agencies in a variety of possible areas to see what they believe they can offer in the way of rental returns and what type of property is likely to be most popular there. Allow for the usual industry over-optimism, however, and be sure to take references. If you are thinking of finding tenants yourself, it is you who will have to decide on your primary market. Most Brits buying a property in France and letting it themselves let it primarily to the British.

Weather is a huge factor in deciding where to go on holiday, but fortunately not everybody has the same idea about what 'good weather' means – the number of people who take summer holidays in Normandy shows that rain is not a total turnoff. That said, in general you're best off picking an area known to be warm and dry, especially during the major British holiday season (July, August and September). May, June and October also offer reasonable letting prospects if you are in an area with a mild climate, and then there is also a (relatively small) market for longer-term lets in areas with particularly mild climates or which are socially desirable. For more details, see the climate charts (p.243), ask at the regional tourist office, or see the websites mentioned on p.15.

Just as important as climate is the ability of your tenants to get **access** to your property, both in terms of where they are travelling from and how easy it is to find. If your guests are British, convenient access to an area means having good access from the Channel ports or a major airport. Travel industry research has shown that 25% of potential visitors won't travel for more than an hour from an airport at either end of their journey. If that figure rises to 90 minutes, the number put off rises to 50%. Though many people are much more adventurous (especially the type who rent property in rural France) and view the journey as part of the holiday (particularly in France, where roads are less crowded than in the UK), if you are within easy travelling distance of a port or major airport, the number of people renting from you will be greater and so will your profit.

Don't underestimate the importance of being able to find your property – navigation in the depths of rural France can be trying, with few people to ask for directions (especially if you don't speak French) and few signposts that are of much help when it comes to locating a rural cottage. The closer you are to a main road the better, although this factor needs to be balanced with the sense of remoteness that many holidaymakers seek. Sending your tenants decent maps and guidance notes ahead of their trip is essential.

It's also useful to be near a **tourist attraction**, whether it be Disneyland Paris, a famous wine region, a well-known château, a prize sailing area, or just a lady in your village who teaches pottery classes (and might refer visitors to you for a small cut of the rent). Bear in mind that, though it may be enough to have one major attraction nearby, where there is lots of competition to let properties it may be better to have several smaller attractions, some of them seasonal – a local abbey might attract a small number of visitors year round, for example, while a flower festival or classic car rally could attract many more for a limited period. Remember that **facilities** such as golf courses or first-class beaches are themselves tourist attractions.

The Right Property

The most important thing to understand about rental potential is that there are thousands of properties in France that are, commercially speaking, impossible to let. A rustic house in a rural backwater may find one or two tenants in

In the Swim

In December 2002, the French parliament passed the Loi Raffarin making private swimming pools (except indoor pools or above-ground pools) safer for both children and pets. Pool owners must install a standardised security system (*dispositif de sécurité normalisé*) before 1 January 2006 or face a €45,000 penalty. This *dispositif* consists of compulsory fencing around the pool (1.10m high with a childproof entrance), reinforced pool covers (which cover the surface of the water and the edges of the pool and must support the weight of an adult), drowning alarms (which detect objects that have fallen in with infrared technology) and pool shelters. Permission to build new pools will only be granted to those who have applied the new security system to their designs.

Keeping Your Cool

Air-conditioning is considered a luxury, and it's true that it's expensive to install and operate (as reflected in your electricity bills). But once you've spent a sleepless night in a warm region at the end of July (you can't open the windows because vicious mosquitoes will turn you into a bloody pulp), you'll run to the nearest appliance store. Air-conditioning is particularly recommended if you are a retiree or expect to have elderly visitors. Some 13,000 deaths were blamed on the summer 2003 heatwave, and many lives might have been saved if more hospitals and private homes had air-conditioning.

the course of a year, but these will not be anywhere near sufficient to generate a sensible return on your investment.

Assessing rental potential is a skill that takes a little time to acquire. There are, however, some good indicators of property that are likely to let well. Most people will be renting your house from a small photograph in a brochure or listings guide, or on a website, and if it **looks pretty** you will get a massively better response. There is also the question of expectations: it may seem like a bit of a cliché, but people going on holiday to Normandy prefer to stay in a traditional Norman cottage with wooden beams and a thatched roof. Brittany Ferries (which has a property rental arm) tells me that some of its properties are so pretty they can find tenants for 50 weeks of the year (an average figure is 16 weeks), and in a test I carried out myself, 80% of people asked chose the same three properties out of 24 shown when I asked them which ones they'd like to rent. Buy a property that will look good in a photograph. You should also bear in mind that, though new houses are generally cheaper to maintain than older ones, they're not likely to be nearly as attractive to potential tenants.

In addition to the considerations on area in the preceding section, you need to take into account the fact that most visitors like to be able to walk to a **village or town** – ideally one with a bar and at least one restaurant, as well as a supermarket, a bakery and other amenities. At the very least, there should be a village no more than a short car ride away.

The tourist attractions near to you, discussed above, will not only determine the number of visitors you get but who they are, and your property should be geared towards them. If, for example, you are near an area famous for windsurfing, your house should be furnished robustly enough to cater for young enthusiasts, and should have somewhere to store gear and to dry clothing. This type of detail will help attract people choosing between your property and that of your neighbour, and will bring repeat custom.

In terms of facilities, think about what would make the place special, and do some market research by asking people similar to those who you want to attract what they would like. The biggest issue is whether to have a **swimming pool** – if you're catering to families, in rural France a pool will dramatically increase bookings, but they are expensive (a decent-sized one will cost around

£10,000–15,000 to construct and about £3,000 a year to maintain). They need not be heated.

Remember that much of your custom can be from repeat visitors and their word-of-mouth recommendations, but only if the property meets or exceeds their **expectations** in terms of the facilities it offers and its cleanliness. Kitchens must be modern, even if they are traditional in style, with a microwave and sufficient cutlery and cooking equipment. Everything must be functioning and in good condition. A washing machine and drier are now commonplace. Bathrooms should ideally have tubs rather than just showers; an en-suite bathrooms for each bedroom is an advantage. Bidets are welcomed by French visitors and give a local feel for Brits. Make sure that there is soap in the bathrooms, and provide towels if you can. Air-conditioning can be expensive to run and maintain but is essential for the most expensive letting properties in the hottest areas. Heating is essential; it should be effective and cover the whole property. Cleaning implements, including a vacuum cleaner, must be provided.

The number of **bedrooms** you offer is very important: in cities you generally get a better return on your investment on properties with one or two bedrooms, whereas in rural areas, or by the seaside, where most guests will probably be families, a three-bedroom property is probably the best compromise. Bedrooms should have adequate storage space and, most crucially, clean and comfortable beds. The only beds that last well in a regularly used property where the guests will be different sizes and weights are the expensive kind used in the hotel industry. They should be protected from obvious soiling by the use of removable mattress covers that should be changed with each change of tenants. Clients prefer bedding to be supplied to having to bring their own. In the living areas, furniture and upholstery should be in good condition and comfortable. Though décor is a matter of personal preference, a 'local' style is often considered attractive.

The property must be spotlessly **clean**, especially the kitchen and bathroom. You may need to 'train' your cleaner, as our expectations of rented accommodation can be higher than what we are used to in our own homes. It is also a good idea to arrange for someone to be present either at the property or in a nearby house to **welcome** your guests when they arrive, to sort out any minor problems or particular requirements of the guests. A 'welcome pack' of basic groceries such as bread, milk, coffee, sugar and a bowl of fruit should be left in the house to greet your guests, and perhaps a bottle of wine and a speciality of the area. Providing a cookbook giving local recipes is a nice touch.

Send guests a pre-visit pack with notes about the area and local attractions (these are usually available free from your local tourist office), a map of the immediate vicinity, instructions on how to get to the property, emergency contact numbers and instructions on what to do if they are delayed. Within the property, a 'house book' should give much more information about local attractions, restaurants and the like, and a comprehensive list of contact numbers for use in the case of any conceivable emergency. It can also act as a visitors' book, which is a useful vehicle both for obtaining feedback and for making future contact direct with visitors who might have been supplied via an agency.

The Right Price

If you are buying a property purely as a business proposition, the price/rental income balance (or return on investment), together with your judgement of how much its value will rise over the years, are your main criteria. If you are also going to use it as your own holiday home, you need to calculate how much time your projected rental return will allow you to spend there. For example, if you bought a one-bedroom apartment in Nice for €250,000, that property might be let for 30 weeks a year and produce you a return (after deduction of all expenses) of 6%. If you bought a two-bedroom apartment in the old town of St-Malo for €250,000 and let that for 20 weeks per year, it might perform equally well, but you could use the latter for 32 weeks a year – 10 weeks more than the Nice property. This and the fact that it had an extra bedroom could make it the more attractive proposition.

As a rule of thumb, cheaper properties produce a better rate of return than more expensive properties, because it does not cost 25 times as much to rent a £1 million house as it does to rent a £40,000 one. There are also usually more vacant weeks with more expensive properties, because there is a smaller pool of possible tenants. In each area and for each type of target clientele there is an ideal compromise of price and size.

In some parts of France there are many estate agents competing for your business and it's easy to compare the prices of the various properties on offer. Elsewhere there may only be one estate agent covering an area, and if he or she doesn't operate from shopfront prices, it may be very difficult to get any meaningful comparison of prices. The only thing you can be sure of is that they will look spectacularly cheap compared to prices in southern England. Under such circumstances, it may be sensible to get someone experienced in letting property to give you a second opinion as to the viability of the project and any projections given to you by the managing agent.

Likely Rental Income

It generally it takes four or five years for a rental property to achieve its full potential. If your property is well located, attractive and clean, you should expect repeat custom rate of about 30% in most areas.

'Target weeks' is the number of weeks you could expect to let an average property provided you did not use it yourself in July or August. The percentage return is the amount you should expect to generate as a percentage of the value of the property, after payment of all agents' fees, water, electricity, cleaning and other outgoings related to the rental period but before taking into account your own personal tax liability. In our experience a reasonably diligent person who is doing his or her best to find tenants and is not relying wholly on a management company, but is not being totally obsessive about the property, can expect to produce roughly the following results:

Area and Type of Property	Target Weeks	% return
Paris – apartment	35	8
Nice – apartment	30	7
Côte d'Azur – villa	25	5
Normandy/Brittany – coastal house/apartment	20	6
Normandy/Brittany – inland	16	5
Atlantic Coast	20	6
Dordogne	16	5
Provence	16	5
Other Inland France	12	4

The figures assume that you have bought a property suitable for rental, that you bought reasonably well, and that you are reasonably efficient in the management and, most importantly, the letting of it. It must be stressed that these are general guides only and will vary significantly from property to property, management company to management company, and owner to owner.

The decision as to whether to price your product only in sterling, only in euros, or in multiple currencies, including US dollars, will be influenced by where you are tax resident and where you hold bank accounts.

Marketing the Property

Properties do not let themselves, but there seems to be no correlation between the amount spent on advertising and the results achieved. As in any other type of business, the cheapest type of marketing is repeat custom and word-of-mouth business, so money invested in making sure that the property lives up to or exceeds visitors' expectations is probably the best spend that you will make. However, in the early years you will have to do more marketing because you have no client base.

Your own contacts are, without doubt, the best opportunity you have for marketing your property in France. Remember how few people you need to rent it out for, say, 25 weeks per year – many people will take it for two weeks or more, so you will probably only looking for 10 to 15 lettings a year. The people who find this easiest are those who work for large organisations, who will almost certainly be able to find enough people to keep their property fully occupied either from within their workplace or workmates' contacts. You have the additional advantage of knowing the tenants, which substantially reduces the risk that they will damage it or fail to pay you. This will leave only a relatively small number of tenants to be found by advertising or other marketing means. The only disadvantage in renting to family, friends or close working colleagues is that you will have to learn how to raise the delicate issue of payment, but given that you are not incurring any marketing costs and, probably, little in the way of property management costs, you should be able to offer them an attractive price. Just make sure that you address the issue when you accept the booking.

But even without people from work, most owners will be able to find enough friends, neighbours and relatives to rent a nice property in France for 10 weeks a year. If you do need to advertise, the **Internet** is the best way of bringing a specialist niche product to the attention of a vast audience at very little cost, especially the significant English-speaking markets in Scandinavia, Germany, the USA and elsewhere. It's an ideal medium for those letting property because it allows you to provide photos and other information about your property and the area in which it is found. It's worth having your own little website, which can serve both as your brochure (saving you money on printing and postage) and act as a way of taking bookings (though not of taking payment unless you're a merchant with a credit card account or are prepared to incur the expense of setting up the facility; otherwise, you'll have to be paid by cheque). If you don't have the expertise to create your site (perhaps using one of the standard template packages provided by the domaine providers), or the time or inclination to learn, a simple but very effective site can be put together for as little as £250.

As well as having your own website, it may be worth listing your property on one of the many **French property websites** to be found, such as **www.french connections.co.uk**, **www.RelaxInFranceOnline.com** and **www.cheznous.com,** especially as these are usually either free or inexpensive. Which one suits you is largely a matter of trial and error.

Except for very expensive properties, **traditional advertising** is too expensive because you only need a very small number of responses. If your property is pretty, you're likely to get good results from the various directories and magazines focusing on properties to let in France, but these only work if they are inexpensive – for a private owner with only one property to let you only have one opportunity of letting each week and so a directory that produces, say, 50 enquiries for the first week in September is not particularly helpful. We have had good reports of results from Brittany Ferries' directory (for property in northern France; see **www.brittany-ferries.co.uk**), *Private Villas* magazine (for upmarket property; see **www.privatevillas.co.uk**), and *Dalton's Weekly* and *Dalton's Holidays* (*see* **www.daltons.co.uk**), but also from flyers on local supermarket noticeboards.

Whatever form of marketing you choose, always stress that your property is clean, modern and well equipped, and make sure you include attractive pictures of the façade and pool. Remember, though, that your marketing is only as good as the quality of the response you give to people making enquiries. A key point is to follow up all leads at once, and then contact each person again after a couple of weeks to find out if they have made their mind up. At about the same time the following year, when they are likely to be thinking about another holiday, send them your details again to jog their memory. Another idea is to team up with other people in the area who are letting properties so you can pass excess lettings on to one another.

Using a Letting and Managing Agent

Managing agents let the property, deal with the cleaning and handovers, pay the bills, look after repairs, and so on, typically for about 20% of the rental – a large portion of your income. They generally operate only in popular areas. In our experience, people who make the most from renting don't use a management company but deal with these things themselves, though usually they still need to employ a cleaner and someone to deal with handovers (this could be the same person; in rural areas it's normally a neighbour). If you don't have the time to do it yourself, bear in mind that it is seldom possible to rely on a management company if you want to let the property to its full potential – owners, through family, friends, workmates and other contacts, are usually better at filling the off-season weeks than an agent (who can, on the other hand, capture passing trade that you would not pick up and redirect visitors from overbooked properties). Consider, too, that agents might not be as discerning about possible tenants as you would be if you were doing the job yourself.

Where letting agencies come into their own is when you want to offer a property on the French market but don't speak French sufficiently well. Your choice of agency is critical – some are excellent and some are little short of crooks (pocketing rent in the hope you won't find out it had let the property because you were 1,000 miles away, letting apartments belonging to agency 'friends' in preference to yours). The key is to check, in the case of a French agency, that staff hold the obligatory professional qualifications (most management services are offered as an adjunct to estate agencies), then ask to see two or three properties the agency is presently managing – if they're dirty or ill cared for, yours will be too, and will not let. Ask for references, too, preferably from other overseas clients, and take them up, preferably by phone; ask referees whether they're happy with the agency's performance and whether the financial projections given them have been met.

Then find out what kind of marketing the agency does (those reliant purely on passing trade will seldom net you good results except in exceptional areas) and ask to see a sample information pack sent to potential tenants – is it professionally done and does it give an alluring image of the property? Visit the agency's premises to check if they are welcoming and busy, and seem efficient.

If this all seems in order, find out how many weeks' rental the agency thinks you will be able to obtain in this area, and how much it thinks it would generate for you after deducting all expenses, including its charges. Make sure that the contract entitles you to full reports showing when the property was let and for what money – insist on a breakdown week by week rather than an analysis by period. Insist, too, on a full breakdown of all expenses incurred in connection with the property. Lastly, make sure the contract gives you the right to dismiss the agency at fairly short notice. Unless you're familiar with French law, it is sensible to get your contract checked by your lawyer before you sign it, as some give you far more rights than others.

Once you've appointed an agency, you need to monitor its performance; a recent meeting of people letting properties in the USA revealed that 30% had changed their original agency because of incompetence or mismanagement, and French agents are no better than US agents. The following steps may sound like hard work, but they will pay off in terms of the income you receive.

First, let the agency know, in the nicest possible way, that you and all your friends in the area check one another's properties every time you are there and compare notes about which are occupied and the performance of your letting agencies. This will deter unauthorised lettings. Telephone the property from time to time, too; if someone answers the phone, make a note of the date and ensure that you receive income relating to that period. Additionally, ask friends to pose as prospective customers and ask for property details every so often, to see how efficient the agency is being, and if you get the opportunity, call in to see the property without warning to see what state it is in. Lastly, study the report the agency sends and check that the money you receive corresponds to the amounts shown in the reports.

The Letting Agreement

If you're letting property, it is vital that you make your tenant sign a proper agreement before they take occupation – if you rely on a verbal agreement or simple exchange of letters, you may find it difficult to recover possession at the end of the period of occupation. The rights of tenants (*locataires*) can surprise the careless landlord (*bailleur*); *see* the box below.

The type of contract you need depends on whether the tenant is taking on a short-term holiday let for, say, two weeks, or whether it is a longer-term contract. If your property is being let furnished to a British person for less than six months, there is no legal reason why the contract should not be made subject to English law, which means that if anything relatively minor goes wrong, such as a dispute about whether the property was in good condition, it can be dealt with back home (if anything serious goes wrong, such as the tenant refusing to leave at the end of the tenancy, French law requires that this be dealt with in the French courts, because only they have the authority to issue an eviction order). If the property is being let to a non-Brit, it is more sensible to have the whole agreement dealt with under French law. And if the property is being let for more than six months, the paperwork must comply with French law and be in French.

Whatever you decide, you should see your lawyer when you start letting properties. He or she will prepare a general tenancy agreement with blanks into which you can insert the details of the tenant. The law changes from time to time, so you should make sure you get this revised every three or four years. In the contract, you should stipulate which items are going to be covered by your household insurance and which are not; the tenants' personal possessions are not normally covered under your policy.

Squatters' Rights

Those letting property in France should be aware that by French law it is much more dangerous to let a property unfurnished than furnished, because in the first case the tenants could acquire the rights to stay on at the end of the tenancy. 'Furnished' means that a house or apartment has all the elements needed to live in it, such as a bed, a table, chairs, a cooker and a fridge.

From a landlord's point of view, the safest type of letting is a short holiday letting of furnished property. A holiday let takes place during the recognised holiday season, which varies from place to place. In non-skiing areas, it generally covers at least the period from June to September.

If a furnished property is taken on as a holiday home for less than three months, tenants' rights to stay on at the end of that period are extremely limited – you are entitled to recover possession if tenant's have another home to go to (or had one at the time they moved into the property).

If your property forms part of a *copropriété* (*see* pp.198–9), your tenants will have to agree to abide by the rules of the community.

Taxation of Rental Income

If you're thinking of letting property in France, you *must* seek tax advice before doing so – the situation is very complex, and there are a number of options available to you, both when you buy the property and subsequently, that will have long-lasting and significant tax consequences. The following is only a very brief discussion of the main issues. Above all, don't make the mistake of many people who own property in France and 'forget' to notify either the French or British tax authorities about the income derived from it – the number of people who are caught rises each year, and they have to pay not only the tax due but also interest on the late payments plus penalties.

Letting your property will produce a tax liability – or at least potential tax liability – both in France and your own country. In the case of UK residents, there is a double taxation treaty that means you do not pay the same tax twice – under international tax law the French government has the primary right to raise tax on income derived from letting real estate (land or buildings) in their country, and if you give the British government a tax return in relation to that income they will give you a full credit for the tax that has already been paid in respect of the same income in France. For instance, if the tax due in England is £1,000 and you've already paid £600 in France, you only have to pay the British tax office the balance of £400. In fact the way the British tax office will calculate the tax and allowances they will give you against the income that you have received means that often you will face little or no tax liability in Britain. (For more on UK taxes, *see* the box opposite.)

Most people who own a home in France and let it on a casual basis will not be treated as a business, even if they let it for the whole or most of the year. For that to be the case, the property would have to either be bought in the name of a commercial company (this doesn't generally include properties bought in the name of an SCI; see p.83), be a commercial property such as a bar, restaurant or shop, or be a residential property run as a business (most commonly if the property comprises more than five self-contained rooms or units available to let for most of the holiday season – typically, a large property divided into six *gîtes*).

Those letting property casually still need to appoint a tax representative in France to deal with their tax affairs, but this is normally inexpensive (about £100 a year for a basic service, £300 if your affairs are complex). You will need to file a tax return with the French government every year, on a self-declaration

UK Property Taxes

Until recently, there was a lot of confusion within the British tax office about whether letting property in France counted as a genuine business activity in respect of which one could claim allowances and, in particular, morgage or loan interest payments against the income received. It is now quite clear that this is the case, though if there is evidence of substantial holiday use you may still find it difficult or impossible to recover any interest charges against income.

If you have rental property in the UK, all income from all those properties (furnished or unfurnished) is put into one 'pool' and taxed as one. Allowable expenses in respect of all the properties are set against the collective income, and the profit (surplus) is taxed under Schedule A as investment income. Accumulated losses are carried forward. The income from your overseas property is now taxed in a similar way, but under Schedule D.

The expenses allowable against UK tax are, in summary:

- Repairs and maintenance.
- Insurance.
- Management costs, including advertising, rent collection, legal charges and the cost of a reasonable number of visits to the property.
- Services supplied free to tenants.
- Local taxes and standing charges for water, electricity, etc.
- Any service charges on the property.
- The cost of running any communal part of the property.
- The upkeep of gardens.
- Architects' and surveyors' fees on maintenance but not improvements.
- Capital allowances on any machinery used to maintain the property.
- The upkeep of roads, ditches, etc. for the benefit of the tenants.

If you have properties in the UK that you let, the foreign properties should be treated as one with the British properties for tax purposes, so losses made in one place should be set off against gains made in another.

basis similar to the new British system – it's your responsibility to make a declaration and to pay the amount due rather than the responsibility of the government to assess you as owing them a certain amount of tax. If you are resident in France, the rental income you receive will be added to any other income in the same category and be taxed as part of that overall income.

If you let part of your main home and the person who rents it is using it as their main home, your income will be tax-free. If you let part of your main home to someone who uses it as a holiday home, approximately the first €800 a year is tax-free.

If you let **furnished property** regularly or habitually (which generally means that it is available to let for much of the holiday season), the letting will be treated for tax purposes as a business activity (*bénéfices industriels et commerciaux*). As such, it is taxed in a number of different ways depending on the amount of income you generate. If your income is less than €16,000 a year, you may, if you wish, be treated under the special scheme known as **Micro BIC**, which means you will only be taxed on half the amount you receive – the other half is treated as an allowance in respect of all the expenses you will have incurred running a property, which you will not have to keep records about or individually prove to the tax office. This scheme is attractive in its simplicity (a rarity in the French tax system!), but you will usually find that it is cheaper to claim the expenses and allowances to which you would otherwise be entitled (under the Micro BIC you cannot claim any extra allowances even if your expenses amount to more than the general allowance). If your income is between €16,000 and €80,000 per year (which is the case for the vast majority of people letting a property in France), you are entitled to have an estimate of your income (*forfait*) carried out by the authorities every two years on the basis of typical industry performance and profits.

If you prefer, you can opt for the normal system of taxation (*régime réel*), which is more complicated and requires you to keep more records but is in many cases cheaper in terms of the tax you will have to pay if you let your property on anything like a regular basis. Under this regime, you take the total income you generated by letting the property and deduct from it all of the expenses in the various categories allowed by law. Most business expenses are deductible, including finance costs and a small allowance for depreciation of the property, but you can't include expenses related to any periods for which you occupied the property or it was available for your use.

Unfurnished lettings are taxed as a separate part of your income, termed property-related income (*revenus fonciers*). You are allowed to make various deductions from your total income, including deductions in respect of local property taxes, management expenses, consumables (such as water and electricity), repairs and insurance premiums, and there is also a miscellaneous general deduction of 14% of the amount received (which rises to 25% in the case of an SCI; *see* p.83). You will need to keep records of your expenditure to show to the tax office if they so require. Again, you can't make any deductions or claim any allowances relating to periods in which you occupied the property or it was available for your use. Once you've calculated the amount on which you will have to pay tax, the rate will be calculated by reference to your family circumstances (*see* p.153).

Other French taxes you may run up against when letting property are **VAT (TVA)**, which in certain circumstances you will have to charge on your rent (not usually when you let furnished accommodation that does not include the provision of meals as part of the rent); and the **local business tax** (*taxe professionnelle*), but only seldom if you are renting out a property you use yourself for part of the year, if it is part of your home, if it is a *gîte* (*see* pp.54–6) or if it is a 'one off' let. It is also possible that you will have to pay a tax locally in respect of **rental income** you generate, called the *droit de bail*. This is calculated, in the areas where it applies, at 2.5% of the total received during the year (which, for some reason, runs from 1 October to 30 September instead of the usual 1 January to 31 December).

Capital Growth

One of the great attractions of owning a rental property is the potential for the asset to grow in value while you enjoy the use of it and a decent income stream from it – few would say that you get as much fun out of 10,000 building society shares as you do out of an apartment in Antibes! The flat in Antibes is also less likely to go bust, or to be taken over and lose half its value overnight.

For some people, the shortlist of places in which they plan to buy a property is governed by the capital growth projected. The British view property as an investment as well as a home, and expect their house to rise in value, if not year by year then at least over time. This was not really a consideration for the French until recently, which resulted in the erroneous perception that property in France does not increase in value, or at least not to any significant extent. It's true that in some rural areas property prices were depressed for many years after the massive depopulation of the countryside in the 20th century (in 1914 80% of French people lived in the countryside, compared with less than 20% now), but even in these areas, especially where property has 'sold out', there have been increases in value – for instance, a cottage in Normandy bought for £10,000 in 1990 might well be worth £40,000 today.

Though property prices in France have not risen as rapidly as in London or the UK generally, many people believe that for the next few years there will be limited if any growth in the British market but substantial ongoing growth in the French market, whether in Paris, the south, or more rural areas. It comes as a big surprise to most people to learn that real estate, both in France and in the UK, has crudely kept pace with the Stock Exchange over the last 25 years. In the 1990s the Stock Exchange romped away, but the subsequent correction/crash has eroded all of that advantage, and over the last five years the Stock Exchange has actually lost in value whereas real estate has risen substantially wherever you bought it. In fact, for most people buying property in France the picture is better than the available figures suggest, because most foreign investors have been buying in the better-performing areas, and buying properties of a type that have increased in value at an above-average rate.

For comparative up-to-date figures on property prices across the various regions see www.immoprix.com (general price indications) and www.seloger.com for more specific information (down to town and street level) and paid-for reports. For Paris by area see www.paris.notaires.fr.

Letting *Gîtes*

Most people think of *gîtes* as outbuildings or cottages attached to or adjoining larger rural properties, often with fairly basic facilities. They were in fact originally set up as part of the movement to encourage rural tourism, and were intended as a sideline activity for farmers, for whom they would provide a extra

---

Gîtes de France

It's impossible to talk about *gîtes* in France without mentioning Gîtes de France, a quango supervised by the Conseil Général. Founded more than 50 years ago, this federation of owners was granted official status by the government in the 1950s, as part of its post-war promotion of tourism to France. Now also promoting B&Bs throughout the country, it has enormous influence both within the market and within government. The figures speak for themselves: it has 42,000 owners and 56,000 properties, and provides 35 million days' holiday a year costing more than €350 million. A fifth of its clients are from abroad, predominantly Britain. It offers different categories of *gîtes*: standard rural ones for occupation by a family; holiday *gîtes* designed for groups of friends or larger families, or, in some cases, for use by students and schools during educational visits; and *gîtes* offering visitors simple weekend accommodation.

From an owner's perspective, joining Gîtes de France, which charges a commission of 12–15%, is voluntary. Our clients who have done so, primarily to take advantage of the marketing opportunities offered by the Gîtes de France printed guides and its excellent website, have had mixed results. You can only join if your property is in a community of less than 5,000 people (this includes huge areas of France), and if you adhere to its rather rigid standards and requirements, including a minimum period for which the property must be open to the public. This and the very Frency bureaucracy involved has led some people to leave the organisation, although there are exit penalties for doing so.

It may help you to make a decision to contact the owners of member *gîtes* in the area in which you're thinking of setting up, to talk to them frankly about their experiences. It's also worth knowing that the organisation is a source of grants to people setting up *gîtes*.

source of income. But while many do fit this description, the definition has now been expanded to include almost any small rural property let as self-catering holiday accommodation. There are about 50,000 official *gîtes* in France but thousands more, often belonging to foreigners, that are let out informally.

The foreign – especially British – love affair with running *gîtes* (at one point more than half of our clients moving to France were intent on setting up a *gîte* business) is over. There were too many people offering this type of accommodation for the market, with the result that number of weeks they could let a place for fell away year by year, eroding profits and rental yields. At the same time, property prices were rising and, especially in the south of France, the dream of buying an inexpensive property and eking a living from it by letting part of it for a few weeks a year was patently no longer achievable. We still have clients looking to run *gîtes*, but nowadays they tend to have done more homework and are more realistic about the potential of their business.

There are many good points to running *gîtes*. They mean you can live in rural France (something you probably wanted to do anyway), invest more of your money in your home (rather than some of your money in your home and some in an investment property elsewhere), take several months of the year off (the work is usually seasonal), and meet a wide variety of people, many of whom will become semi-regular visitors or even friends. The work is also less 'hands on' than running a B&B – you still have to take bookings, maintain and repair the property, and deal with the handover (including cleaning), but you don't have to provide meals or clean rooms daily, and the guests are not living in your own home. Guests also tend to stay longer in a *gîte* than a B&B (the average stay in a *gîte* is one or two weeks; in a B&B it's about three days). Best of all, there is no barrier to entry – you don't need to have any qualifications, and you don't even need to speak French. All you need, in fact, are some outbuildings that can be converted into simple accommodation.

Ther disadvantages are also numerous, however. Most importantly, it's difficult to make a living from them. In an oversaturated market, you have to choose your location very carefully and become adept at marketing if you want this to be your sole or main source of income. This could involve, for example, targeting specific UK-based leisure markets (sailing clubs, hikers, birdwatchers, golfers, etc.) or business markets (such as organisations that like to take their sales or development teams somewhere remote to thrash out ideas, small law or accountancy firms looking for somewhere to hold an annual partners' strategy meeting, or businesses looking for somewhere special to entertain clients). Families are an obvious market, or, if you have small *gîtes* without a swimming pool, you may be able to carve out a niche catering to Brits house-hunting in your area, who need a good-value base rather than the usual holiday facilities.

Beware that the government has started to crack down on the holiday rental market, and in some places *gîte* owners must now pay a *taxe séjour* (a fixed amount per head of guests per week, previously limited to hotels) to the *commune*.

You certainly won't be able to make a living from a single *gîte* – most people consider that they need three or four units. According to Gîtes de France (*see* p.54), the average *gîte* is occupied for 43.4% of the time that it is available (*not* 43.4% of the year), which equates to 17 weeks a year – many of our clients report less. The average weekly rental charged is €387 in high season and €259 in low season, though there are significant variations between prices in different areas and between different properties. From this income, you have to deduct all of your expenses. Remember, too, that your income will be very seasonal.

In terms of formalities, you need to register your business with the Chamber of Commerce, and if you're living in a small village (anywhere with a population of less than 10,000), you have to obtain permission to let your property commercially if your income is going to exceed €23,000 a year or your rental income constitutes more than 50% of your total income.

Tourism

With the vast – and ever-growing – number of foreign visitors to France each year, the tourist industry represents a dynamic potential market for small businesses. Though the chances of an overall decline are minuscule, it is worth studying tourism figures in the various regions to see which areas are booming and which have had their day. Apart from the fields listed below, you could organize walking tours, bike tours, wine-tasting trips or hot-air-balloon trips.

Running a B&B

B&Bs, or *chambres d'hôtes*, are, along with *gîtes*, a mainstay of foreigners setting up business in France. As with running *gîtes*, this industry has few barriers to entry, can be satisfying if you like dealing with people, and allows for a lot of time off, as the work is often seasonal. And you can target English-speaking guests until you've learnt enough French to widen your horizons.

As with all property, though, you must buy the right place in the right place at the right price (*see* pp.40–45). In addition, this can be hard, unglamorous work – cooking breakfasts, cleaning, washing, stripping three or four beds and perhaps preparing dinner for four guests means days are long. Sometimes it will seem that your life is not your own – unexpected guests may turn up at 10pm, and expected guests turn up late, in the small hours, or not at all. Your public may have a small budget but it has high expectations – in-room coffee facilities are en-suite bathrooms are expected these days, but fitting bathrooms into attractive older properties can cause major headaches, and take up space where you could have lettable rooms.

Buying an existing B&B can be expensive (many are overpriced), as can the marketing required to get your B&B known – there are lots of people with the same dream and a finite pool of guests, with oversupply a particular problem in the south of France. Those who want to branch out into providing dinner too (in which case the business becomes a *table d'hôte*) need to be aware that *chambres d'hôtes* are rooted in the agritourism industry and are therefore encouraged or even obliged to use fresh local produce and offer local recipes.

In terms of formalities, you must register with the Chamber of Commerce and comply with hygiene regulations. If you have more than five bedrooms to let, you become a hotel and have to comply with a lot more regulations. It's also possible to register your B&B with Gîtes de France (*see* p.54), which means that you not only display their logo and appear in their guide but are also likely to receive preferential referrals from the local tourist office. On the downside, the organisation is very prescriptive when it comes to how your business should be run, especially how your rooms should be presented.

Running a Hotel

The numerous foreign-run, owner-managed hotels in France (mainly by Brits or Americans) tend to be small, specialist establishments. The advantages and disadvantages of running a *gîte* (*see* pp.54–6), a B&B (*see* pp.56–7), and a restaurant (*see* p.61) also apply to hotels, but there are other factors to take into account. Running a hotel certainly has more glamour, especially in a larger enterprise where the owner can delegate some of the more boring and menial day-to-day tasks to their staff. If the hotel is running well, it is a very satisfying line of work, especially if you lay on special functions and become part of the event and the local community, or when you realise that you are helping people to have a good holiday as well as contributing to the prosperity of the area.

However, this is also a cut-throat occupation demanding considerable management skills; if you don't run it efficiently and maintain a firm direction of events, the hotel is unlikely to prosper. The hours are generally long and the work hard. As in any country, there are a lot of regulations with which you have to comply, including those for health and safety, licensing, hygiene, pricing and services, disabled access and employment. You need to seek good professional advice early on, but such advice is not easy to find.

Buying a hotel can also be expensive, even allowing for the lower price of property in France. You can reduce the cost by only buying the business (*fonds de commerce*) and not the building, but this does have drawbacks (*see* pp.103–4).

Running a Campsite or Caravan Site

Camping is very popular in France, both with the French and with tourists, especially those from northern Europe. As a business proposition, it's something you'll either love or loathe. The major draw is that it allows you to live in the French countryside or on the coast, and in glorious isolation for up to 10 months a year, since the business is generally extremely seasonal (most sites derive 60–70% of their annual turnover from the months of July and August,

Case Study: The Hoteliers

Nearly 20 years ago, Roger Farrell-Cook and his wife Suzanne bought a house in Aviernoz, Haute-Savoie, with a characteristic slanted Alpine roof and thick walls set against the snow-capped peaks of the Parmelan mountains and surrounded by meadows and wild flowers. Geneva is 45 minutes away, and they are close to the Rhône, Chamonix, Mont Blanc and the Italian border.

'The idea was to have a *pied-à-terre* but the house was too big so we decided to open a hotel.' The result was Hotel Camelia (**www.hotelcamelia.com**), with 12 guest rooms. The couple had no major problems starting their own business in France.

'We decided we wanted to welcome people to this beautiful part of the world and the rest was easy. Maybe the bureaucracy and paperwork were a bit more than I expected,' explains Roger, 'but there are no major difficulties provided you accept the norm.'

The process, he adds, was made easier thanks to Suzanne's excellent French. Over the years, this successful business has grown to include a restaurant and space for seminars thanks to the friendly and hospitable nature of its owners, and their dog Alpha Tango, who has become somewhat of a local celebrity. He takes guests for walks, rather than the other way around. Roger celebrates his native roots when Hotel Camelia throws what he calls its English theme night.

'We sit around and drink English beer and eat English food and then I start singing English songs – but none that I'd care for you to hear right now.'

although there's a steady flow of Dutch, Belgian, British and German campers between Easter and October). When you do have customers, they are (hopefully) having a good time, so the atmosphere is congenial.

It's an expensive business to set up, though – you'll generally need a minimum of £200,000, plus somewhere to live (if this is on-site, allow at least another £100,000). Creating a new site is not for the faint-hearted: the bureaucratic process can take at least 12 months and the cost of installations to comply with EU regulations is very high. And then, even with a following wind, it will typically take three or four years for a site to become profitable.

Planning permission is not always easy to obtain, particularly in the more popular tourist areas or areas of outstanding beauty. It's usually conditional on the site being, in essence, invisible – that is to say, the tenants and caravans should be screened from the view of anybody driving past or engaged in activities in the area. If you are thinking of applying for planning permission, get good professional advice at the very earliest stage – certainly before you spend any money on the project, as it might come to an abrupt end at that point.

As well as planning consent, you will need permission to construct the site, and that will dictate the facilities you have to include – in addition to those required for small sites (*see* below), you must provide hot showers, a common room for guests, and proper waste disposal facilities. To obtain a top star in the rating system, you also need to provide facilities for washing clothes, emptying waste tanks for caravans, and so on. All of this is pretty expensive.

Many existing sites that are for sale are either in the wrong place or owned by people reaching retirement, who set up with the minimum of capital and lived off the business for a number of years but are seeing their income diminishing because they haven't invested in the site to keep up with the competition. Camping is not, as many people believe, a poor man's holiday – most people who camp do so for the freedom and the chance to be in the open air, and will pay for quality in the right place (although you should always allow space for backpackers wanting a place to lay their heads at a sensible price). And clients are becoming more discerning – there is little doubt that the *hôtel plein air* ('open-air hotel'), consisting of fully equipped chalets or mobile homes in an attractive setting with access to natural attractions, is the camping of the future.

Obtaining finance to buy an existing campsite can be tricky – it depends on the declared turnover of the business, the length of time it's been trading, and the previous business experience of the buyer. The main problem is always turnover – as with most cash businesses, the declared figures are rarely true, but banks will only lend against a declared, positive track record. It seldom makes sense, even if it is possible, to borrow more than 50% of the purchase price.

As with every type of business, marketing is the essential ingredient for success, and each site has a different target clientele to satisfy. It takes special skills to keep all age groups entertained and obtain the highest possible expenditure per camper through on-site shops, restaurants, bars and entertainments, and through running organised tours – these are where the real profits can be made. Service is all-important: staff must speak the languages required and create a good atmosphere (and may need the people skills – or physique – to deal with 'interesting' visitors), and facilities must be clean.

Licensing requirements depend on which category the site falls into; your plans and projected facilities will be checked out by the *préfecture*. At the top end, beach/sea/sun sites (*camps de tourisme*) are, as the name implies, within easy reach of a beach and have a great deal of on-site entertainment, especially for kids. This can be very profitable, and is indeed becoming big business, but you have to run a slick, professional outfit to achieve maximum volume in a very short season (often 7–10 weeks). Substantial capital and continuous investment is required to maintain a share of this very competitive market. The most profitable are sites created 15–50 years ago, when land costs were negligible, but if they come on to the market today the land value often makes the total purchase price seem too high to give a satisfactory return on investment.

As a *camp de tourisme*, you can either apply for permission to run a site for a maximum of two months a year (typically July and August, when you would normally expect to generate up to 70% of your annual income), or apply to have it open for up to six months per year, in which case you are permitted only a very low density of pitches per hectare (typically, you have to provide 150 square metres a pitch, whereas campsites open for two months a year can operate from as little as 25 square metres per pitch, though 50 is more common).

Rural sites (*aires naturelles de camping*) are situated inland, preferably within easy reach of a good tourist route, natural attractions such as mountains and lakes, and historic towns. They are generally more low key than coastal sites, offering 20–75 larger pitches and peace and quiet, with an emphasis on the environment. They often have a family atmosphere, and for the owners become more of a way of life than seaside sites, opening all year round or at least from May to October. Even if the site itself closes for part of the time, if it's well placed its bar and restaurant can remain open throughout the year.

At the most basic level, there are tiny sites limited to a maximum of six pitches or 20 people at any given time, with no permanent caravans. These *terrains de camping déclarés* have to be registered with the local town hall (*mairie*) and, depending on the place, are subject to greater or lesser degrees of regulation. You will always need full toilets, linked to the mains drainage or a proper septic tank, a shower block with sinks, outdoor lighting, some form of hard surface to walk on, especially around the communal areas, and a supply of electricity for site users. These are often as an adjunct to another activity, usually farming (in some cases they can only be run by people operating an active farm).

There are a growing number of campers who rent a permanent pitch on a campsite for their own caravan or mobile home, and visit more than once a year, letting it the rest of the time to cover costs. If you, as the campsite owner, manage rentals for them, you need to register this too.

Catering

Bars

Back in the late 1980s, I had so many clients buying bars – mainly in Spain – that I had a special spreadsheet on my computer. The clients would tell me how much money they had, and I would tell them when they would go bust!

Those days are over, but opening a bar is still a dream of many British people of all ages and from all walks of life. The prospective bar owner tends to want to open the business either in a tourist resort such as St-Tropez or in a small rural town or village. Few look to the cities, except Paris.

The advantages of this type of work are that there are no formal barriers to entry, and that the work can often be congenial. If however, like most of our clients, you've never run a bar before, you need to think long and hard about going into this line of business – as the cliché goes, it's usually better on the customers' side of the bar than the owner's. Bars are expensive to set up but tend not to make a lot of money – in villages and small towns, surprisingly little can cross the counter, while in large towns, especially in tourist centres, expenses can be high. This is part of the reason for very high failure rate – in the case of my clients, well over 80%. Add to that the fickleness of the public – today's trendy bar is tomorrow's waning star and the following day's liquidation, although this is not a consideration if you run the only bar in a village. On the other hand, in tourist areas your customers may want a themed English pub, complete with fake ploughshares and inn signs, rather than the chic traditional café/bar you long to run.

Selling alcohol requires registration with Customs and Excise and a licence from the *mairie*, but in most areas the number of licences issued is limited, and there are seldom any 'extra' licences available. This means that you have to buy the licence, and usually an existing business to go with it – and bars are usually expensive to buy. A Category 4 licence (a full bar licence permitting you to sell all kinds of drink) can cost €30,000 or more; if you want to be a *bar-tabac* (a pub with a special area or kiosk selling cigarettes, and perhaps other tobacco products) an extra licence is required. Running a bar also usually involves preparing food, and compliance with the usual hygiene and smoking regulations.

If all this doesn't put you off, think of the long hours, especially in tourist areas and Paris – not only are you up late, but you also have to rise early to do your shopping and set up for the day. The stress of it all leads many to drink their assets – for Brits, at least, owning a bar is a fast track to alcoholism and divorce.

Restaurants (*Restos*)

In the top 10 business schemes among foreigners, setting up a *resto* is the most curious – mainly because those who entertain the notion have seldom run a restaurant, or even worked in one, before. *Excusez-moi?* This is France, home to the best cuisine in the world. *Bonne chance!*

That said, opportunities do exist – the number of restaurants in France is growing, as is the appetite for non-French fare, so a foreign-owned restaurant, if the food is good, can be chic and do well. This includes British cuisine, which is currently fashionable. Bear in mind, however, that the French public can be very demanding, and that you will need to speak good French, even if your primary aim is to cater to English-speaking tourists.

This can also be very hard work with long hours – between serving lunch and dinner (and possibly breakfast too), you have to find time to do your administration and buy all your provisions (which, in France, involves much more than a quick visit to Tesco). Then there are a mass of detailed regulations to comply with, dealing with everything from health and safety, hygiene and disabled access to the types of alcoholic beverages you can sell (a *grande licence* means you can serve all alcoholic drinks with food). Thankfully, alcohol licences aren't restricted in number in the way bar licences are (*see* above). Compliance with regulations is ensured by means of regular inspections.

Shops (*Magasins*)

Shops are an interesting option offering a huge range of possibilities. Most of our clients start out with ideas of specialising in selling items from their own country, or in providing things that expats from their country miss, such as baked beans or Marmite. But this is only really viable in Paris and places with high concentrations of expats or a trendy cosmopolitan clientele, and even then you may find your local supermarket has beaten you to it (and can beat your prices). You may need to look instead at servicing the general needs of a local community, whether it be French people or expats.

The type of product to be sold is your main consideration, and your focus should be on capturing a niche market or tapping into a local market where competition from the *grandes surfaces* (hypermarkets) with their vicious price-slashing is not going to be troublesome. A careful study of local market conditions is essential, as is the ability to speak French.

The pluses to this kind of career include civilised working hours (though remember that the work doesn't stop when the shop is closed) and the fact that you become part of the local community, especially in small towns. Certain regulations need to be complied with, particularly those concerning health and safety and access to the premises (and perhaps other regulations according to the nature of the goods you're selling), but these are modest indeed alongside many other commercial activities.

Commercial leases in France are granted for nine years, with three-yearly reviews, which are index-linked unless there have been changes to the property. The lease is automatically renewed after nine years, providing the tenant has behaved and paid on time. At this point, the rent is reviewed at market price; this may involve a court deciding on a fair amount. If the landlord wishes to terminate a lease after the nine years (or the next nine years), he or she has to

> ### Case Study: The Deli
>
> One of our clients, who'd worked for a major construction company, managing multi-million-pound projects around the world, decided he wanted to 'change his life' and open a 'delicatessen in the sun'. He was very particular in terms of what he wanted, which included teams of draughtsmen to prepare the most detailed designs for his shop. What he failed to take into account was the difference between running workmen on a multi-million pound dam project and running a team of local workers in rural France, and he ran way over schedule and budget.
>
> I happened to be in the area on the day it opened, and called by to say hello at 1pm. A sign on the door said 'Closed for Lunch'. There was no recognition of the fact that a food store might get valuable custom at lunchtime, or that potential French clients might be put off by or not understand a sign in English only. The business lasted three months, and the client lost a lot of money.

> ### Case Study: The English Grocers
> La Perfide Albion in the town of Saintes about an hour north of Bordeaux was set up, at least in part, to cater for the large number of Brits living in the area. Among its *spécialités anglaises* are English jams and chutneys, traditional biscuits, teas, beer, jelly (the bestseller), baked beans, Worcestershire sauce and Marmite – the last two even feature on its shop sign at 11 rue de l'Arc de Triomphe (**t** 05 46 94 24 98). Although business has been brisk, its owner, Nathaniel Waugh, is the first to admit that it's Brits rather than the French who often turn their noses up at the treats lining the shelves – many expats come in merely to tell him that they want to 'live like the French', or to look at the china, furniture and artworks that are also for sale. Still, somebody – British or French – must be craving the likes of Cadbury's chocolate, digestive biscuits, mint sauce, Branston pickle and PG Tips, for there's another English grocer, Plummers, not far away in the town of Gémozac (**t** 05 49 90 78 58).

give at least six months' notice, and the tenant is reimbursed the value of the goodwill of his business, which can be a lot of money.

As a prospective buyer, much of your time may be wasted by the fact that businesses in France will not generally give out accounts and financial information prior to your visit.

Translating

There's a huge demand for translation from French into English – and vice versa, but the basic principle is that that you should translate *into* your own native language. The quality of much of French-to-English translation in documents from French companies or on the Internet shows how much room for improvement there is, and there's a lot of scope for self-employed translators working freelance for one or more companies. That said, there's nothing to stop you translating from English into French more casually for English-speaking people who need simple documents translated into basic French or verbal translations.

Official translators (*traducteurs assermentés*) are sometimes required, for instance to translate formal documents for the office of the notary or in court, or to translate certificates of qualification. It's not too difficult to become one – precise formalities vary from place to place but it is usually awarded on the basis of experience and perceived ability rather than a written examination. In theory, judges can designate anyone of their choice (subject only to legal restrictions) as an *expert-traducteur*, but in general they appoint people from the *liste officielle* compiled by the Court of Appeal. Appointment to the list is for a probationary period of two years, then renewed for five years.

Court work can be sporadic, but on the whole this is an interesting, if often demanding, career that allows you to work where and when you want, usually at your own pace. It's also reasonably well paid, particularly if you translate for major commercial organisations. There is lots of work available in the major cities, but this is balanced out by the large number of potential translators.

Secretarial Work

There are lots of opportunities for bilingual secretaries in France; although many such roles are salaried, a significant of people work freelance, either through recruitment agencies or as their own business (some stretch the concept of freelance to all but breaking point). Secretarial work is generally well paid, and it often allows you to work flexible hours and from home, so it's ideal for those trying to juggle work with the demands of a family. Depending on the job, you may find yourself stuck at home on your own typing up endless transcriptions, or sitting in an office meeting interesting people and further improving your French.

The French national unemployment service's website, **www.anpe.fr**, can be a good source of contacts for those looking to break into this field.

E-Commerce

On the face of it, e-commerce, defined by the European Commission as 'any service normally provided for remuneration, at a distance, by electronic means and at the individual request of a recipient of services', and by the World Trade Organisation as 'the production, distribution, marketing, sale or delivery of goods and services by electronic means', gets round almost all the problems associated with living in France – you don't need business premises, you don't need to speak French, you don't need to become embroiled in the French administrative system, and you don't necessarily need to get involved with French taxes. But though this is an interesting option for someone wishing to run a business in France, e-commerce gives rise to its own set of problems, as well as requiring considerable technical skills and a good business and technical model.

The particular issues requiring attention include the legal status of your business, compliance with European directives on the subject, and the appropriate registration for tax for both the business and you personally. The tax situation is still a little vague and badly understood by tax officials in France, though the transactions are low-profile and so less likely to come to their attention.

The EU has created a huge legal framework covering all sorts of issues in relation to e-commerce, but the e-commerce directive is intended to supplement other parts of the existing law relating to 'information society services', including the data protection directives, the distance selling directive and existing European consumer protection legislation. It's all incredibly complicated, and the constraints of space mean we can only offer a very brief guide.

The **e-commerce directive** states that the 'information service provider' (and its website) must comply with the law in the EU state in which it is 'pursuing an economic activity using a fixed establishment for an indefinite period' (the country of origin rule). However, direct e-commerce transactions (see box above) may easily be effected through websites on 'off-shore' (non-EU) servers without being subject to the restrictions of European laws.

The **distance selling directive** requires the e-trader to provide the buyer with full information about the transaction prior to the conclusion of the contract, including the vendor's precise identity, the main characteristics and price of the goods or services, the payment terms, the right of withdrawal, the delivery costs, the duration of any limited offers, and the minimum duration of the contract where it involves recurrent deliveries. The buyer has the right to withdraw from a contract without penalties and without giving any reason for its withdrawal within a period of at least seven working days.

Under French law, the place of taxation of a direct e-commerce transaction depends on where the e-trader 'resides' and where the transaction is realised, as well as where the beneficiary is 'established'. Most of the double taxation treaties signed by France (see p.145) state that the country can't tax the profits of the enterprise of another country unless that enterprise carries on business in France through a 'permanent establishment' situated there. In this respect, its position with respect to income tax is similar to one with respect to VAT, where both employees and equipment (or a place of business) are required.

The place where the contract is performed also has VAT consequences under French VAT rules. The **VAT directive** says that a supply of goods and services within an EU member state by a 'taxable person' ('any person who carries out in any place any economic activity') shall be subject to VAT.

It's worth noting that general **development grants** are available for this kind of business. See pp.110–15 for information on grant aid.

> *Online, Offline: Beyond the Jargon*
>
> An indirect e-commerce transaction takes place when a vendor and a buyer conclude a contract via the Internet but perform their contractual obligations (for example, the delivery of goods or the performance of services, and payment of the purchase price) by means other than the Internet ('offline'). So the purchase of tangible goods always constitutes an indirect e-commerce transaction. This is also true of the supply of tangible goods in connection with the delivery of a service (such as the delivery of an airline ticket to a buyer).
>
> A direct e-commerce transaction is where a vendor and a buyer not only conclude the contract but also perform all their contractual obligations via the Internet ('online'). This is only possible if the goods purchased are intangible or the services are performed exclusively through the Internet or by other electronic means – this includes the purchase of software, films, music or information (such as the contents of a book) that are downloaded by the buyer.

Art

The French like artists nearly as much as they like farmers, and there is often significant aid available to a person wanting to set up in business as an artist, whether it be painting, sculpture, music, acting or circus performing, particularly if they are already recognised in their field. There's even a special Ministry of Culture and Communications website for foreign artists wanting to work or set up business in France, **www.artistes-etrangers.com**, with some useful links.

The position is less rosy for aspiring or part-time artists – there have been cuts in the French budget for art and culture, with total investment in the arts now not permitted to exceed 1% of the state budget (though the regions may provide additional funding if they have it). The criteria for artists receiving unemployment benefits have also been made more onerous – they must have worked a total of 507 hours in the previous 10½ months to receive benefits, and they will receive money for only eight months.

Gardening

There is substantial demand for English-speaking gardeners among British and other English-speaking people whose French isn't sufficient to deal with local workers, especially those with big gardens, those who are too old to do their own, and – most significantly – those who are absent for much of the year or who have investment properties with gardens that need to be kept in a good state. Such an enterprise would be considered a regular non-regulated business (see p.81). There is scope for earning a reasonable living from catering to the expat community, and you may also enjoy a better climate than 'back home'.

At a grander level, there are a number of British-owned garden centres, some in popular English-speaking areas and others competing with the French for French clients; see pp.62–3 for a discussion of running a shop in France.

Farming

About one-third of the total area of France is taken up by farmland, and the French respect farmers and agricultural produce in a way that has long since disappeared in Britain, if not quite in Ireland or the United States. The French government supports its farmers politically and, through the Common Agricultural Policy, financially, which has led many foreign farmers, most of them under the age of 35, to set up there. The French government encourages this by making grants to suitable applicants, with the type and extent of assistance varying from region to region. Most of it is available in areas that have suffered huge depopulation over the last 100 years (particularly the last 30 or 40 years), which, luckily, often happen to be places where foreigners want to set up, such as much of the central portion of France. These areas are also

Case Study: Grape Expectations

Bud break? Veraison? Double cordon? Bunch rot? Phylloxera? Drip line? Root-stock? Sometimes starting a new life means learning a new vocabulary to go with it. This was certainly the case for Patricia Atkinson, whose first professional incarnation was as a PR manager with an international bank in London. Her husband James worked as a financial consultant, and both flirted with the idea of leaving the rat race for the French countryside.

The couple eventually bought a property outside Bergerac in the Dordogne region, of which 4.5 hectares were planted to vine. Both around 40 years old at the time, Patricia and her husband hoped to make a few barrels of wine as a hobby, although they knew nothing about viticulture, and spoke only a few words of French. Before long, however, James grew ill and as the couple's savings dwindled, Patricia started to see her grape-growing hobby as a means for survival. Single-handedly she tended to the vineyard, pruned, learned to drive a tractor and operate a sprayer, and eventually mastered the techniques necessary for producing a quality crop. 'The French have great respect for people who work,' she says. 'It was very confusing at first and there was a steep learning curve. Learning French was essential.'

Thus marks her second professional incarnation as a *vigneron*. The couple eventually split, but Patricia's heart was too deeply rooted in the vineyard to leave what she had worked so hard to create. ('I had grown new muscles where I didn't know I had them.') She bought additional land to expand the vineyard and worked on marketing her merlot, cabernet sauvignon and cabernet franc. Her wines caught the attention of top retailers and appeared in Michel Roux's Waterside Inn, a three-star Michelin restaurant in Berkshire. Today, Patricia's winery, the Clos d'Yvigne (**www.cdywine.com**), produces some 70,000 bottles per year, of which two-thirds are exported to the UK market.

An inspiring story? Random House thought so when they bought Patricia's book *The Ripening Sun*, describing how she reinvented herself and detailing life on her vineyard. In her third professional incarnation as an accomplished author, a new vocabulary is the fruit of an excellent harvest.

where the land is cheapest. Those who have no previous experience of farming but are tempted to set up as farmers in France should think again, however – it involves long hours of back-breaking work in all weathers for minimal financial reward (most farmers in France make a very modest living of €20,000–30,000 a year). For amateurs, it's likely to end in ruin. This applies less to 'gentleman' or hobby farmers who are only really after a house, and for whom the question of profit or loss is academic, though even these have one or two obstacles to cross when trying to buy a farm in France.

Buying a farm is quite a lengthy process, and it is vital to get good professional advice from the outset to avoid wasting lots of money and time. Fortunately, there are several sources for such advice, from both the French government and other authorities and from private enterprises. Your first port of call should be the **town hall** (*mairie*), where staff know everything that is going on locally and can often be extremely helpful (in small towns where resources are limited they can take some time). Secondly, the **Chambre d'Agriculture**, which exists at departmental and regional level, has masses of information; see **www.paris.apca.chambagri.fr** for contacts. You should also contact the **Ministère de l'Agriculture, de l'Alimentation, de la Pêche et des Affaires Rurales (MAAPAR; www.agriculture.gouv.fr**) and the **Société d'Aménagement Foncier et d'Etablissements Rural (SAFER; www.safer.fr**), which lists properties for sale, offers a full range of consultation services, and has detailed records of land prices over many years, broken down into categories of land, including vineyards, and analysable by *département*, by region or nationally.

Still, this is a job that you can do with a limited command of French (though a knowledge of technical French is needed to converse with vets, suppliers and fellow farmers), and you will find that French farming communities can be very welcoming places, especially if you go to one of the depopulated areas where few foreigners have settled.

Your first step is to decide what type of farming you wish to pursue. In today's market, this involves a consideration of the average financial returns for each category, and consideration of the grant aid available (*see* pp.110–15). Make sure you take into account the threat to the continuation of the Common Agricultural Policy, or, at the very least, likely reductions in the payments made to farmers in western Europe. On the other hand, there are several ways in which you can maximise the income from your farm, including agritourism or other agribusiness, plus agencies that encourage alternative uses of farmland.

You then need to locate a suitable farm. There are agents specialising in agricultural property, or specialist websites such as **www.repertoireinstallation.com**, but in major rural areas most general estate agents will be able to locate farmland for you. A good farmer will be able to evaluate the quality of that land; the city slicker who has decided to become a farmer may not. It may also be sensible to take advice from someone local experienced in the type of agriculture you wish to pursue, who can guide you away from potential problems.

It's at this point that the fun begins. You may find that your farm is subject to various rights of preemption (*droit de préemption*), which could be contractual, relate to rights registered at the land registry, or arise by virtue of somebody's previous employment at the farm or in a number of other ways. If you wish to buy farmland, you have to obtain prior clearance by SAFER that they do not want the property or, at least, wait until their time for accepting the purchase right has expired. This is work that will normally be dealt with by the notary, but it is very important that you ensure that it has been done properly, and that the notary also eliminates the other rights (those of the *mairie*, tenants, and so on).

As part of the process of buying a farm, you need to deal with all of the matters necessary when buying an ordinary house, plus agricultural matters such as the state of the land in winter and summer, the adequacy of irrigation, the adequacy of access, the amounts of EU quota available for your chosen area of activity, the grant aid available, and other state aid and subventions. If, as is likely to be the case, you are also buying stock and machinery, you need to take these into account.

You are likely to need finance, for which expert guidance is essential, especially if you have no previous experience of running a farm. If you proceed with the purchase, you need permission from the agricultural department of the *département* to run the farm. Then you need to register for social security and other taxes; for the former there's a special entity, the Mutuelle Sociale Agricole. As you might expect, the social security payments and taxes demanded of farmers are at the lower end of the spectrum.

In addition to 'standard' French grants available to all industries (*see* pp.110–15), a number of special subventions are available to farmers. The state-sponsored **Centre National pour l'Aménagement des Structures des Exploitations Agricoles (www.cnasea.fr)** distributes public funds relating to almost all aspects of agriculture in France, including the installation of young farmers, the transfer of farming activity, and the modernisation of farms. The non-profit **Association Départementale pour l'Aménagement des Structures des Exploitations Agricoles (www.adasea.net)** assists rural development by issuing the contracts needed to carry out farming (*contrat territorial d'exploitation* or **CTE**), dealing with the transfer of undertakings between farmers, encouraging long-term farming (i.e, by assisting in the transmission of farmers from one generation to the next), and by helping farmers with feasibility studies, applications for finance and more general state aid and specific farming aid. It can also help farmers in their sometimes complicated relationships with the state, especially to do with regulations governing farming. For example, after a recent dry winter it gained permission for farmers in 77 *départements* to use their set-aside or fallow land for feeding animals. It also helps farmers who are finishing their working careers. The departmental agency of the Ministry of Agriculture, Food, Fisheries and Rural Affairs, called the **Direction Départementale de l'Agriculture et de la Forêt** or **DDAF (www.ddaf. cher.agriculture.gouv.fr)** covers many of the same areas of activity.

Small parts of these organisations' websites are translated into English, but there are also specific information sources for foreigners, most notably **Terres d'Europe SCAFR (Société de Conseil pour l'Aménagement Foncier Rural)**, 91 rue du Faubourg Saint-Honoré, Paris 75008, which is part of SAFER. Note also that one of the French Common Agricultural Policy's priorities is to promote the setting up of farms outside families to ensure the satisfactory renewal of farmholders, and its online guide to setting up as a farmer in France (**www. terresdeurope.net**) is indispensable preliminary reading.

Medicine

French healthcare is said to be the best in the world, but it's also a bureaucratic nightmare and an unsustainably expensive system, partly because French people are entitled to treatments that are not available under the British National Health or US insurance. Within the sector, however, there's enormous resistance to change, and there is little doubt that it will remain well paid as a profession, with working conditions that generally far exceed those of the UK.

The qualifications for doctors, general nurse, midwives, dentists, veterinary surgeons and pharmacists have been co-ordinated at EU level, allowing you to practise in any other EU country, though you normally have to validate your qualifications and prove that your command of French is sufficient.

Doctors

To work as a physician in France you need to be an EU resident or of Andorran, Tunisian or Moroccan citizenship, hold a medical degree issued in France or another country included on the list established by EU regulations (including the UK and Ireland) or any other degree obtained in a university of an EU country (where studies started before 20 December 1976), and hold a certificate stating that you have worked as a physician for at least three consecutive years, or for five years after graduating. You must also register at the **Tableau de l'Ordre de Médecins Français (www.conseil-national.medecin.fr)**. The rules of professional conduct (*déontologie*) are stated on the *ordre*'s website. The **British Medical Association (www.bma.org.uk)** can advise British and Irish citizens.

Other physicians, including those from the USA, have to register as first-year medical students. If they are accepted, they can obtain a *dispense de scolarité* covering the first and second cycle of study (*premier et deuxième cycle d'études médicales*) if they pass an exam covering the items taught during those years (basic sciences, including a wide range of health sciences such as anatomy, pharmacology, virology, immunology and cytology, healthcare provision, and core medical theory). They then have to follow the third cycle, which gives students the choice of doing an *internat* (residency) for two and a half years, resulting in a degree in general medicine, or competing for an internship position and specialising in a particular area of medicine after four to five years' further study. The national examination for specialised studies involves amassing an incredible amount of knowledge (six years' worth of medical studies), and practising problem-solving and critical thinking. It touches on more than 300 medical subjects broken down into three parts: a four-hour session of 200 multiple-choice questions, a two-hour session of 150 clinical cases (multiple choice), and six hours of eight diagnostic and therapy reports. Successful entrants into the full-time internship programme can work towards one of seven different diplomas. The final step to becoming a *docteur en médecine* is the completion of a thesis, the preparation for which may take a few weeks or a couple of years. You can then set up your office.

Nurses

Any European nurse (that is, one who has followed at least 10 years of primary and secondary school and at least three years of professional training, of which a third was theoretical teaching and at least half was clinical teaching) is technically free to work in the EU state of their choice, as an employee, a self-employed professional or a company. For further details, see **www.infirmiers.com**.

In practice, there are some hurdles to jump. First, you need to validate your nursing diploma with the **General Direction of Health**, the only institution in France authorised to deliver the certificates of conformity with the European requirements. You have to send a photocopy of the diploma (for the UK, a certificate of admission to the general part of the register delivered in Northern Ireland, in Wales, in Scotland and/or in England by the appropriate licensing body; for Ireland, a certificate of 'registered general nurse' delivered by An Bord Altranais, the nursing board); proof of marital status and nationality; a statement of all preceding employment (for any diploma dated before 29 June 1982); a certificate of character and good standing; a medical certificate testifying to your good physical and mental health; and proof that you have a sufficient knowledge of French (for this you must contact the Direction Départemental des Affaires Sanitaires et Sociales or DDASS of the area where you want to work). The authorities must answer your request within three months.

In the USA, the CGFNS (Commission on Graduates of Foreign Nursing School, 3624 Market St, Philadelphia, PA, 19104) will provide all the information necessary and take care of the organisation of the examinations of equivalence.

Dentists

Dental qualifications held by the nationals of EU countries are recognised in each member state. Each EU country has a designated information centre to advise on registration/licensure, and on any special internal requirements. In the UK this is the **General Dental Council** (**www.gdc-uk.org**), in Ireland the **Dental Council of Ireland** (**www.dentist.ie**).

Foreign dentists in France must register with the French Dental Association (**Conseil National de l'Ordre des Chirurgiens Dentistes**; **www.ordre-chirurgiens-dentistes.fr**) and provide proof of qualification, a letter of good standing and proof of fitness. The General Dental Council or Dental Council of Ireland has to certify many of these papers, so make sure to contact them as soon as possible. The French Dental Association's website has details of the conduct of dentistry in France.

Osteopaths

Osteopathy, a way of detecting and treating damaged parts of the body such as muscles, ligaments, nerves and joints, is now an official health practice, but the educational requirements, practice rules and legitimate scope of professional activity have not yet been harmonised within the EU.

The European Centre for Higher Training in Osteopathy in Paris (**Centre Européen d'Enseignement Supérieur de l'Ostéopathie** or **CEESO**; **www.ceeso.com**) can grant the qualification required in France. Its Registre des Ostéopathes de France provides guidelines in term of deontology and ethics and has issued a quality logo (**MROF**) for osteopaths who have been properly trained and act as ethical professionals, displayed in osteopaths' offices.

Masseurs/Masseuses

This area became quite complicated in January 2005, when the Court of Appeal in Versailles (by way of a judgment on an appeal from a criminal conviction for working as a masseur without the appropriate qualification) confirmed that any massage, whether for therapeutic ends or not, comes under the jurisdiction of the regulated profession of *kinésithérapeute* (medical masseur/masseuse), including various treatments that would not normally be thought of as massage (some cellulite treatments, for instance).

Those from an EU state or another qualifying state who have completed a qualifying course can work as a *masseur-kinésithérapeute* without the French diploma, but the French authorities can insist on an aptitude test, possibly accompanied by a period of traineeship of up to three years. *Masseurs-kinésithérapeutes* must, when they start work, register their qualification and authorisation to practise at the local *préfecture*, stating the areas of practice that they pursue. For more informations see **www.kinelegis.com**, the website of the **CNKE** (**Compagnie Nationale des Kinésithérapeutes Experts**).

Chiropractors

Chiropracty (neuromusculoskeletal manipulation, especially of the spinal column) has been recognised in France since 2002. You need to follow a six-year full-time course to become a registered Doctor of Chiropractic (*chiropraticien diplômé*). There is no Europe-wide acceptance of qualifications, however, making the situation rather murky for non-French residents. For guidance, contact the **Institut Franco-Européen de Chiropratique** (**IFEC; www.ifec.net**) or the **Association Française de la Chiropratique** (**www.chiropratique.org**), which are more trade associations than approved and regulated bodies. The former is growing, and played a significant part at the World Federation of Chiropractors Congress in Paris in 2001.

Complementary Medicine

The basic principle of freedom of movement and of work within the EU applies to complementary medical practitioners such as herbalists (*phytothérapeutes*). Acupuncturists and homeopaths must be registered doctors.

Complementary medical practitioners technically have the freedom to establish their own business in any EU member state they so desire, but the problem that surfaces here is whether their business (which will be classified as a liberal profession or *profession libérale*) is regulated – most complementary medical spheres of activity aren't. It's a bit of a Catch-22 situation in that, though your profession might not be a regulated one, you will almost certainly be required (as in almost all cases in France) to be a member of some professional organisation or other, despite the fact that there may not be an association appropriate for your needs or one that will accept you into membership

Associated Medical Activities

Orthophonistes (speech and language pathologists), *orthoptistes* (ophthalmologists), *ergothérapeutes* (occupational therapists), *psychomotriciens* (cognitive behavioural therapists), *pédicures-podologues* (podologists), *opticiens-lunetiers* (opticians and glasses makers), *audioprothésistes* (hearing-aid specialists), *manipulateurs d'électroradiologie médicale* (radiology technicians) and *techniciens de laboratoire d'analyses de biologie médicale* (medical laboratory technicians) are all regulated paramedical professions and part of the French healthcare system. Care assistants, auxiliary nurses, childcare nurses and one or two other specific areas are subject to special regulations.

To obtain an authorisation to practise, you must be an EU resident who has gained a suitable professional qualification in your home country, but that country has to be one that regulates the profession in question (if it doesn't, you have to have worked in the profession for at least two years). Citizens of EU member states who have obtained a relevant professional qualification in a third party state (for example, the USA) can practise if they have also worked for at least three years in the profession concerned. Those from outside the EU must gain the French qualification in France.

You have to apply for recognition of your qualification to the **Ministère de la Santé, Direction Générale de la Santé – Bureau des Professions Paramédicales**, 8 avenue de Ségur, 75350 Paris Cedex 07. If your qualification is not considered sufficiently close to the French qualification, you will have to enrol to qualify in France but can apply for a full or partial exemption from study. The rules are complicated and depend on the profession you're seeking to join.

Note that there is no exemption on the basis of previous experience or study for the *diplôme d'état de technicien en analyses biomédicales* (DETAB).

Continuing What You Did at Home

Many people who have decided to go to live in France instinctively think about starting afresh career-wise; indeed, doing something different from what they've been engaged in for the last 10 or 20 years constitutes much of the attraction of moving in the first place. Others may be emigrating for a new way of life or for an increased quality of life but want to continue with a form of work that they have enjoyed. The latter has a number of advantages – it's one less adjustment to make, you are experienced in your field and may even be quite senior within it, and you will probably, at least initially, earn more money this way. It may also be a way of staying in contact with colleagues and friends in your home country.

The increasing numbers of people in this second category in turn fall into two sub-categories – those who want to continue in their former line of activity and carry on servicing pre-existing customers, and those who want to cater to new customers in France. Among recent people who have relocated to France but pursued their old careers supplying the same people are computer software writers, computer helpline workers, accountants, scientists, day traders on the financial markets, and business consultants. What they all have in common is the ability to work from almost anywhere – either their business can be done by phone and e-mail (with the odd visit to see clients), or they deal with a physical product that is small enough to be shipped cheaply wherever necessary.

Continuing your old occupation with new French clients can be more complicated. Much hinges on whether you have the level of French necessary to service them professionally; if you don't, then, unless you have special skills that are in short supply locally, few French clients will use your services in preference to those of a French person with whom they can communicate freely. Exceptions to this are when British, Irish or US companies based in France need

Case Study: the Dental Technician

Adam ran a successful business manufacturing dental plates and false teeth for local dentists from his small workshop in an unprepossessing part of Sheffield. When he and his wife relocated to the Charente-Maritime to indulge in their twin passions for sailing and walking, he simply put his equipment in the back of a transit van and drove it to his new home. He continued to carry out the same work for the same clients, receiving orders by e-mail or by fax (as before) and despatching them by courier. Deliveries took 24–48 hours longer than they had in Sheffield, but he discussed this with his customers and they worked around it.

Those in a similar position must remember, as Adam did not (at least to begin with), to import their equipment officially, to register their business in France, and to declare their income to the French tax authorities rather than continuing to pay British tax.

> ### Case Study: The Hotline Consultant
> George worked for a computer firm based near Reading, providing hotline asssistance to its customers. He'd been working for the company since the mid 1980s and knew their range of specialist products inside out – indeed, when it came to one or two of the older products, he was the only person in the office who remembered that the company had sold them and knew how they worked. He wanted to take early retirement in France but also to do some part-time work to supplement his pension and keep himself mentally stimulated. His first idea was to set up a small business servicing computer hardware for the large number of retired Brits and Americans in the south of France, who would value him for his English-language skills. But when he told his employer about his project, they suggested that he continued providing their customers with hotline assistance from France. Even if he spent an hour on the phone to a customer, it would only cost £3–4, while the firm would save the cost of deskspace and all of its associated expenses. If George couldn't resolve the problem over the phone, he could access the customer's computer using remote-control software, just as he had in Reading.
> This all worked exceptionally well, not least because the firm's customers got to deal with the same person who'd been helping them for years, which gave them a sense of security. Now, a few years down the line, advances in communications technology, especially the introduction of software making George's international phone calls free of charge, make this an even more viable option.

fluent English-speakers – one Scottish computer specialist who spoke little French spent months updating the networking systems of American businesses in Paris, which largely involved talking to staff in the main office in Houston. Other areas of activity worth considering in this context are web design (perhaps working alongside French web designers to make English-language versions of their sites), IT consultancy and teaching English as a foreign language (TEFL; see p.168).

Of course, there is absolutely nothing stopping you from combining these approaches, or from starting off servicing existing British customers or American customers and gradually building up your French language skills and a French customer base.

Other Small Business Ideas

- **Accountants or solicitors**: Few French accountants are familiar with foreign tax laws, especially when complicated situations involving both the UK and France arise, perhaps to do with inheritance laws or double taxation treaties.

- **Art or furniture restoration**: Many foreigners, especially in small towns, open labs where they can concentrate on paint-stripping and the like.
- **Business services**: Your English-language skills could be put to use by those seeking to organise conventions, seminars or logistics (e.g. transport and accommodation) for businesses. This may be a thriving field for experienced consultants.
- **Computer technology**: There is always a need for people versed in the latest hardware and software – especially webpage-designing programmes such as as Dreamweaver or Flash that are sold in English. You could open a studio or consultancy for building web pages or managing websites.
- **Estate agents**: Qualified English-speaking agents with regional knowledge to help Brits buy French property are always in demand.
- **Health foods**: French are increasingly attracted to 'health foods', resulting in a need for organic groceries, frozen yoghurt shops and vegetarian restaurants.
- **Relocation services**: Many entrepreneurs make money from precisely what you're seeking to do: work and live in France. Relocation or expatriate consultants can help foreigners wade through bureaucratic procedures such as getting a work permit, or setting up a lease to let property. They can also help change ownership of a car and give tips on how to save on one's electricity or gas bill.
- **Schools**: Some foreigners open English-language kindergartens, others target French students who need help preparing for exams or writing CVs in English, or adults seeking tuition in fitness, pottery or painting.
- **Theatres and art galleries**: The French have a soft spot for the arts. Why not contribute to the entente cordiale by creating a space in which non-French and French artists can showcase their craft side by side?
- **TV services**: Many expats open small businesses to help them install television satellite services for Brits who can't live without the BBC or SkyNews.
- **Wedding services**: The laws governing foreign weddings in France are complicated, but the popularity of 'destination weddings' continues to rise. You could cater to engaged couples looking for a wedding venue, photographer, florist, caterer and chauffeur.

Setting Up a Business in France

First Steps 78
Taking Advice **78**
Choosing a Structure **79**
Licences and Registration **86**
Planning 87
The Business Plan **87**
Your 'Life Plan' **95**
Working from Home 96
Relating to a 'Parent' Business 96
Setting Up Your Own Business or Buying Into an Existing Business 102
Raising Finance 106
Ways of Delaying Full Financial Commitment **106**
Grants and Aid **110**
French Banks and Loans **116**
Acquiring Business Premises 116
Employing Staff 118
Summary: A Step by Step Guide to Setting Up Your Business 121

First Steps

The process of setting up a business in France sounds horrendously complicated, but if you were a French person setting up, say, a restaurant in the UK, you would find it just as complicated. The main problem is not so much the complexity but that you are not familiar with the organisations and structures involved, so relatively minor issues can seem overwhelming – for instance, if you have lived in the UK a long time, you will find it relatively easy to locate the town hall, VAT office, Inland Revenue office, Environmental Health Department or whatever it might be, whereas in a strange town in France you will not.

Taking Advice

Your very first step in setting up your own business in France is to discuss your idea with your lawyer and/or accountant, who can advise you on assessing the potential market and the existing competition, and on preparing a business plan. They may have years of experience and may be able to tell you, off the top of their head, whether something you're trying to do is impossible or almost certainly doomed to failure. They can also tell you whether you need specific permission to set up your business. A lawyer is also needed if you intend to buy or rent premises from which to run your business, or want to buy a business. Additionally, you will need to give some early consideration to the taxation and other issues that will determine the form of legal ownership of the business that is most appropriate in your case. You will have to consult a financial adviser to obtain loans, grants or a mortgage. A financial/business adviser can also help focus the business on your personal circumstances.

Before appointing any adviser, check on their level of experience and make sure you're comfortable with them – if you have an adviser whose general approach to life is totally different from yours, you're not likely to appreciate the reasoning behind the recommendations they make.

Unless your business is to be large or complicated, about 90 minutes should suffice for the initial meeting, so it won't be expensive (whereas setting off down a dead end without taking advice may well be). It should leave you with a

Chambers of Commerce

To British, American and Irish people, 'chamber of commerce' suggests a relatively modest enterprise, whereas *chambres de commerce et d'industrie* in France are key parts of the state's machinery for governing business. They are well funded and very active, and have considerable power.

Contact with your chamber of commerce or chamber of tradespeople (Chambre de Métiers de l'Artisanat/Maison des Entreprises) is an essential step for anyone thinking of setting up a business in France, particularly given their extensive and very helpful websites (*see* pp.239–40).

list of further actions to take to progress your idea to the point where you have a workable business plan. You may be lucky and have only one or two small items to take care of; more often, it's such a long list that six months or more can elapse before a client is ready for a second meeting to finalise plans.

In the meantime, there may be further research your advisers can be doing, especially if you are the first person undertaking a particular activity. You may require more detailed tax advice than they were able to give at the preliminary meeting, or more research may be needed to assess the best legal, tax and practical structure for the ownership and exploitation of your business. This can be agreed after the initial meeting, and a budget fixed.

Choosing a Structure

The business structure you will choose depends on your professional activity and desired tax liability. They range from small businesses for self-employed people to large businesses with plans to be publicly listed. Before you begin, consult your local Chambre de Commerce et d'Industrie (CCI) or Chambre de Métiers et de l'Artisanat; *see* box, left. They offer literature and courses on starting a business, including the CCI's English-language *Setting up a Business in France for Non-French Nationals* (€7).

Your choice of structure for your business is of great importance, first because if you choose the wrong structure, this can severely hamper the growth of the business, and it can be costly to restructure later on. Secondly, the structure determines the formalities needed to register the business, the degree of personal risk you assume and – last but not least – your tax liabilities.

It is more likely that simpler, cheaper structures will be used by smaller businesses, but that is a matter of practice, not of law. Structure is something on which you should always take professional advice, but before doing so (or before taking the advice), make sure you read as much as possible of the material that is available on websites such as **www.pme.gouv.fr**, **www.apce.com** and **www.francebritishchamber.com**.

What is best for you will depend entirely on your own personal circumstances and, in the case of joint ventures, the personal circumstances of your partners. What follows can only skim the surface of a very complicated situation. Seeking early professional advice about the appropriate structures and how best to put them in place will save you a lot of money.

Sole Trader/Proprietorship (*Entreprise Individuelle*)

This is the business structure most foreigners choose, as it is relatively simple, informal and flexible. Sole proprietorships are businesses under the control of a single individual, who has total liability for its assets and liabilities, so it is suitable for small businesses involving little or no financial risk or large investment.

Size of Business

The French 'translation' for the British acronym **SME** ('small or medium-sized enterprise') is **PME** (*petites et moyennes entreprises*); outside the EU they're often known as **SMB**s ('small and medium-sized businesses'). In 2005 the EU introduced a new common definition of SMEs, purportedly to help avoid the unfair allocation of aid caused by governments meaning something different by the term. However, the result actually makes things more complex.

It divides businesses under the SME umbrella into 'Micro', 'Small', 'Medium' and 'Other' on the basis of their number of employees, turnover and size of their balance sheet. Micro businesses have fewer than 10 employees and an annual turnover and balance sheet of less than €2 million; 'small' ones have fewer than 50 employees and an annual turnover and balance sheet of less than €10 million; and 'medium-sized' ones have fewer than 250 employees, an annual turnover of less than €50 million and a balance sheet of less than €43 million. Anything above this is 'Other'. SMEs also have to conform to certain criteria of independence that basically forbid them from being linked to another enterprise with a view to splitting its activities into several parts, thus creating several small and medium enterprises that can unfairly benefit from the rules.

To complicate matters further, the French are still widely using their old definition of PMEs (fewer than 20 employees and a turnover of less than €5 million). They also have the peculiarly French category of TPE or tiny enterprise, which is not well defined.

'Small' and 'medium-sized' enterprises account for 99% of EU enterprises and provide about 65 million jobs within the Union. The French website www.pme.gouv.fr has lots of information about the creation and transfer of ownership of such enterprises and the structural options.

It's important to note that the categorisation of your business as a PME or a **TPE** does not make any difference to the choice of structures available to you when it comes to setting up the enterprise. These are simply shorthand labels helpful for administrative purposes.

The Loi Dutreil of 2003 (*see* p.5) was a significant breakthrough in that it allows, in certain circumstances, for the proprietor of an *entreprise individuelle* to declare in front of a notary that he or she wishes to run the business on the basis that their home is immune from seizure from creditors. There are quite a few formalities associated with this, including the registration of that declaration at the Land Registry and the publication of the fact that you have made the declaration, but it is a useful facility designed to encourage more people to set up in business in this simple manner without risking destitution if it goes wrong. You can also protect some of your assets by registering them in the name of your wife or partner, but you need to make sure that your 'matrimonial regime' does not include community of assets (*see* pp.197–8).

If you start a sole proprietorship, you report all profits and losses on your personal French income tax return and pay income tax as an individual on the profit generated by the business as well as any other sources of income you enjoy. You will also be liable to pay VAT (assuming you cross the VAT threshold) and social security payments once you are registered, but you can choose to pay a fixed reduced social security rate of €2,580 for the first year of the life of the business and €1,874 for the first half of the second year instead of the fixed contribution of about 35% of your total earnings before tax. (See pp.127–56 for more about your personal tax liabilities.) That said, you benefit from none of the protection afforded to salaried employees or to businesses registered with the Chambre de Commerce, and unemployment benefit is an optional extra. For sickness, retirement and family benefits, you have to register with the appropriate entity.

There are four basic classifications of *entreprise individuelle*: *professions libérales*, *commerçants*, *artisans* and *professions agricoles*.

The ***professions libérales*** are what we would think of as the 'classic' professions and includes doctors, lawyers, architects and accountants, although there is no exhaustive list. In fact, about 70% of French workers operate within the *professions libérales*, and many activities included under this category would not be seen as professions in the UK or USA. In essence, if you are selling something intangible or a service, you are likely to be in a *profession libérale*.

Professions libérales are split into '**regulated**' (*réglementées*) and '**unregulated**' professions (*non-réglementées*), though all are subject to general regulation. The 'regulated' professions include the traditional professions listed above plus many more, on the basis that you need to have a specific qualification in order to undertake them. Some are regulated under the EU general systems directive; others (including doctors, nurses, midwives, pharmacists and vets) under sector-specific directives. The EU has attempted to compile a list of all regulated professions and the equivalency rules for each, see: **www.europa.eu.int/comm/internal_market/qualifications/regprof/professions/dsp_index.cfm**. For more on the recognition of qualifications, *see* pp.157–9.

Commerçants are shopkeepers and traders, hoteliers and landlords – people who buy or sell goods or specified services deemed not to form part of the *professions libérales*. The formalities and regulations associated with being an individual trader depend on the nature of the activity – the rules relating to running a hotel and a shop differ, for instance – but in all cases be prepared for a significant amount of regulation, inspection and general interference from the various organs of the state and its quangos. *Commerçants* register with the Chambre de Commerce, not the Chambre de Métiers (*see* p.124).

Artisans loosely translate as craftspeople – generally, they make things or work with their hands. It would be a mistake, however, to think of them solely in the sense of stonemasons, potters and so on – the list includes taxi firms, transport companies, ambulances, homecare workers, cleaners, jewellers, musicians, advice services, car mechanics, cooks and lingerie manufacturers. Setting up a business as an artisan is not the same as working in one of the activities – it's a lifestyle choice that involves investing in an enterprise run on a human scale.

There are four basic hurdles to cross to have your business registered as that of an artisan. First, the activity in which you wish to engage must be one of the 250 or so listed as *artisanale* on the **Nomenclature d'Activités Française de l'Artisanat (NAFA)**. Secondly, at the time of its creation the business must have fewer than 10 salaried employees. Thirdly, you may be required to have a professional qualification if you wish to engage in one of the following activities:

- The maintenance and repair of vehicles and machines.
- Construction.
- The maintenance and repair of buildings.
- The installation, maintenance and repair of equipment with fluids or equipment used for the production of food or the heating of buildings or for electronic installations.
- Chimney-sweeping.
- Healthcare or cosmetic care outside the scope of the medical or paramedical.
- Making dental prosthetics.
- The preparation or manufacture of fresh meats.
- *Rôtisserie*.
- Butchery.
- Running a *charcuterie* or fishmongers.
- Ice-cream manufacture.
- Certain activities relating to animal care and veterinary care (*activités maréchal-ferrant*).

Any person wanting to run a company that carries out any of these activities must have the relevant qualification (the CAP or a diploma equivalent in status) or working experience of at least three years acquired as a self-employed or salaried worker in that field.

Historically, most artisans have worked as sole traders or in the form of small groupings or co-operatives, but more and more are now working through the vehicle of a limited company (*see* pp.84–6).

Entreprises agricoles are related to farming but extend also to forestry, fish-farming and other such activities, which are regulated by the Chambre d'Agriculture. *See* pp.66–9 for information about foreign farmers in France.

Partnerships

Partnerships as we are familiar with them under Anglo-Saxon law are little used in France. When they are, they are normally set up in the form of a *société en nom collectif.* As in the case of a sole proprietorship, partnerships have no capital requirement, and the profits and losses are passed on to the partners, who are also responsible for any debts that are incurred.

The transfer of ownership of any of the following partnership entities is normally subject to transfer tax of 4.89%, though there are exceptions. The taxation of income and gains is dealt with on pp.127–56. Partnerships can be set up for a maximum of 99 years.

Société en Nom Collectif (SNC)

This is an organisation formed by two or more people, who can contribute as much or as little as they wish. They are treated as sole traders for many purposes but they are collectively responsible for all the debts of the business. Each individual is taxed on their share of the partnership profits as if the partnership did not exist. Management of the entity is by a director/partner chosen by all of the partners; they need not be a partner in the business. The manager has the right to bind the partnership.

The constitution (and dissolution) of a *société en nom collectif* is registered with the commercial court (*tribunal de commerce*). The rules relating to its management are fairly simple, and the costs of running it are quite a lot lower than those associated with a commercial company. The other main advantages of an SNC are that it is fiscally transparent and very flexible. The downside is the unlimited liability.

Société Civile Immobilière (SCI)

This type of partnership is used for the purposes of owning property and must have at least two members. It is governed and managed in much the same way as the SNC. It is invisible to the tax office in the sense that the income and capital gains of the *société* are treated as the incoming gains of the members who are part of it.

Britons setting up a *société civile immobilière* need to be aware of three main issues. First, they are limited to real estate and can therefore be used to own and let unfurnished property but not furnished accommodation such as a *gîte*. In the latter case, the SCI, if it owns the property, will have to let the house to another entity – either an individual or a company – and that entity will have to let the property to the tenant, which confuses the tax situation a considerable degree. Secondly, if you are resident in the UK, the use of a property you own through an SCI can give rise to some unfortunate tax consequences in the form of a charge to tax of a so-called 'benefit in kind'. If you are deemed by the British authorities to be either the director or shadow director (someone who pulls the strings but is not technically a director) of the SCI, you will be treated as having received the benefit in kind every time the company allows *you* to use the property without your having to pay for it. The third issue is that SCIs are quite expensive to set up – they typically cost approximately €2,000–2,750.

The main attractions of this form of ownership are the fact that for non-residents in France the shares can pass to whoever they like on their death and not be caught up in the French inheritance system, and the closed ownership and great flexibility it offers. The main downside is the fact that it cannot engage in commercial activity.

Société en Commandité par Actions (SCA)

This is a form of limited partnership with active and sleeping partners. The active partners (a minimum of one) have unlimited liability; that of the sleeping partners (minimum three) is limited to the capital contributed. The minimum capital necessary is €38,100, and a statutory auditor is required. The partnership pays corporate tax rather than enjoying fiscal transparency.

This structure is little used but does have a place, thanks, in the main, to its great flexibility in terms of raising capital.

Société Civile

This is a non-trading entity that can, however, be used for transactions involving real estate or agriculture. The management and taxation are similar to the other forms of partnership.

Société d'Exercice Libérale

This special type of partnership set up within the liberal professions (see p.81) is common among doctors and lawyers. The main feature by which it differs from other partnerships is the fact that it can be charged corporation or company rather than individual tax, which may result in a lower tax bill. The partnership can employ non-partner staff.

Société de Fait

This is a *de facto* partnership that has not been constituted in accordance with the law but arises by the mere activity of the people in it. If two or more people get together and, without any paperwork, engage in a commercial activity in what would appear to the authorities to be a partnership, then they will be treated as such. The most likely way in which a *société de fait* will arise is where two people jointly own a property in France and let it. If you are in this situation or likely to be so, it's important to get good advice as how to minimise your tax liabilities because the company (although it doesn't exist) has to pay corporate taxes on its profits, instead of the individual 'partners' each being responsible for their proportion of those profits and paying simple income tax on them.

Limited Companies/Corporations

By forming a corporation, you're protected against liabilities that are incurred by the enterprise, except where the original investment is concerned. If the corporation goes bankrupt, shareholders' personal effects cannot be taken to pay off debts.

There are different kinds of corporations, each with its own set of capital requirements. You generally need at least two members, and you must contribute the capital prescribed by the law as a bare minimum. All can be managed by a single director or board of directors, and all can be fully foreign-owned. They are subject to income tax, TVA and corporation tax.

The setting up of the company must be registered with the clerk of the commercial court and advertised in the *Journal Officiel*, and the company must be registered with the Registry of Commerce and Societies. It must have an official registered office, but this can be – and often is – a home. The directors must meet various minimum requirements regarding their previous conduct and their ongoing conduct *vis-à-vis* the business. If the company is engaged in activities that are restricted and regulated, the directors must be qualified to pursue them.

Entreprise Unipersonnelle à Responsabilité Limitée (EURL)

The *entreprise unipersonnelle à responsabilité limitée* forms an exception to the general rule stated above in that it only comprises one person. The main reason for creating an EURL is to enjoy limited liability rather than the unlimited liability of the sole trader, and it is simple and cheap to set up and run – the minimum capital required is €1 and the cost of setting up is usually about €300. If your business grows to take in more 'partners', it is very easy to turn it into a SARL (*see* below). The owner of the business (the shareholder) is not treated as a salaried employee, which dramatically reduces the amount of social security contributions he or she has to pay. It can be set up so as either to be fiscally transparent or so that it pays corporate taxes, which can be an advantage.

On the downside, the company has to abide by certain rules of conduct. If it does not, it will lose its limited liability and be reclassified as a sole trader.

Société à Responsabilité Limitée (SARL)

The most popular form of corporation is the *société à responsabilité limitée*, a privately owned standard small limited company ideal for small businesses or shops. Cheap and simple both to set up and operate, it must be formed with 2–50 shareholders, and a managing director (*gérant*) must be appointed who is held financially accountable if managerial fault is found (the other shareholders are only responsible for the value of their shares).

A yearly audit is not required unless profits exceed certain pre-established limits. On a sale of the shares, French transfer tax is payable at 4.89%.

Société Anonyme (SA)

This is the equivalent of the British public limited company (plc) – its shares can be (but don't have to be) listed on the Stock Exchange. Its greater cost and complexity make it better suited for larger operations (the minimum capital requirement is €38,100). The minimum number of shareholders is seven, and it has a management structure intended to provide the necessary supervision to protect shareholders' interests.

Société par Actions Simplifiées (SAS)

This is a smaller version of the SA, designed, as the name suggests, to be simpler to operate. Its flexibility and less complicated operating requirements make it interesting for joint ventures (there must be at least two companies as shareholders, with a minimum capital of about €250,000 each, plus a minimum capital for the company of €38,100), but it is not generally used by small businesses. There is also a 'one-man band' version, the **SASU**.

Société Coopérative Ouvrière de Production (SCOP)

This workers' co-operative is a special form of SARL or SA where at least 51% of the shares are owned by the people working in the business. It has a certain number of tax advantages for people in that situation.

Foreign Companies

There is nothing to stop you doing business in France through the vehicle of a UK-based company or one elsewhere in the EU (in some cases, you can do business through a company registered in a non-EU state), but there are limits as to your activities. And if that company has a permanent establishment in France, it is going to be treated, sooner or later, as a French company for tax purposes and will be liable to taxation on (at least) all of the income generated in France. It will also be liable to pay social security contributions to its staff engaged in activities in France. If you are thinking of using a non-French company for your business purposes in France, take detailed tax advice before doing so.

Licences and Registration

Special permits and licences are needed for various types of business. To sell *brocante*, for example, you need two licences: the first is to sell used furniture and the second is to sell from a moveable stand (as opposed to a shop in a fixed location). There is a special office at the **Préfecture** that issues these licences.

The next step is to call the **Centre de Formalités des Entreprises (CFE)** to set up your business. Before you make the appointment, make sure your paperwork is in order and that you have copies of any provisional licences. At the appointment, you choose the business structure you want (*entreprise individuelle*, SARL, EURL or whatever). You must deposit an amount of money equal to the amount of your liability. Bring other documents, such as your marriage licence and residency papers. You should leave the meeting with provisional papers allowing you to start your business, and a week or two later receive confirmation by post that your business has been registered. To set up a more complicated business, seek professional help from an accountant or solicitor.

Note that before they can apply for their permits and licences, **non-EU citizens** need to apply for the right kind of *carte de séjour* at the Préfecture, or change the status of the one they have. If you are setting up, say, as an antiques dealer, you want a *carte de commerçant étranger*. To get it, you must fill out a 15-page questionnaire (*dossier de carte de commerçant étranger*), which you must submit together with a business plan complete with financial statements. The Chambre de Commerce et d'Industrie offers a five-day course, '*Cinq jours pour entreprendre*', that explains how to fill in the forms and the questionnaire. You should receive your *carte* about four to six weeks after application.

Planning

People thinking of moving to France and setting up business there would be well advised to make two different plans, both in writing. The first, the business plan, is essential – not legally but practically, since if you don't do it your business is much more likely to fail. The life plan is probably even more useful in that it will save you from forgetting critical issues in the fog of your move.

The Business Plan

A business plan is simply a way of saying how you will get from where you are now to where you want to be in the future. It doesn't have to be long and complicated – few businesses need more than 50 pages, and a small one can usually be reported in 10 pages of text plus financial statements. Research has shown that businesses with a plan are much more likely to survive – and grow much faster – than those without a plan. A plan will also help you keep track of the business once it has started – everyone gets wrapped up in the day- to-day running of their business, but you need to stand back regularly and review its progress against your targets, assess what customers think and check that profits are being made.

> *Six Good Reasons for Preparing a Business Plan*
>
> • To avoid wasting money – you need to identify whether the new enterprise will be viable.
>
> • To persuade your bank or other funders to lend you money – most banks require a business plan before considering a loan application.
>
> • To open a bank account. Some French banks now require a rudimentary plan before opening any business account
>
> • To support grant applications – many organisations require business plans as part of the application process.
>
> • To help you and your staff understand what's required for success.
>
> • Because the first step towards creating a successful new business is to state clearly what you want to achieve, how and when.

Key Principles in Preparing a Business Plan

- Keep it as simple as possible, tailored to the needs and size of the business.
- Give yourself time to think through the plan, to develop it, and to discuss it with others.
- Be positive but not over-optimistic.
- Be completely honest – ignoring or hiding any major problems may run you into serious difficulties later, and you won't get away with it.
- Talk to others who are already running similar enterprises. Use their best practice to help your business, and find out what problems they had to overcome.
- Involve whoever will be working with you in the new enterprise, e.g. partners or staff.
- Don't underestimate the time it will take to set up the new venture.
- Don't underestimate how much is needed to fund the business, i.e. to cover capital costs and day-to-day running costs. Many new enterprises cost a lot more than expected because not all the costs had been identified at the outset.
- Focus on what customers want, and how to market to them.
- Identify the skills you and your staff need to be successful.
- Think about what makes the new enterprise 'tick', and how competitors will respond to you.

Though they are absolutely essential, there is a lot of nonsense spoken about business plans, and a whole industry has grown up around the preparation of them. That said, producing one according to the generally approved structure (there is no standard format) will both help you and make it more likely that you will obtain the necessary finance and other assistance for your business. If you deviate too much from this structure, the person reading the plan may find it difficult to understand, and this in turn may stop them from studying it in detail or lead them to conclude that you are not sufficiently knowledgeable to produce a business plan and therefore unlikely to be successful in business. Even at the best of times, business plans submitted to venture capitalists are almost all rejected.

The first principle is prepare your business plan yourself – no one else will understand your ideas as you do, and if you don't have major input into the plan, you will not understand or be able to explain it, and you may not fully understand the risks involved. It's your money, so make sure you stay in control. That said, you must take good professional advice, and your lawyer and accountant should be able to help with the financial forecasts and advise you on the tax implications and structural requirements of your new business. Other specialist professional advisers may also be necessary.

Before you prepare the plan, think through the following points:

- Who will read the plan and why?
- Have you researched the idea fully?
- Will the business or project be viable?
- Do you have the necessary skills to run the project? If not, how will you get them?
- Have you considered what legal, regulatory and training requirements you may have to meet?
- What will the legal status of the business be?
- Where will the business be based?
- Who will your customers be?
- What will you need to buy and how much will it cost?
- How much capital can you invest and how much will you need to borrow?
- Would someone experienced in the field and independent put their money into the project?

A British Business Plan

Most of our clients start off by preparing a British-style business plan, which differs greatly from French plans, because they are familiar with the structure. This is not wasted time – the exercise of preparing the British plan will greatly facilitate the preparing of the French plan, and the thought processes will be useful to the development of the business.

The report will, typically, include sections similar to those set out below, though there are no rigid rules.

Executive Summary

This could be a detachable page stapled to the front of the plan, which would allow it to be tailored to different audiences by changing the emphasis slightly – this doesn't mean that you should tell people what you think they want to hear, but that different people will be reading the plan for different purposes and have slightly different expectations of it. First impressions count, so make sure it is positive, realistic and well presented. Keep it to a maximum of one or two pages.

- Summarise the key points from each section of the main report (so write this last, after you have produced the main sections).
- Use tables and graphs to summarise the financial details.
- Try to capture the essential elements of your new venture, and convey why you are enthusiastic about it and how you plan to make it a success.
- Outline what you are trying to achieve by undertaking the new venture; what is the rationale behind the project?

• End with a 'summary of the summary', specifically designed for use by banks or other lenders. How much do you want to borrow? Why do you want to borrow? How will you be able to repay the interest? When will you be able to repay the loan? Could you survive a reversal of fortune? What security do you have for the loan? Why (from your point of view and theirs) is this project worthwhile?

Performance of an Existing Business

Briefly describe the size and nature of any current business that you are thinking of taking over. Include its legal trading status (e.g. partnership, limited company, see pp.79–86) and any links to other businesses, for example as part of a group of companies.

- Summarise the performance of the business in terms of profit and loss.
- Give accounts for the last three years.
- Give a statement of assets and liabilities.
- If the business has any current underlying problems, explain what you are going to do to address them.
- State the current strengths, weaknesses, opportunities and threats.

New Product or Service

- Explain what your new product or service is.
- Explain what your customers will get that they cannot get elsewhere.
- Lay out the disadvantages or weak points.
- Assess your customers' future needs.

Marketing Plan

Summarise your market research:

- What is the market you will be selling to?
- Which segments of the market do you plan to target, e.g. local customers, families, retired people, expats?
- How large is each market segment?
- What are the important trends? Is the market growing, static or declining? What is the evidence to support those trends?
- What is the likely demand for your product/service?
- What research have you undertaken to assess the market? Attach results.
- Who are the likely customers (what categories or segments do they fall into) and where are they located?
- Do you have any customers already waiting? If so, who?
- Identify who will be responsible for implementing the marketing plan, indicate who has helped you to prepare it and name the sources of the key information.

The Competition
- Who are the competitors and what do they offer?
- How will your service/product be better or differ from your competitors'?
- Why will customers come to you rather than your competitors?
- Are there other businesses similar to your proposal operating in the local area? If so, what effect will your project have on their business? How are they likely to respond?

Legislation
Where legislation will have a major influence on the new venture, explain how you plan to comply with it.

Pricing
Outline your pricing policy in relation to that of your competitors and the quality of your product/service. How do you plan to respond to changes in market conditions?

Promotion and Branding
- Give details of how you plan to distribute, promote and sell your product/service. Include a timetable of marketing activities for up to the first three years. Indicate how much you expect to spend on each item.
- Provide information on any test marketing you have undertaken.
- Explain how you will promote your product, e.g. leaflets, advertising, direct mail, the Internet.
- Explain how you plan to brand your venture, and assess the importance of marketing material and packaging.

Project Costs
Summarise the costs associated with setting up the new enterprise, with reference to detailed quotations if available. Cover the main elements of the capital investment programme, explaining how they contribute to the overall plan. You should include all of the capital costs. List the main items of expenditure, clearly stating the project costs and the timing of the investments.

Projected Sales
Clearly state your sales targets for the first three years. Don't be over-optimistic – consider when you will really start selling, whether seasonality is a factor, the proportion of enquiries likely to turn into sales, the volume you will be able to sell, and the length of time it will take to collect payment.

Project Funding
Indicate how the project costs are going to be funded, show the amounts that are to be sourced from personal funding, from any investors and from grants. They might include:

- Your own resources, such as cash reserves or sale of assets.
- Borrowings, such as an overdraft facility, commercial loan, mortgage, loan from private individual or business, etc.
- Investors: who; how much; do you have proof?
- Other private contributions, i.e sponsorship or gifts in kind.
- Grant aid: identify the claims that you would like to make.

Financial Projections (Spreadsheets/Graphs)

- Provide a three-year cashflow forecast. Some people panic at the thought of producing a three-year forecast, but it's important to understand that, although it needs to be as accurate as possible, the current year is always going to be more accurate than years two and three. When making forecasts, you have to consider, in particular, how you're going to treat the impact of taxation and inflation, but unless there are special circumstances in your case where, for example, your products or sales prices are going to vary in value by much more than prevailing inflation, it seems simpler to cast everything at today's prices (at least in periods of relatively low inflation). Similarly, if you look at profit before tax, the only real question is whether, after tax, there will be enough left to live on and make the exercise worthwhile. You do not need to have a detailed tax projection to make that rough and ready calculation.
- Give details of the key assumptions that underpin your cashflow and profit forecasts (e.g. prices, volumes, timing, growth, etc.), and explain how they relate to your marketing plans, in order to show that they are realistic, accurate and achievable. A realistic sales forecast is necessary to underpin the financial figures.
- Provide forecasts of annual profit/loss and changes in the balance sheet. Comment on how you assess the future viability of the business.
- Assess the sensitivity of the budgets, e.g. the impact of any shortfalls in performance on profit, cashflow and the amount you need to borrow. Indicate how the business will be financially monitored. If applicable, indicate who has helped you to prepare the forecasts.

Management and Staffing

A business enterprise will not succeed if the management or staff do not have the skills or desire to make it a success. You should:

- Outline the key business managers and staff, setting out their roles and their skills.
- Provide details of how you plan to manage the business, who will be the project manager during the set-up phase, any external help you have enlisted, any plans for recruiting new staff, and who will be involved in the day-to-day operations.

- Outline who will manage the different project areas, i.e. finances, grant claims, construction, operation.
- Set out what experience they (or you) have to manage these areas of the project.
- Indicate, in cases where skills need to be developed, the training or work experience you plan to undertake, and when.
- Set out the job descriptions or skills required of any new employees you will be taking on.

Assessment of Risks

There are risks in any new venture. Identify your key risks, and explain:

- What impact they would have on your business.
- What the effects on your budgets will be given the best- and worst-case assumptions (i.e. make a sensitivity analysis).
- How you plan to overcome or minimise the impacts of these risks.
- What your exit strategy will be if all else fails – how will you close the business and maximise its sale value?

In addition, if you're applying for a grant, cover the issues specific to that.

Project Milestones

This covers what you need to do to implement your project successfully. You should set out the key steps you need to take, together with target dates to complete those stages.

Appendices

It can be useful to add a number of appendices to your business plan. They can save space in the plan itself. Typical items to include could be:

- **The CVs of all key personnel.**
- Copies of all documents referred to, especially market research.
- Organisation charts.
- Audited accounts for any business you are taking over, preferably covering the last three years.
- Copies of any existing marketing materials.
- A glossary of all the terms used in the plan.

A French Business Plan

The typical headings for a French plan reflect fundamental differences in culture between France and the UK, though the purpose is the same, and so is the importance. As is the case with the British business plan, the French plan allows for a great number of permutations in terms of its content. However, most plans begin by focusing on the **individual** who is presenting the plan or who will be in charge of the venture, on the assumption that, if they are not suited to business, the enterprise is bound to fail. This 'personal and professional balance sheet' (*bilan personnel and professionnel*), which can be attached to the business plan, sets out your experience and qualities.

Typical headings would be:

Ambition	Emotionality	Organisational Skills
Anxiety	Decision-making	Perseverance
Authority	Reasoning	Punctuality
Attitude to Criticism	Fidelity	Presentation
Capacity to Work	Frankness	and Appearance
Outside Interests – Nature and Extent	Ability to Persuade	Relations
	Attitude to Risk	Resistance to Stress
Clarity – Having a Global View	Imagination	Health
	Attitude to Money	Sense
Leadership	Working as a Team	of Responsibility
Communications	Intelligence	Practical Skills
Self-knowledge	Intuition	Willpower
Concentration	Judgement	Attitude
Effectiveness	Self-control	to Travelling
Elocution		

Following on from this analysis would be a summary of your education, starting at secondary school level and detailing the subjects that were studied and the results of all examinations. Then you would list all training taken after degree level, any languages spoken and any overseas work experience. You would also, at this point, give a working history, stressing the relevant professional experience you have acquired. As a result, this document is a combination of self-analysis and CV.

The business plan itself also has a different emphasis – it's seen more as a file (***dossier***) supporting the application being made, and is more generic than a British plan. **Typical headings** for the 'file presenting the project' (*le dossier de présentation du projet*) would be:

Definition of the Project and its Characteristics	Pricing Policy
	Distribution Policy
Economic Background	Communication Policy
Analysis of the Sector of Activity	Sales Targets
The Competition	Material Factors Relating to the Workplace – Premises, Machinery, Staff, Necessary Expenditure
Stakeholders	
Suppliers	
Clients	Financial Statements
Market Study	Choice of Legal Structure

Beneath each of these headings, there would be a number of detailed **sub-headings**, which are often set out according to a standard format.

For example, the **financial statements** will usually contain exactly the same headings for any business within the same sector. Those analysis headings are different from those that you would normally apply within the UK. The plan will also include a cashflow statement (*tableau de trésorerie*) and financial statement (*tableau de financement*). These stress how different the French form of accounts is from the more free and easy Anglo-Saxon form. There will also be a calculation of the break-even point for the venture and a separate calculation for the need for ongoing cashflow.

Mark your business plan 'confidential', and if you're concerned, ask the recipient to sign a non-disclosure agreement. It is generally not a good idea to number the plans: if you send somebody number 97, it suggests that 96 people have already turned you down.

Business Plan Software

There are quite a few software products for the preparation of a business plan on the French model, but you need a pretty detailed knowledge of both the system and the French language to reply to the questions that lead to the finished documentation. One good example is from EBP Logiciels de Gestion (**www.ebp.com**). A business plan package costs about €50 and can be downloaded or bought from many outlets in France, including hypermarkets such as Auchan.

If you're competent with spreadsheets, that software could be of assistance because it produces, semi-automatically, documents with lots of impressive graphs, charts and so on. If you're familiar with Excel, however, it is probably simpler to work directly in Excel and Word.

Your 'Life Plan'

If anything, this is even more important than your business plan. It's for your own benefit and no one else need see it, but just putting the issues down in writing will help you focus on the decisions you need to make, including:

- Where will you live? *See* pp.178–210.
- How much income do you need to survive? *See* p.35.
- What will you do about healthcare? *See* pp.228–32.
- What will you do about education for your children? *See* pp.233–6.
- What will you do about transport? Are you going to take your car with you or buy another one when you get to France? *See* pp.222–6.
- What will you do about your furnishings and possessions?
- What are you going to do about any savings you might possess?
- What are you going to do about a pension? *See* p.232.

There are clearly a wide variety of topics that could be covered under this heading, and you need to come up with a detailed plan as to how to deal with each. For example, in connection with the education of your children, what documentation will you need to have the children admitted to school?

Working from Home

Working from home has been permitted for sole traders for some time, but, since the Loi Dutreil of 2003 (*see* p.5), this applies equally to the representatives of companies who wish to work from home.

You need to register your business as being one that you are conducting from home. If you are working from home or using part of your home for business purposes, your business registration and tax forms will automatically generate an enquiry from the Centre des Impôts (tax office) requesting information on the proportion of your floor space that you use for business purposes. Take advice when completing this form, or you could find yourself with a hefty tax bill. For more on business premises, *see* pp.116–18.

Relating to a 'Parent' Business

If you want to maintain a British or other foreign business but carry out some business activities in France, a range of options is open to you, and you must tread carefully – making the wrong choice can have costly consequences. If, for example, you start off by setting up a local branch office and then decide that a better model would be a completely self-contained French business, the transfer of the business undertaking from the branch office to your new independent business will be taxable.

Beware, too, of the temptation to run your business in France 'notionally' in the name of your British business when, in effect, the activity is a French activity pure and simple. This is often attractive for people wanting to set up a new business in France who are frightened of the complexities and administrative issues and feel more comfortable with the British equivalents, but, though you might get away with it for a while, the authorities will almost certainly catch up with you. The law is clear: if you are carrying out any commercial activity in France, you must have a French structure of some kind, however simple, and pay the requisite taxes and social security in France.

Local Representative Office

A foreign firm that wants to look for business in France and promote its products or services can start simply and then proceed to set up a formal representative or liaison office (*vitrine/bureau de liaison*). It may then acquire its own or rented premises, recruit a further employee in France or second an employee to France to represent it. Liaison offices may conduct only non-commercial operations, such as prospecting, advertising, providing information, storing merchandise, or other operations of a preparatory or auxiliary nature. Such offices are not separate legal entities. They may draw up purchase orders, but the parent company must accept the orders, issue invoices and agree any contracts.

Liaison offices are not permanent establishments with respect to tax laws. They are not subject to corporate income tax or VAT, but must pay certain local taxes and payroll taxes. Registration with the trade register (**Registre du Commerce et des Sociétés**) is optional except in the case of banks and insurance companies. The major advantage of doing so is that it gives you the right (in most cases) to automatically renew a commercial lease for office premises. The disadvantages are that: if the manager of the liaison office is a foreigner (non-EU), he or she must obtain a foreign trade card (*carte de commerçant; see* pp.154–6); the foreign company must file annual financial statements with the trade register as a branch; it must as a principle pay the business licence tax (*taxe professionnelle*); and there is an increased risk that the liaison office will be reclassified as a permanent establishment (branch) for tax purposes, with the consequent requirement of paying corporate tax. If you do register, you must supply: the decision of the board of directors or other competent body authorising the establishment and appointing the individual representative of this office in France; personal documents concerning this representative (passport, attestation of the absence of a criminal record, etc.); company articles and by-laws; and proof of its right to the use of premises in France (a lease or contract with a business centre). All these documents must be translated into French by an official translator. Registration takes a week from the date when documents are filed.

The liaison office must be registered with the **Institut National de la Statistique** (**INSEE**), the **local tax office**, and, if it has employees, the **URSSAF** (Social Welfare Benefits and Family Subsidies Office). These registration formalities are handled automatically by the **Centre de Formalités des Entreprises** (**CFE**) if the liaison office is registered with the trade register; otherwise, they must be handled directly by the manager of the liaison office.

Liaison offices are only a temporary solution. If they become lasting arrangements, the tax authorities or courts may deem them to be permanent establishments or *succursales* (*see* below).

Salaried Representative ('Agency Office')

A foreign company may employ one person in France, to whom it pays a salary plus amounts corresponding to the related social security and other levies, which the employee is responsible for paying on to the bodies concerned. The employee representative usually has the status of a salaried employee and is hired by the foreign company under a French employment contract, with the employment governed by French law. Alternatively, the representative can be a foreign employee assigned to France by the foreign business entity for a limited period of time. He or she must comply with the rules applicable to residence and work permits.

If representatives visits customers and has a certain degree of autonomy, they will have the advantageous status of a **VRP** (travelling salesperson). To qualify, the representative must:

- be an individual working as a salaried employee for one or more employers and never for his or her own account.
- conduct activity only and exclusively as a commercial middleperson, and visit current and potential customers in order to obtain orders for goods and/or services for his or her employer(s).
- benefit from a degree of autonomy in organising visits to customers.

Regardless of nationality, the representative must be registered as a VRP and hold a professional ID card (different from a *carte de commerçant*) issued by the appropriate Préfecture. At the termination of the representation contract, the VRP is entitled to compensation – usually the equivalent of two years' salary – in place of the statutory compensation for dismissal applicable to all salaried employees.

If the employee representative has the power to agree/sign contracts, the formalities applicable to a branch apply (*see* opposite). If the employee is a non-EU foreigner, he or she will then have to apply for a foreign trader card (*carte de commerçant*) in his or her capacity as manager of a branch. If the employee representative does not have the power to agree/sign contracts, the formalities applicable to a local representative office apply (*see* pp.96–7).

Salaried representatives of a foreign business are deemed, for tax purposes, to be a permanent establishment of the business in France. As a result, the foreign business must pay French corporate tax and VAT (TVA) as a branch on the profits generated by the activities of the salaried representative. It will also have to pay other minor business taxes.

If the company grows to have its own premises and/or employs two or more people in France, it must be officially represented by a liaison office, a branch or a subsidiary.

Branch (*Succursale*)

If a company conducts industrial or commercial activities in France, it must set up a branch office or subsidiary. 'Commercial activity' is any activity involving the signing of documents or contracts by an employee or representative of the business and/or taking other steps that bind the foreign company. Examples include contracts for direct sales in France, or contracts for providing services to a customer of the company.

The creation of a branch office entails no great formalities. The head of the branch office must nonetheless hold a business permit for foreign residents (*carte de commerçant*) unless he or she benefits from waivers applying to nationals of EU member countries or holds a residence permit (*carte de séjour*).

If you're going to open a branch in France, you must register it at the local **Registre du Commerce et des Sociétés** (through the local **Centre de Formalités des Entreprises** or **CFE**; *see* pp.86–7). There are various formalities attached to this registration: you have to give the registry copies of the constitution of the company, proof of the current registration of the company in its own country, details of the latest annual accounts for the company, and the details of the person who has legal responsibility for the affairs of the company in France – i.e. the manager of the local branch. In most cases you also have to produce proof of the right to occupy the place in which the business trades in France – generally a leasing agreement or a title deed for the premises it occupies.

Branches are considered permanent establishments for tax purposes. They are required to keep, and file with the tax authorities, financial statements for their business activities conforming to French accounting principles, and they must be able to provide the French tax authorities with a translation of such financial statements if they are prepared in a foreign language. They are, in either case, required to file tax returns in France and pay social security payments in France in respect of their France-based staff and activities.

The branch is subject to French corporate tax on its profits, whether distributed or undistributed. This tax is generally calculated on the basis of the deemed net profits that would have been generated by an independent company performing the same services. However, in certain cases, the French tax authorities may allow the total 'French' net profit to be valued automatically at a percentage of the total overall amount of the charges made.

The branch will also be liable to French VAT and other business taxes.

If the company is taxed on its worldwide income in its country of origin, the profits or losses of its branch office are included in its taxable income at home. This has no effect on the tax liabilities of the branch office in France (the French get first crack at the money), but, under the relevant double tax treaty (*see* p.145), you can often set your French tax liability off against your 'home' liability.

Branches are usually the preferred form for foreign companies' first serious activities in France. They are headed by a legal representative and operate like agencies that report to their British or other overseas headquarters. There are no legal restrictions on their decision-making powers or operating procedures, other than those that apply to everyone in France. They may conduct all the activities of an industrial or commercial company but are not separate legal entities. If they encounter financial problems, the parent company bears unlimited joint liability for their debts.

There is no hard and fast rule about when a business activity ceases to be a representative office and becomes a branch. If the local office has the right to conduct business essentially independently on behalf of the company (for example, if it has the right to enter contracts on its own initiative and without the documentation being signed off at the head office or the home office) or if it issues invoices, it is likely to be treated as a branch office. Essentially, the difference between a branch and a liaison office is one of where tax has to be paid. It is not necessary to have a formal French legal structure for the business to become a branch.

Self-contained Business

The most suitable legal form for a self-contained business varies according to the strategy involved. Criteria usually taken into account include the cost of the operation, the presence or absence of financial investors among the shareholders, and confidentiality. If they don't already have one, limited liability companies are required to appoint a statutory auditor as soon as they meet any two of three criteria – sales of €3,048,781 or more, a balance sheet total value of €1,524,391 or more, and a staff of 50 or more. Seek further advice before deciding which of the following options will be best for you.

Subsidiary (*Filiale*)

A subsidiary is wholly or majority-owned by another company, including an overseas company. Almost any structure valid in France can be a subsidiary. The subsidiary company becomes a separate legal entity when it is entered in the company register (Registre du Commerce et des Sociétés). The founders are personally liable for their legal commitments during the set-up phase, which are then assumed retroactively by the newly incorporated company.

A subsidiary in France must register as a French entity. It is then subject to all the tax and social security rules that apply to any other French entity, including the payment of corporate income tax and VAT in France.

Independent French Company

This entity in France may have the same shareholders or many of the same shareholders as your British or American company but is officially unrelated to it. This can give you greater freedom in the way you trade, but there are regulations governing activities between related parties not formally linked.

Relationships Between an Overseas Company and its French Branch or Subsidiary

These can fall into several legal categories. The subsidiary may be an agent, acting only on behalf of the parent, which itself signs the sales contracts. The position of the subsidiary is perfectly clear, since it only receives a commission, while the profits generated by sales in France are taxed in the parent company's home country. Great care should be taken in drawing up the 'agency contract' between the parent and subsidiary, since this determines the tax treatment of profits made by the parent company.

A subsidiary may also act as a distributor – that is, it buys the products from the foreign parent company and resells them in France. The profits it makes in this way are declared and taxed in France. Royalties may be payable to the parent. They are taxed in the country where the parent company is located.

Taxation is not the only consideration in drawing up the contract between the parent and the subsidiary. If the subsidiary plays a significant role in organising distribution or is involved in after-sales services, a distribution contract is preferable from a legal, commercial and tax point of view.

The transfer pricing of goods must, by law, take place at proper market prices. Payments may, however, be made from one company to the other for various types of services supplied, provided they are actually rendered. Such payments include: management fees, patent and brand royalties, and interest on shareholders' loans (for tax purposes, a ceiling is set on interest rates and the amount of shareholders' loans may not exceed a certain proportion of the subsidiary's capital stock). The impact of such charges on the 'bottom line' can be considerable, as it can shift the tax liability from country A to country B, and if, for example, country A has a tax rate of 40% and country B a rate of 12%, the effect is dramatic.

Importing Funds into France (and Getting Them Out Again)

Most activities likely to be carried out by a British company active in France or a French company funded by British finance are likely to be specifically outside the scope of exchange control or any other regulation. For example, the formation of a company or branch requires no specific consents relating to exchange control, and if you have several companies in the same group, you generally do not require permission to restructure those companies or move investment from one company into another. Nor is consent usually required for changing a company's share structure or increasing the level of an investment, for loans, guarantees, security and so on from one company to another, for direct investment in property-holding companies, or for the acquisition of land.

If you decide to sell up and go home, you may find that some notification issues arise, but that is unlikely. In general, you need only tell the authorities what you are doing by way of a simple declaration.

Setting Up Your Own Business or Buying into an Existing Business

In some cases, people have no choice about this – for example, if you want to buy a bar, you will almost certainly have to buy an existing business, because there is a severe restriction on the issuing of new licences to serve alcohol in bars. In other cases, you need to take the advantages and disadvantages of each option into consideration.

If you are buying an existing business, somebody will have already done most of the work, and you will only have to deal with the generally simpler paperwork involved in transferring the ownership of the various licences and of the equipment. You will also have the benefit of an existing client base, and the business will be known in the area. All things being equal, this should lead to a faster development of your business. With cashflow coming in from day one, you should very quickly be able to move into profit.

The downside to taking over an existing business is that, if it has been failing for a number of years (which is why many businesses are being sold in the first place), it can take a long time to undo a bad reputation, however good your services or product. Additionally, many businesses come with existing staff who may need substantial retraining and a shift in attitude. Most importantly, it is a truism that when you buy a new business, you seldom get good surprises – you may pay for it on the basis that it has a track record of a certain level of income, but the day after you take it over the main customer deserts you to go elsewhere, sometimes to another business being set up by the seller of your business or one of their friends.

Generally, our clients who have started their own businesses have been more successful than those who have taken over existing businesses, but this probably reflects their greater entrepreneurial skills.

Setting Up a New Business

Once you have established that the business you wish to set up can be started freely (for example, it is not a bar), it's a relatively straightforward but bureaucratic task to do so. If you set up a new business:

- **Make sure you have the necessary qualifications.**
- **Acquire any premises necessary.**
- **Register the business with the appropriate authorities. What you need to do depends on the nature of the business and the nature of the corporate or other structure you are adopting.**
- **Register the business for tax, social security etc.**

Buying an Existing Business

Taking over an existing business involves risks in any country: you can be taking on the debts of the existing business at the same time as its assets; the employees could have significant claims in the event of redundancy, or might be useless or dishonest; there may be a lot of dissatisfied customers who are likely to leave; and the lease for the premises could be due for renewal or a rent review, and the rent could increase substantially.

The first thing you need to do is make sure whether the business is worth buying – this is trendily known as 'due diligence', which means nothing more than finding out whether what you have been told about the business is true. It can be a complicated, time-consuming and expensive process, especially if you are buying a major business. But even if you are buying a small one, for example a café, bar or small shop, the cost might not justify the expense.

Fortunately, there are some monetary shortcuts you may be able to use. The first is employing your own spy – for instance, if you are buying a bar and the seller tells you that it has 100 customers a night and takes €2,000 per week, you can recruit a friend or relative to go on holiday to the area and visit as a customer. If they tell you that there are four customers a night and the bar took €30, you will know there is something seriously wrong.

The second is to check that the business is legitimate and properly registered by verifying its business identification number or SIREN (*see* p.124) on **www.infogreffe.fr**, which can also supply you with a lot of information about the company concerned for a modest fee. The number should be displayed on the business's advertising materials if you don't want to ask the seller. You also need to check if the business has everything necessary for its continuation – for example, does it have the necessary intellectual property licences for any services it is using, and does the equipment belong to it or is it rented?

Valuing a Business

A business's value depends on a number of factors, including whether it owns or rents the premises (*les murs*; the walls) from which it trades; whether it has certain equipment; and whether it has existing stock (a café might have food in the freezers and drinks on the shelf, for instance). All of these items can be valued and a price agreed for them. Over and above that price, you will have to pay something for what, in Anglo-Saxon culture, is known as goodwill.

In France the concept is rather wider, and is known as the ***fonds de commerce***. This is totally independent of all other assets. Even if the business closed its premises and moved to a new location with a new building, new equipment and new stock, it would have a certain value. That is because, all things being equal, its existing client base would follow it and the business would be able to reach profitability faster than would otherwise be the case.

The valuation of the *fonds de commerce* is complicated and a matter for careful and skilful negotiation. The first problem is that, in France, the accuracy of accounting records is sometimes not as great as you might expect. If you were going to buy a shop in the UK or USA, the first thing you would ask for is the audit of accounts for the last three years. If the shopkeeper told you that, nudge, nudge, wink, wink, there was a certain amount of money that went under the counter that had not been declared in the accounts and that amounted to, say, 10% of the turnover, you might be prepared to accept it. If they told you that only a third of the true income was recorded, you would probably be very sceptical. In France (particularly in rural areas), there is more likelihood that the business's official figures differ dramatically from the true figures, which makes the valuation process that much more complicated. That said, it is becoming more and more difficult to deceive the tax office.

There are, in any case, various ways to check the likely real performance of any business. First, figures showing the likely income of a particular business within the different sectors are generally available from local chambers of commerce. If you find that an average income declared by a restaurant is €5,000 per month, for example, these figures are at least a starting point for checking whether the figures you're being told are even vaguely realistic.

The second set of figures that is interesting is the readily available statistics as to the likely percentage of the gross turnover of a business that is retained as profit at the end of the year. These are, again, broken down by sector. For example, if you are a builder or electrician, you might realistically expect to retain about 30% of your turnover as gross profit; if you run a restaurant it might be 20%; and if you run a food shop it might be 15%. If an owner claims that their restaurant is retaining 35% of gross turnover as profit, you need to be very suspicious. Equally, if they tell you it is only retaining 10% as gross profit, the restaurant is probably running very inefficiently and it is likely to take you a long time to nurse it back to health and profitability.

Once you have got to the bottom of the facts, you will then be in a position to assess how much you are prepared to pay for the *fonds de commerce*. Though this is a matter for negotiation, there are some guideline figures available at **www.cession-commerce.fr**, which has a calculator to help you assess the value of the *fonds de commerce*. The information on the value of businesses by sector and region is quite detailed, and the site asks you a series of other questions about the business before coming up with a suggested value. It is also full of other useful information about buying businesses in France.

This is a very useful guide for you to start your negotiations, but do not follow it slavishly, and do take professional accountancy or legal advice before making an offer. Double check that you are clear about all the background facts. Does the lease have a long time to run at its current rent? Are there any debts? Are there any employees with significant redundancy or any other entitlements? Is the business up to date with its social security and tax payments?

Purchasing a Business

The purchase of the *fonds de commerce* is dealt with in a similar way to the purchase of property (*see* pp.179–209) and formalised by the notary. The precise terms of the sale agreement are negotiated between the parties and there is a more or less standard format for agreements. Once you and the seller have signed the deed of transfer of the business (*acte de cession de fonds de commerce*), there are further formalities to attend to – you need to register the transfer of ownership with the tax office, publish the transfer of ownership in the official journal for the area in which the business is located (*journal d'annonces légales*), register the business with social security, pay the taxes associated with the transfer of the ownership (normally at a rate of 4.8%), pay the notary's fee (typically another 3% of the price paid), and register the new ownership at the **Registre du Commerce et des Sociétés**.

Be aware that any person or entity can challenge the right of the seller to sell the business or claim that they have certain pre-existing rights against the business. These rights should be clarified and eliminated by your lawyer before you complete the purchase of the business.

Franchises

Franchising has become more and more popular in France. The basic concept is that you set up your own business with the assistance of the person offering the franchise (the franchisor), which typically involves a manual showing you how to implement a system of work that has been proven and is well established, the supply of raw materials, centralised advertising, the use of a common design or logo, training, and discounts on any equipment needed.

Many franchise businesses on offer in France are US-based, but a growing number are European. Good franchises can be particularly useful in a country where you are less familiar with business practices, while many French people set up franchises because of the guidance and support they get from the franchisor. However, one of the main comments made by people who have started up franchises is that they underestimated the amount of restrictions placed on their freedom. These restrictions are inevitable but can be irksome. For example, you might not be able to expand your business outside a certain area; you have to follow the marketing systems of the franchise; you have to sell at least in marked measure the franchise products; you will probably have to stick to opening hours laid down by the franchisor; and you will probably have to abide by the dress/uniform code of the franchisor. Nor do franchises come cheap. The approximate minimum for a franchise in a small enterprise is €30,000; this can rise to €1 million or more for McDonald's, Mr Bricolage or InterSport.

Among websites covering franchising are **www.british-franchise.org**, **www.franchisebusiness.co.uk** and **www.whichfranchise.com**, which are a good guide to the pros and cons. Among the France-specific websites, see in particular **www.franchise-fff.com**. To find out about people who have tried various franchise operations in France, see **www.observatoiredelafranchise.com**.

Joint Ventures

Starting a business with somebody with local contacts, local language skills and some finance is an attractive option, allowing you to avoid many of the problems associated with setting up from scratch. However, joint ventures are said to be a bit like marriages – you should not go into them lightly, and they can be extremely expensive and difficult if it comes to divorce.

If you're thinking about a joint venture, it is particularly important to get good legal and accountancy advice and to make sure, before you go very far down the path of setting up the venture, that you are truly comfortable with all aspects of your colleague's attitude to business in general and to this business in particular. Pay particular attention to the legal structure you choose for the venture, because that in turn has a bearing on the control mechanisms. You need to be clear that you will have the right to veto any activities of which you disapprove strongly, and you will have to concede that same right to your partners.

Joint-venture vehicles can be loose and unofficial associations that become companies, special companies set up to operate a business and owned by the participant companies in such proportions as they see fit, or official groupings of companies using the European Economic Interest Group (EEIG) as a model. The latter were designed to promote cross-border activity between like minded companies in the EU but can be used effectively within a single country; for more information, see **www.europa.eu.int/scadelus/leg/en**.

Raising Finance

Ways of Delaying Full Financial Commitment

There are two big financial problems for those setting up in business in France – you have no income, and you have a lot of expenses. Continuing to work in your old job can be an attractive option – at the very least, it allows you earn a salary and run the business 'on the side' until it builds up enough volume to pay for your keep. This is perfectly legal. You set up the structure for your business in France in the usual way, complying with all the requirements of a business, including the payment of tax and social security on your earnings, and you also contribute towards social security through your job if it is based in France. If your job is based in the UK, you will be contributing partly to the social security system in the UK and partly to French social security (depending on your circumstances, you may get a partial credit for these indicated payments).

While this option helps maintain the cashflow, however, it does little about the expenses of launching a new business. Luckily, there are certain steps you can take to test the waters as far as your business idea is concerned without going to the expense of setting up and registering your business – this can be done in addition to continuing to work or in place of it. The advantage is that, if you find you have made a ghastly mistake and the business is not going to work, you can pull out without incurring all of the set-up costs (or the expense of closing the business).

The three basic ways of doing this, described in detail below, share a key element – that the creator of the business delegates all of the administration (and aggravation) of the business to a third party, receiving in return what is, in effect, a salary, set-up grant or share of profit. In each case, you use the commercial registration and VAT numbers of the entity of which you have become a part. The measures were spurred or created by the 2003 initiatives to encourage small businesses (*see* p.5), and, because they are relatively new, the practices relating to them and even their availability varies from region to region. None comes free: in each case, you will be paying part of your earnings to your 'host'. Whichever structure you may be thinking of incorporating, it is important to discuss the situation thoroughly with the people offering the facility – you need to understand precisely what you are letting yourself in for in their particular organisation, and how long you are likely to remain there.

What these entities offer is, if anything, even more valuable to the foreigner setting up in business than to a native-born French person, since the former's need for ongoing advice and assistance is substantial, and the cost of this advice may be a lot lower here than from other sources.

Salaried Self-employment (*Portage Salarial*)

This option is open to people who have previous experience in a particular line of work – references are almost always required before you are accepted into the organisation. The idea is that you can launch your business without having to deal with all of the paperwork associated with it by becoming a member of a special type of entity that takes you under its wing, deals with all of the legal and administrative tasks associated with running a business, invoices your clients on your behalf, receives payment on your behalf, and then pays you what is, in effect, a salary after deducting its share to cover its expenses.

There are *portage salarial* schemes for people offering professional or intellectual, manual or commercial services. You (*le porté*) are responsible for finding your clients and providing the services they need. All the enterprise does is deal with the administration and act as your legal shield.

If you are going to such an entity for a project of known duration and revenue, you agree the split between you. If you go to them with an idea that will continue indefinitely, you arrange what are effectively frequent salary reviews reflecting the success of your venture. You concentrate on the business and the society concentrates on paying social security and professional registrations, accounting and so on. In addition, it may offer advice and assistance, preferential rates for marketing or other expenses, and bulk-buying facilities that enable you to buy a letterhead, equipment and so on at reduced rates.

The amount of your turnover that the society will take is normally 5–15%, and they will also pass on your social security costs, and tax costs if they are responsible for paying those (most aren't). You will generally receive about 50% of the gross income of your business after deduction of their commission and of social security. Happily, you retain all of the unemployment and other benefits that come with salaried employment, and these are slightly better than they are for the self-employed, even in France.

This is such a new activity that it is not recognised under French labour law, so be very careful when choosing the society with which you are going to work. Speak to other people who are working with the society you are considering and ensure that they are satisfied. Further information is available from **www.guideduportage.com**, the **Fédération Nationale du Portage Salarial (www.fenps.fr)**, the **Syndicat National des Entreprises de Portage Salarial (www. portagesalarial.org)**, and the **Union National des Entreprises de Portage Spécialisées (www.uneps.org)**, which was set up in May 2005 to deal with activities previously excluded from *portage salarial*, such as estate agency and architecture.

Shelter (*La Couveuse*)

This involves becoming part of an organisation that will permit you to work on your project with the view to discovering whether it is truly suitable for you and whether it is going to work, and if necessary to redefine it before going public. It is generally intended for people who are just starting up and who are probably going to be entitled to some form of state aid while doing so – women rejoining the workforce, long-term unemployed people, young people, people with disabilities, and so on. It allows them to start a business without having to make substantial investment and without having to set up the legal structures necessary to own their own business. At the end of your period of 'shelter', you either go back to salaried employment and leave the scheme, or you open your own business in the normal way.

The entity looking after such business carries out all the accounting and admin in much the same way as in a *portage salarial*. To the public, the business appears to be yours, but you operate it behind a protective screen that absorbs much of the day-to-day aggro. Where *la couveuse* differs from *portage salarial* is that, as well as providing the framework within which your business operates, it provides collective training and support, typically for one day or one morning per week.

You can remain part of such a scheme for 6–36 months. The criteria for joining vary from scheme to scheme and place to place. Generally, however, you can't join if your own skills or if the project you want to set up are in an advanced state. The project does, however, have to be well defined and feasible, and to be confirmed as such by professional opinion. This means you will generally need to have prepared a business plan (see pp.87–95), although occasionally people with no more than a reasonably well-crafted idea are accepted.

In addition to administrative backup, *la couveuse* offers certain facilities, which vary from place to place but are more or less what you would expect from a serviced office – telephone lines, meeting rooms, faxes, photocopiers, and so on. Very often, *la couveuse* will also be able to introduce you to providers of finance and other services. Further information is available at **www.uniondecouveuse.com** and **www.synergiescreateurs.org**.

Cooperative of Business and Employment (*Coopérative d'Activités et d'Emplois*)

The main purpose of a co-operative is to permit the people taking part in it to share their experiences in a structured way. It also reduces or eliminates the paperwork associated with the creation of a business.

The Coopérative d'Activités et d'Emplois (CAE), which has been around for a number of years now, is of most interest to people who think they have a good business idea but are not really sure if it's going to fly. The sorts of functions that it performs for its members are more or less the same as those of the *portage salarial*. However, as co-operatives vary in the types of members they have, they can also supply services directly related to those members' needs – if, for example, you had a co-operative with a number of potters as members, it could provide a shared oven or wheel.

People can join the co-operative in two ways. Some will join when they have no more than a vague idea as to what they want to do, signing a business creation partnership agreement (*convention d'accompagnement partenarial à la création d'activité*), which permits them to proceed with the development of their project and to commence production. During this period, they preserve their original status, which might, for example, be unemployed or salaried employee. The point at which this relationship changes depends on the co-operative but is normally triggered when the fledgling business attains a certain level of turnover. The person running the business then becomes an *entrepreneur salarié* (salaried businessperson) and is remunerated pro rata according to his or her turnover in the previous month. From that turnover, all applicable social security contributions will be deducted, as will the entrepreneur's share of the expenses of the co-op (typically about 10% of turnover).

Businesses share the VAT number and commercial registration of the co-operative, which deals with billing, accounts, salaries, and so on. It also provides one-to-one training and analysis of the business, helps it with its strategies, marketing, fixing of objectives and so on, and generally acts as its best friend.

This aid is normally very personalised, with the aim of showing you how to deal with all eventualities.

As well as enjoying the aid and shelter offered by the *portage salarial* and *la couveuse*, you can enjoy the networking opportunities that come from being a member of a cooperative. Co-ops may have a range of different activities being carried out within their remit, but members feel part of an entity and can draw on each others' strengths and experience.

After a while, the entrepreneur either flees the nest to set up alone or becomes a permanent part of the cooperative movement, continuing as a **Société Coopérative Ouvrière de Production** (**SCOP**; *see* p.86). To learn more, see **www.cooperer.coop** and **www.scop.coop**.

Grants and Aid

France's vast public spending brings with it the need for lots of taxes, but these taxes in turn mean there is a great deal of grant aid sloshing around. In fact, sometimes it seems that there is so much grant aid that it must be a rarity for anybody to have to do anything without some form of public subvention.

France has no qualms about claiming its entitlements to any EU grant going, and there is a lot of money available, particularly because of the country's nature, size and large percentage of rural/agricultural land. There is also grant aid from the French government, in a wide range of different forms at regional, departmental and *commune* level. If these don't bear fruit for you, grant aid is available in particular parishes or historic regions, or for those pursuing an activity supported by a professional organisation or some charity. There are grants available for tourism, particularly in rural areas, for disabled business people or businesses that are going to cater for the disabled, and for restoring historic buildings. In some places, there are even grants available for people for whom no other grants are available!

It is well worth taking professional advice to see what you may be entitled to, especially if you don't have a perfect command of French and a good understanding of the French system, though such advice is hard to come by and tends to be quite expensive.

A word of caution: grants usually come with conditions attached, which might significantly reduce your freedom of choice or operation. Sometimes they can involve you in incurring considerable expense in order to qualify for the grant in the first place (there was a case not long ago where the cost of complying with the grant would have been more than the cost of the grant). Or sometimes the rules can be plain stupid. This was the case with a client opening a small hotel in a historic building in France, who was offered substantial grant aid (about 30% of the project cost) if they increased the size of the bedrooms by about 3cm. Given that the walls were about 75cm thick, this was no easy task, and the client decided to proceed without the grant aid.

Grant aid can come in different forms. Sometimes it is a cash subvention, in other cases it may be a tax or social security 'holiday' or vouchers entitling you to certain services at no cost or reduced cost. Or sometimes it may come in the form of access to facilities provided by the organisation concerned. In addition to all of this, there are also low-interest or interest-free loans available in certain cases, although these tend to come in small chunks and involve a lot of planning, preparation and paperwork.

An exhaustive list of all of the resources available is outside the scope of this book, and you should also bear in mind that these change all the time. In particular, we don't deal with the grants available at a very local level – from the *commune* or parish or on an industry basis. To find out about these, ask your mayor, a local accountant, your Conseil Régional, or the Chambre de Commerce, Chambre de Métiers or Chambre d'Agriculture if you are in a sector governed by them. If you are involved in tourism in a rural area, go to the tourist office. Or try searching the Internet.

EU Grants

Note that grants from the European Union are only available to registered companies or other legal entities and not to individual traders.

European Social Fund and European Development Fund

The European Union has made vast amounts of money available in its attempt to raise standards of living and the economy in its more backward regions, but the regulations are, as you might imagine, immensely complicated. The EU website (**http://europa.eu.int**) or the French Euro Information Office (**www.travail.gouv.fr**) will help you find the detailed rules.

Essentially, there are various tests to see whether a region benefits from any entitlement to European aid under these headings. Only if the part of the country where you live can benefit can you start to think about whether your business can benefit. Such tests include whether the area suffers from high unemployment or is performing below the average from an economic point of view. Very large areas of France come into one or more of the categories, since many of the rural areas are relatively poor.

There are three zones that are of particular importance in this context – the *zone de revitalisation rurale*, the *zone de redynamisation urbaine* and the *zone franche urbaine*, each of which benefit from special tax breaks and other incentive schemes. We will see the way the zones operate when we come to look at some of the individual grants and incentives available later in this chapter.

National Grants and Other Aid Packages

People setting up businesses in deprived areas, young people, long-term unemployed people, women returning to the workforce and people with disabilities are hugely favoured when it comes to French grants, but they can be advantageous to everyone.

Departmental Grants for Young People (FDIJ)

These grants for the creation of new businesses, typically of around €7,500, are available to young people who are unemployed or who have precarious employment, to the long-term unemployed whatever their age, and to students who have finished their course. A committee assesses the viability of projects presented to them in the form of business plans and certain extra documentation. For more details, contact the **Direction Départementale du Travail et de l'Emploi** for the *département* where you are going to be setting up in business.

Launch Grants (*Bourse Défi Jeune*)

These grants are for young people aged 18–25 to set up businesses or projects that are going to create something new. Amounting to about €1,500–2,200, they are awarded every two years, with a committee choosing from among the applicants, who must be sponsored by a business for a sum at least equal to the grant. More details can be obtained from the **Direction Départementale de la Jeunesse et des Sports** of the *département* where you are thinking of setting up, or from the **Association Défi** (t 01 40 31 17 17).

Aid to the Unemployed Creating a Business
(*Aide aux Chômeurs Créateurs ou Repreneurs d'Entreprise*; ACCRE)

This grant – of just over €4,400 – is for people receiving unemployment benefit who are either setting up a business or resuming a business already started, either individually or in groups. If it doesn't succeed, the money is not repayable. The business must be set up according to a structure approved by the grant organisation; at least 51% of the capital must belong to those applying for the grant; and the business must be started within at most three months if it is new or two months if it is a relaunch. The beneficiary will not have to pay any income tax until his or her profit exceeds 120% of the state minimum wage, and is exempt from paying social security for one year. Note that the fixed budget for this type of aid runs out quite early on in the year so you need to get in early. Contact your local **Direction Départementale du Travail**.

Those in receipt of this grant are also eligible for 'grants for the unemployed creating employment' (*majoration pour les créations d'emploi*) if they create a salaried post for an unemployed person within six months of setting up the business. The person must not be a member of your family, and it must be an indefinite (i.e. long-term) full-time post or several part-time posts that are the equivalent of one full-time post. The grant is typically about €22,000.

Advice Vouchers (*Aide à l'Innovation*)

These are available to creators of businesses qualifying for the ACCRE or FDIJ (*see* above) during the first year of the activity to help them resolve financial legal, commercial or certain other problems related to their business. The creator of the business must pay about the first €15 per hour of the price of the consultancy and must present a detailed bill from the approved organisation concerned. The 12 vouchers of about €75 each must be used within 12 months, or returned if the business ceases. Contact the **Agence Nationale pour l'Emploi**, **departmental employment and labour office** or local **chamber of commerce**.

Aids to Services Leading to Innovation (*Aides aux Services de l'Innovation*)

This is available to businesses or persons creating new processes or products (or, occasionally, improving an existing process or product), after consideration of the quality of the innovation, its scientific or technological interest, its commercial and financial possibilities (particularly relating to export), and the needs for financing of the applicant. It can account for up to 50% of the qualifying expenses, to a limit of about €75,000. Contact the **Agence Nationale pour la Valorisation de la Recherche** (**ANVAR**; t 01 40 17 83 00).

Aids to Industrial Innovation (*Aide à l'Innovation Industrielle*)

This is for research establishments and people setting up businesses, and includes market studies, feasibility studies, technical studies, legal studies, intellectual property registration, export studies, issues relating to the adaptation of the product or service to foreign markets, prototype building, research expenses to secure new partners, and start-up expenses. A preliminary consultation with ANVAR (*see* above) is followed by an assessment by technical and financial experts. There are various levels of grant but they are all substantial, amounting to 75% of the expenses involved up to about €60,000. Multiple applications can proceed simultaneously, and grants can be cumulative. The expenditure under this category has been enormous.

Aids to Export (*Aide à l'Export du CODEX*)

Available to businesses with a turnover in excess of about €4.4 million looking to increase exports, this takes the form of assistance in the creation of associates overseas or new overseas companies and in co-ordinating existing grants and other financial means available. Preference is given to projects in the newly industrialised parts of Asia and Europe. Shareholders must invest a sum at least equal to the amount of the grant (approximately 25% of the cost over a period of three years). For more information, contact the **Comité de Développement du Commerce Extérieur** (**CODEX**; t 01 40 24 81 99).

Regional Grants and Assistance

Some French regions are more generous than others in the number of grants given, the sums available or the conditions applied to grants. If you are going into business with a view to maximising your grant aid (this is not necessarily the most sensible of bases for making your decision but one that is adopted by some people, including some very big companies looking for major grant assistance), choose your region with care. As a general guide, look for regions that are remote, poor or have suffered an economic crisis, such as a major car plant closing down.

The following grants and their terms change particularly frequently.

Regional Enterprise Creation Grant
(*Prime Régionale à la Création d'Entreprise*; PRCE)

This grant is available in Alsace, Aquitaine, Bases-Normandie, Champagne-Ardennes, Corse, Franche-Comté, Limousin and Nord-Pas-de-Calais, to aid enterprises newly created in these regions and likely to generate employment in order that they can equip themselves. The business must agree to create a number of employees defined by the region, who must be employed under full-time, long-term contracts and in full accord with the fiscal and social security rules applicable. Various other conditions may be added relating to the nature of the activity and the business's financial health. The likely amount you'll receive is about €22,000, but this can be paid several times. This grant can be added to the regional employment grant (PRE) and the grant for the improvement of the region (PAT); *see* below.

For details, contact the **Conseil Régional** or **Préfecture** for the region.

Regional Employment Creation Grant
(*Prime Régionale à l'Emploi*; PRE)

This grant, available in Alsace, Aquitaine, Auvergne, Basse-Normandie, Champagne-Ardennes, Corse, Haute-Normandie, Limousin and Nord-Pas-de-Calais, is to assist enterprises creating and maintaining employment following their creation or resumption. The enterprise cannot have a turnover of more than about €44 million per year or be related to a subsidiary of a larger enterprise. It must also fall within an area of activity specified by the various regions. The amount generally depends on the number of employees, up to a limit of 30, and can go up to about €6,000 per employee. It cannot be obtained at the same time as a *prime d'aménagement du territoire* (*see* below).

Contact your **Conseil Régional** or **Préfecture** of the region for more details.

Reduced Rate Loans

All regions can award loans (generally repayable) at reduced interest rates or to award aid in part-payment of interest charges paid to third parties, though these have largely been replaced by the PRCE and PRE (*see* above). They are available to new businesses that are going to create employment; these must generate 30 employees following their creation or 10 employees following a relaunch or a restructuring (other conditions may apply depending on the region). Amounts vary from region to region. Contact the **Conseil Régional**.

Individual Grants for Advice (*Fonds Régional d'Aide au Conseil*; FRAC)

This is for payment for the outside advice necessary for the development of a business (usually small or medium-sized), with the areas covered by the advice defined by the region – it is usually related to commercial matters, productivity, organisation of the business and human resources. The business must have been officially created and registered, and must be newly created or restarted. The amount varies from 50 to 80% of the cost of the advice, with a ceiling of about €30,000.

Contact your local **Chambre de Commerce et d'Industrie**.

Discounts on the Purchase or Renting of Industrial Buildings
(*Rabais Pour l'Achat ou la Location de Bâtiments Industriels*)

Any business needing additional space can apply for this grant, which is assessed and fixed by the individual regions but in certain cases can be as much as 25% of the market price.

Grants for the Improvement of the Region
(*Prime d'Aménagement du Territoire*; PAT)

This grant is for major projects or research by businesses with a turnover of in excess of about €75 million making investments that will create or maintain employment of a minimum of 6–20 employees (defined by the sector of activity concerned) in certain disadvantaged regions of France for a minimum of three years, with the employment governed by long-term, full-time contracts. Amounts vary.

For more details, contact the **Délégation à l'Aménagement du Territoire et à l'Action Régionale** (DATAR; **t** 01 40 65 12 34).

Regional Development Funds
(*Fonds Européen de Développement Régional*; FEDER)

The list of *départements* in economic difficulties where this is currently available is under review but at the time of writing comprised Aisne, Ardennes, Corse, Charente-Maritime, DOM, Gard, Loire, Loire-Atlantique, Meuse, Meurthe-et-Moselle, Moselle, Nord-Pas-de-Calais, Saône et Loire, Seine-Maritime, Somme and Tarn. It is aimed at businesses benefiting from national or regional aid setting up in one of these *départements*, and the amounts, decided on a case-by-case basis, are potentially huge. Application is made individually to the relevant commission in the *département* concerned.

More information is available from **DATAR** (*see* above).

Regional Export Aid (*Fonds Régionale d'Aide à l'Exportation*; FRAEX)

This grant to finance the studies and services needed in connection with the development of exports is available to enterprises with a turnover of less than about €20 million per year, on condition that they accept a consultant's report and export French products. The maximum amount is 50% of the global cost of the project, or about €40,000 per year, but there is a maximum for each category of expenditure (i.e. for a diagnostic report it is about €15,000; for the adaptation of products to foreign markets about €22,000).

French Banks and Loans

French banks are highly sophisticated, modern establishments. While it is true that most offer a more modest range of products than their British or American counterparts, this is part of the culture and should not necessarily be seen as a weakness. Generally, French banks operate relatively simple lending structures, and you need to go to a pretty high level in the bank before anything more complicated will be considered. The second issue is that many people moving to France settle in rural areas, where bank managers have relatively little autonomy (even in big cities this can also be the case), so if you are looking for a significant loan, your case will be decided elsewhere.

A further issue that needs to be noted is that if you don't have the funds in your account with which to honour a cheque, it can result not only in criminal prosecution but also in the complete withdrawal of banking facilities.

Bank Services

French banks all offer pretty much the same services, as is the case in the UK, and these are set out on their websites. That said, it still makes sense to shop around to see whether a particular bank can offer a service that might not be readily available from a competitor, or to find the one that can offer the lowest charges on, for instance, bringing in funds from the UK.

Choosing a Bank

If you don't speak French, it's worth looking for a bank that has two or three English-speaking staff or even a dedicated section for foreign customers, such as Crédit Agricole's Britline. In rural areas where English-speaking staff are few and far between, this will probably be your main consideration, irrespective of the services the bank offers. Otherwise, you will probably find that there is only one bank in your nearest small town, and it is a good idea to use it – it will help you integrate into the community, and the bank manager may be able to introduce you to other key players in the area. It's even more important to make a friend of the clerk who serves at the counter, who can help smooth away some of the administrative hassles that will inevitably come your way. Don't underestimate the importance of being able to park near your bank, either.

Acquiring Business Premises

The premises from which you will run your business should be a key part of your business plan (*see* pp.97–95), particularly if you are in a business where your trade is sensitive to the location, such as a restaurant, a bar, a car-hire firm or any type of shop.

Renting Premises

Renting a property reduces your requirement for cash and gives you the flexibility to move when your business grows. The disadvantage is that when you get to the end of your lease, the landlord could refuse to extend it, and could, in the worst-case scenario, let it to a 'friend' who wants to set up an identical business to yours. When negotiating the terms of the lease, it is vital to gain the owner's agreement that he or she will not try to compete with your business either during or after the end of the lease, and to establish who is going to be responsible for the repairs to the building. Make sure you take sound legal advice when taking on any commercial lease.

Commercial leases in France are generally for a period of nine years, sometimes longer. The typical arrangement is the '3-6-9 lease', which means that the rent is reviewed after three years, and again after a further three years, in line with inflation. Leases can either be general – permitting any type of business – or business-specific (*bail exclusif*), which means that if you want to change from, say, a butcher's to a clothes shop, you need the consent of the owner, which can be complicated, and sometimes expensive. It is, therefore, important to make sure that your premises still have some time to go on their original lease, that there is no rent review pending, and that the categorisation of the lease is suitable for your immediate and future requirements.

If you're unsure as to your longer-term requirements and the premises are not of great importance to you, you can take short-term possession of serviced offices, or rent other premises 'at will' (*bail précaire*). The latter is only permitted in certain circumstances, such as when the premises are likely to be demolished or the owner may require them again for personal use at very short notice; it cannot last more than two years.

If you are in one of the liberal professions (*see* p.81), you can opt for a professional lease (*bail professionnel*), which is more flexible than a standard commercial lease. Technically, it must run for six years, but it can be cancelled with six months' notice in writing. There are also special forms of lease for those in the liberal professions who wish to live and work in the same premises.

Buying Premises

Buying your own premises has a number of advantages. You are completely in control of your environment, and any repairs and improvements made accrue to your benefit. If the premises go up in value, this perk can often offset any losses you make if the business proves unsuccessful. The two main drawbacks are the cost and its implications on your cashflow, and the fact that if your business expands and you need to move somewhere bigger, it's expensive to do so – the cost of buying a property in France is typically about 9% of the price of the property; the cost of selling one about 5%.

If you are buying premises for business, you need to be even more careful than if you were simply buying a house to live in, especially when it comes to planning consents and any restrictions on your freedom to use the premises for the purpose intended. There will usually be a land use plan that dictates how all of the land in an area is to be used. If you want to construct, for example, a caravan park or campsite (see pp.57–60), you need to make sure the land has permission for this, and this can be a time-consuming process. If you want to build on land or extend a building, you need to make sure that this will fit within the scope of the agreed PLU (*plan local d'urbanisme*).

Even if you just want to update, say, a shop, to make it look more modern and trendy, you need consent to alter the façade. In some places, particularly key urban locations or the centre of villages, you may find there are significant restrictions on your freedom to do as you please.

Working from Home

Both sole traders and companies can now work from home, if they attend to the various formalities, including official notification of the landlord. There are, however, some restrictions protecting your neighbours' interests – you're not allowed to receive customers or take deliveries of goods there. Nor can you start a business at home and then move out, leaving the business to continue there – you'd first have to apply to convert the building into commercial premises.

Sometimes there could be a clause in your rental lease or in the rules of your community precluding you from working from home. These will be overruled by law for the first five years of operation of your company, but your right to use the premises would eventually come to an end.

Those working from home can now make a declaration to the effect that it cannot be seized by their creditors in satisfaction of their business debts; this must be registered at the land registry and published.

Claiming some of the costs of running your home as business expenses for tax purposes can be complicated and needs to be discussed with your accountant.

Employing Staff

The most important thing to say about employing people in France, particularly your first member of staff, is to treat it seriously. If you get the formalities wrong, it will come back to bite you, and bite you savagely, especially if you have to fire someone. You would be well advised to talk to a lawyer specialising in employment law as soon as you start thinking about taking somebody on.

In terms of finding staff, in addition to the methods available in the UK, the French government's employment service, the **Agence Nationale pour l'Emploi** (**ANPE**; **www.anpe.fr**) is excellent.

The formalities involved in employing someone in France are much more rigid than in Anglo-Saxon countries. A standard form notification (*document unique d'embauche*; **DUE**) must be completed and returned to the **URSSAF** (the Social Welfare Benefits and Family Subsidies Office) at least a week before an employee starts work, which registers them for social security and employment insurance and with the local health and safety organisation, and which satisfies certain statistical requirements.

Your workers have the right to belong to a trade union, but few actually do.

Contracts and Permits

The *document unique d'embauche* means that official written contracts of employment are not legally necessary in most cases. They are needed for certain short-term contracts (*à durée déterminée*), or if you're looking for special subsidies, for example for the employment of long-term, full-time staff.

Short-term contracts can only be used in limited circumstances, such as when an employee is replacing a permanent worker on a temporary basis, or when you are expanding your workforce temporarily to deal with a surge in demand or where the work is seasonal. They must generally be for at least six months unless the work is seasonal, and can be no longer than 18 months in most cases. If the employer fails to comply strictly with the rules for short-term contracts, the contract is automatically converted into a permanent full-time one, though the employee can still cancel on the same terms originally offered to him or her – if they're given another job, for example, they could break the contract simply by giving one month's notice. As ever, it is vital to get legal advice when dealing with employment contracts. For work permits for foreign employees, *see* p.170.

Budgeting for Staff

When budgeting for staff, you need to think carefully not only about their salary but also about their holiday entitlements and social security cost. People in France think of their salary in terms of so much per month rather than so much per year, and you have to get into this way of thinking. Since the introduction of the 35-hour week, the old system of having a standard monthly salary but an entitlement to 14 rather than 12 salaries a year is gradually disappearing. There is a minimum wage in France, the SMIC. The complexities of French social security law and the high – sometimes crippling – cost of employing staff is a huge disincentive to the growth of employment in France.

Working Hours

The now-famous French 35-hour week is a bit of a misnomer – in most cases, employees are now on what boils down to flexitime. They can be required to work up to 39 hours a week (and, in times of crisis, more) and can take back the additional hours by way of increased holiday entitlement. There are also some sectors of the French economy where the 35-hour week is totally ignored.

Holidays and Other Leave

All employees have the right to a minimum of five weeks' paid holiday a year, plus official public holidays (*see* p.246) and weekends. Holiday is normally taken between 1 May and 30 October each year, and employees can take their whole holiday during that period. They can also take holidays outside that period, but if they're required to do so by their employer they are entitled to extra – two additional days if they have to take more than six days' holiday outside the official period. Employers have the right to forbid an employee taking holiday for more than four weeks at a time. Other leave entitlements generally depend on the sector of the economy in which you work and the strength of its unions.

Benefits

The cost of social security in France may be high in terms of what the employer has to contribute, but for the employee the benefits are excellent. The State makes no provision for the sickness benefit for the first three days of absence but this is usually covered by the employer.

Maternity benefit amounts to 16 weeks on full pay (six weeks before and 10 weeks after the birth), which can be increased in special circumstances. The father is entitled to 11 days off on basic sick pay.

For pensions and retirement, and for more on both sickness leave and maternity/paternity benefits, *see* **Working in France**, pp.161–74.

Training and Education

The French are extremely enthusiastic about training – massive grant aid is available for it, in many sectors of the economy there is a requirement for staff to undertake certain amounts of training per year, and many categories of employment subvention carry with them the requirement for substantial training. Consult your Chambre de Commerce and trade association for full details of what is available or required.

Dismissal and Redundancy

This is a very difficult area, with half of all dismissals ending up in front of employment tribunals. As an employer, you therefore need to comply absolutely with the procedures laid down, and remember that the burden of proof is on you. Most employers simply pay the compensation (typically, 10–20% of the monthly salary per year of employment) because it's easier.

Where there is a genuine need for redundancies, there are set procedures that you need to follow to the letter – you must produce a plan showing how you are attempting to save jobs, and you are under a legal obligation to re-employ the staff if the situation improves within one year. Redundancy payments can be substantial – typically, 20% of the monthly salary per year of employment but sometimes considerably more. For more information about the issues surrounding dismissal and redundancy, see **Working in France**, p.172.

Summary: A Step by Step Guide to Setting up Your Business

- **Make sure you're legally permitted to carry out your chosen type of business.**
- **Make sure you have the necessary qualifications and that they are recognised.**
- **Consult your Chambre de Commerce et d'Industrie.** Even if it turns out it is not the proper body to regulate you, staff there will be able to tell you what is.
- **Contact any special bodies that are relevant to your type of activity.** For example, if you are going to establish a farm, contact the Chambre d'Agriculture; if you are going to start a shop, the Direction Départementale de la Concurrence, de la Consommation et de la Répression des Fraudes (DDCCRF); if you are going to set up some sort of craftsperson's business, the Chambre de Métiers; if you want to set up an estate agency, one of the professional bodies. Take whatever advice such bodies have to offer.
- **Make a final plan with your accountant as to the best tax structure to adopt.**
- **Make a final plan with your lawyer as to the best legal structures to adopt.**
- **Contact the tax office to check that it is happy about the situation generally.**
- **Decide where you are going to base your business.** If you are a sole trader (see pp.79–82), there is no longer any overarching restriction on your working from home, but there are restrictions on what you can do from there (for instance, you will not normally be permitted to run an engineering or industrial type business, to take deliveries there or to do anything else that causes nuisance to your neighbours). If you're a company, you can generally work from your manager or chairperson's home for two years.
- **Hire a manager if relevant.**
- **Open a bank account.**
- **Decide on the name of your company.** This important question should have been considered in your business plan, but now is the time to come to a final decision, because changing it at a later date becomes complicated.
- **Read up on or go on a course about anything that is causing you worries at this stage.** France is awash with courses, and if you registered as unemployed before you started to set up your business, you will probably be entitled to some assistance towards the cost.

- **On the basis of what you read or learn, consider whether you need any more one-to-one advice.** This is available, often cheaply or at no cost, from the chambers of Commerce, Tradespeople or Agriculture, or other organisations.
- **Make any final revisions to your business plan and financial projections.** It's worth getting it reviewed one last time by your lawyer and/or accountant unless you are absolutely certain of its content. They should be aware of what you're trying to do, so the review should not take long or cost very much.
- **Present yourself at the Centre de Formalités des Entreprises (CFE).** Your professional advisers can tell you where to go, or go on your behalf. There, you fill in the necessary **application form** and submit it; the CFE, which is intended to be a one-stop shop, distributes the form to the various other entities to whom you would have previously had to go. You will have to produce a declaration, sworn by you, that you have not been in trouble with the police. Non-EU citizens will need a declaration from the police force in the country where they previously lived, as well as a *carte de commerçant (see* pp.154–6 and 170–71). If you require any professional qualifications to register the business, you have to produce certified copies of those qualifications together with sworn translations. You will need to produce proof of your right to occupy your business premises (a copy of your lease or title deeds) and a copy of your marriage certificate or divorce certificate if applicable. *Note that the declaration made to the CFE is of vital importance – if you get it wrong, you will be trading illegally, with all sorts of unfortunate consequences. If you do make a mistake you have two weeks in which to correct it. You really should get professional advice before you submit the form, even if it's only a very simple business you're setting up.*
- **The CFE will give you a receipt known as the** *récépissé de création d'entreprise*, **which does not allow you to start work but does permit you to start placing adverts and obtain official letterheads and the like.**
- **Quite quickly, you will get a document, the Kbis, from the Régistre de Commerce et de Sociétiés.** This means your business is registered and you can start trading.
- **You will probably still not have received your official business number or SIRET** (*see* p.124), **which can be a pain if a potential customer is asking to see it. Until it arrives, your only option is to state that your SIRET is** *en cours* **(being processed).**
- **While all this is going on, you will have been directed by the CFE to the social security and other organisations you need to register with.** This never goes smoothly, and you should, whenever possible, allow yourself plenty of time. Do not (as one of our clients did) arrange a massive opening party for your new restaurant until you have got all of the paperwork.
- **If anything changes – for instance, you move your office or alter a key feature of your business – you need to report the changes to the CFE within a month of their taking place.** A form for doing most such things is available from the CFE.

Red Tape

Registering Your Business 124
Social Security 125
Taxes 127
Should You Pay Corporate or Personal Tax? 127
Corporate Taxes 128
Personal Taxes 142
Immigration and Work Permits 153
EU Citizens 153
Non-EU Citizens 154
Citizenship 156
Professional and Other Qualifications 157
Provision of Services 157
Establishment 158
Getting Your Qualifications Recognised 159

Registering Your Business

In France, the spiritual home of bureaucracy where everything must be officially recognised and the correct piece of paper used, every business must be registered. This causes considerable frustration not only among foreigners but also among some French people. It can be mitigated but not avoided.

Someone wanting to pursue an activity must find out if it is subject to **formal training or qualification requirements** (see pp.157–9). Many activities require qualifications, and it is illegal to engage in them without them. A qualified person can engage in the activity as an employee (*salarié*) or as a self-employed or freelance person (*travailleur indépendant*). There are limits to the degree to which you can legitimately work as the latter; sometimes your activity will be deemed salaried if you work almost wholly for one company. The difference between being salaried and self-employed has many consequences for tax and social security contributions, and, for non-EU citizens, regarding work permits and visas.

In France, businesses are categorised as tradespeople (*artisans*) or businesses – a plumber will be a tradesperson, a person selling taps from a shop will be a business, and a plumber working from a shop will remain a tradesperson. This is significant because tradespeople register with the Chambre de Métiers et de l'Artisanat, and businesses with the Chambre de Commerce et d'Industrie; see p.81. Farmers register with the Chambre d'Agriculture.

Having registered, you obtain your **SIREN** and **SIRET** (business identification numbers) – essential documents for any business operating in France. The Labour Code (*code du travail*) requires that this number be used in all publicity materials and most business documents intended to bring the attention of a service or product to somebody's notice. Non-compliance will net you a fine of €7,500. The SIRET number comprises two parts. The separate SIREN number, allocated by the National Statistics Office (INSEE), comprises nine digits if you are in a liberal profession (*see* p.81), nine digits followed by the initials RCS if you are a business, and nine digits followed by the initials RM and a further three digits if you are an artisan (*see* p.81). This is followed by the SIRET: five digits that identify your geographical location. A business with a single SIREN number can have a number of separate SIRET numbers (up to 9,999) for branches in different locations.

You will also receive a **VAT (TVA) number** comprising your nine-digit SIREN number preceded by the code FR for France and a two-digit check key number. In addition, you will have a code known as an **NAF**, which refers to the category into which your business has been included. There are 702 categories overall, and if it isn't in the list, it doesn't exist.

You also have to register for social security and medical assistance; who with depends on the status of your business. Your business status might also require you to register with certain other entities.

Social Security

Social security contributions, which account for a very large part of the income generated by the French government, are only paid by tax residents (*see* pp.144–5). They're deducted from the figure for gross income before tax is calculated. The main social security office is the **URSSAF (Union de Recouvrement des Cotisations de Sécurité Sociale et d'Allocations Familiales)**, which has a website, **www.urssaf.fr**, with a chart showing how the system is organised.

People employed in any EU member state are subject to its social security legislation even if they are residents of another state, with a few exceptions (such as navigation and air travel, or when the duration of the work does not exceed 12 months and the employee is not deemed to be replacing another person who has completed his or her posting). Hence, if you are working for your business in France, you pay social security and other social charges in France. There are special regulations for different business sectors, and payments are also collected and administered differently depending on your sector.

Social security contributions are hefty – the employer's and employee's contributions together typically amount to 67% of the latter's salary. There is also an extra contribution of 0.5%. Investment income bears a supplemental contribution of 2%. There is a reduced level (6.2%) for pension income.

These contributions should not be underestimated. They apply in many circumstances where you would not think you would be liable for social security payments, and can easily add 10% to your tax rate on investment income, increasing it from, say, 42% to 52%.

The high level of social security contributions and, in particular, the way they increase dramatically after the second year of a business's life (*see* p.81) is said to contribute to the large number of businesses that fail in their third year. This is aggravated by the cessation, in their third year, of tax reductions enjoyed by new businesses. To alleviate the problem, the government introduced an alternative option for payment of social security contributions in 2000 – you can defer your obligation to pay the contributions due in the first year and pay them monthly over the ensuing five years.

Who Do You Pay and How Much?

There are multiple organisations to which you may have to pay your social security payments and that then administer those payments, depending on the business sector in which you're engaged. When you register your business at the **Centre des Formalités des Entreprises** (**CFE**; *see* pp.86–7), one of the tasks they perform is to forward your paperwork to the appropriate social security agency, who will then contact you to tell you how and where to make your social security payments.

There are four main regimes offering health insurance, pensions, unemployment benefits and family income support to four main employment categories, each differing in its scope of activities and the benefits paid:

- The *régime général*, which concerns 80% of French citizens and covers salaried employees in trade and industry.
- The *régime agricole*, for farmers, fieldworkers and anyone who works in the agricultural sector.
- The *régimes spéciaux*, covering various categories of employment, from civil servants to railway staff.
- The *régime autonome*, dealing with the self-employed.

If you are in salaried employment, your employer will register you with the **Caisse de Sécurité Sociale d'Assurance Maladie** a week or so after you start work. Social contributions, amounting to about 20–25% of your net salary, will be deducted from it each month. This is topped up by an additional 35–45% contributed by the employer. The self-employed handle their own registration with the URSSAF. The amount due is calculated annually and contributed in four payments a year.

If you are a sole trader (*entreprise individuelle; see* pp.79–82) or if you run an EURL (*see* p.85) or are the majority director of a SARL (*see* p.85), you enjoy lower initial payments and deferred payment options. For the first years of your business, you pay contributions at a fixed rate because, up to that point, your actual income is not known. You pay a basic contribution and an additional contribution to provide for your pension, which varies depending on the sector in which you work. In the first year, your basic contribution will be €1,227. If you are a *commerçant* (*see* p.81), your extra contribution will amount to approximately €1,250; if you are an artisan (*see* pp.81–2), to about €2,800. In the second year, you pay a basic contribution of €920 for the first half of the year. From that point on, your contributions will reflect your actual earnings. In each case, you will also have to pay the additional contribution for your pension.

This money is distributed by the URSSAF to the **Agence Centrale des Organismes de Sécurité Sociale (ACOSS)**, who redistribute it to the different offices, or *caisses*, that pay out the various social security benefits to employees. The **Caisse Nationale d'Assurance Maladie des Travailleurs Salariés (CNAMTS)** is the national healthcare *caisse* for salaried employees, while contributions from the self-employed go to one of 31 **Caisses d'Assurance Maladies Régionales (CMR)**, which are controlled by the **Caisse Nationale d'Assurance Maladie des Professions Indépendantes (CANAM)**. Reimbursements for medical treatment are paid out by the **Caisses Primaires d'Assurance Maladie (CPAM)**, and family income support is dealt with by the **Caisses d'Allocations Familiales (CAF)**.

For information on your entitlement to state benefits, *see* pp.228–32.

VAT (TAV)

France's largest single source of tax revenue, VAT, is in essence a tax paid by consumers for goods and services. For companies, it is a neutral tax – they collect the VAT on their sales and deduct the amount of VAT that they have paid on purchases of goods and services. If companies have paid more VAT than they have collected, the difference is refunded to them on request. Exports of goods outside the EU are completely exempt from VAT.

The standard French VAT rate on sales of goods and services is 19.6%, but there are also reduced rates. Residential lettings are not subject to VAT. The rate on medicines is 5.5% or 2.1%. The rate on food products and certain agricultural products is 5.5%, as is the rate on books, most hotels, public transport, newspapers and magazines, and certain leisure activities (including restaurant bills!).

Taxes

All tax systems are complicated, but the French system is one of the most byzantine, complex and subtle in the world – and, just to confuse you, it changes every year. Before you panic, bear in mind that most foreigners setting up a business in France have limited contact with the system's more intricate realms, including those letting holiday homes (*see* pp.50–53). That said, it's helpful to have some understanding of the way the system works and the taxes you might face. It's also a good idea to learn some of the words and concepts that seem familiar but that have a fundamentally different meaning in France (*see* the glossary on pp.249–58).

Books (and long ones at that) have been written about French taxation. What follows does little more than scratch the surface of an immensely complex subject. It's intended to allow you to have a sensible discussion with professional advisers and to help you work out the questions you need to ask them. It is no substitute for obtaining individual professional advice.

Should You Pay Corporate or Personal Tax?

If you are a sole trader or a partner in certain categories of partnership (*see* pp.79–86), your business affairs will be treated as fiscally transparent, which means that the entity engaged in the business is not taxed separately – the income of that business is treated directly as being the income of the sole trader or the partners concerned. If you run your business through a limited company or any of the other mechanisms explained on pp.79–86, you pay French **company income tax** (*impôt sur les sociétés*; **IS**). If that company, in turn, pays any money to you as an individual, you pay **individual income tax** (*impôt sur le revenue*; **IR**) on it.

- Mr A and Mr B are in a simple partnership (*see* pp.82–4). Mr A receives 60% of the profit, Mr B 40%. This income is simply added to any other income they may have (e.g. from property rental, from shares they own, or from their pensions) and taxed under the personal taxation rules.
- Mr A and Mr B are shareholders in a SARL (*see* p.85). Mr A has 60% of the shares, Mr B 40%. The company will pay corporate income tax on its profit calculated in accordance with French law. What is left over after payment of the tax can either be retained in the company (in which case no further tax is due) or distributed as a dividend to the shareholders, in which case the amount distributed will be added to the shareholders' other income and taxed in the normal way.

It can come as a bit of a surprise to Anglo-Saxons that in France you can, in some cases, choose whether to pay taxes as a company or as an individual. This decision is made at the time you register your business and is a crucial decision, meaning you should take advice from your accountant or lawyer. If you decide to pay personal tax, it is relatively straightforward to convert to paying company tax at a later date, but once you have done so you can't convert back, or it becomes very complicated and expensive to do so.

The basic situation is as follows:

Entreprise individuelle	IR
EURL	either
SARL	IS
SA	IS
SAS	IS
Partnerships	IR (generally)
Limited partnerships	IS

If you decide to pay tax by way of personal taxation, there are three different bases upon which you can be taxed, and you will need to choose the most appropriate.

Corporate Taxes

The taxation of companies in France is less nightmarish than the taxation of individuals, probably because corporate tax does not carry as much political baggage and there are fewer sacred cows – businesses and businesspeople are more accepting of reviews of the tax system than the public.

Note that, because of lack of space, the exemptions detailed over the next few pages can never be comprehensively listed, and the rules related to those exemptions are always more complicated than it has been possible to convey. The following is an overview illustrating some of the issues involved when it comes to exemptions, loopholes and accountancy practice.

Certain aspects of French corporate tax are governed by a three-year cycle by which you can get little or no tax in years one and two but then be hit for large amounts in year three. Unsurprisingly, large numbers of French businesses fail in year three (some are re-established in year four and start the process again!).

Tax Evasion

Not declaring your full income to the tax office is illegal, and there are substantial penalties for those engaged in significant evasion. That said, it is rife in France, particularly in small businesses, and people sometimes find it hard to avoid when trying to keep their business competitive. For instance, your full-time shop assistant might ask to be treated as a part-time worker to avoid the very high social charges she would otherwise have to pay, and this would have the benefit of reducing the social charges you have to pay too. However, in order to do this, you have to pay part of the wages in cash, which means in turn that you must also have 'black money' coming over the counter otherwise you will not be able to account for it.

Foreigners are particularly at risk if they engage in tax evasion. If your business is successful, jealous rivals may denounce you to the tax authorities, even if their own practices are a little grubby (between competing French businessmen in the same places there is often a certain *esprit de corps*).

In any case, tax evasion is becoming harder, particularly in the light of EU directives on money-laundering and anti-terrorist legislation. Set up your business in full compliance with local rules, however much it might hurt when you have to sign the cheques for the tax and social charges, and however much you might resent the fact that your local competitors are being a little less ethical.

Honesty Pays

If you don't voluntarily declare the tax you owe and pay it, the government can issue you with a demand to submit a return. If you don't do so within 30 days, they will estimate your liability, and such estimates are not normally generous to taxpayers. Proving that the estimate is wrong is a major (and thus expensive) task. You also have to pay interest at the current rate on the amount you owe (0.75% a month compounded, at the time of writing), and a penalty ranging from 10% to 80% depending on how late the payment is.

Lest you think you can slip under the radar, be aware that the tax office can assess your tax for any period up to three years previously. The resulting bill, including interest and penalties, can make your eyes water! Make a proper declaration each year rather than running this senseless risk, especially given that for most people the tax properly payable is modest. Nor is it sensible to underdeclare: if you claim less income and tax payable than the government thinks you should have to pay, an assessment will be issued and, once again, you will have to prove that it is wrong.

The Freelance Scene

There are many foreign 'freelancers' in France, a lot of whom don't declare their status to the French authorities. Perhaps they write travel articles on France for British publications out of their French summerhouse, in which case they probably pay taxes on their income back home and don't expect or want French social security benefits or any of the other 'perks' of paying taxes in France. Rather than being 'illegal', you could argue that these people were on a very productive 'holiday'. But too often foreigners – especially those who work for other foreigners – opt not to set themselves up for business in France on the grounds that they are registered in the UK. If they're caught, they not only face fines and the confiscation of their equipment – they could face time in prison.

The moment a self-employed person begins to do business in France, and earns an income in the country, he or she needs to make their status known to the French government. This includes people selling *brocante* at a travelling antiques fair, official translators, people installing satellite TVs for foreigners, builders, repairers and artisans. Here are the basic things you need to know.

In France, the term 'freelance' refers to any individual who is responsible for is or her income and for generating business and clients. A freelance operates under the independent worker status (*travailleur indépendant*). As such, you are responsible for all social charges and benefits associated with your income. That means you will have to make contributions to France's social security system, retirement funds and health coverage. You also need to keep the following in mind:

- Your sales figure is your gross income. You will end up with roughly 40% of that figure as your personal income or 'salary'.
- The contributions you make to social security will equal roughly 40% of your total net income before income tax.

Accountants (*Experts Comptables*)

In France the certified public accountant has a similar role to his or her British, Irish or American counterparts, reviewing and assessing the accounts of companies for the tax authorities, and perhaps giving an opinion on a company's accounts and records or on general management issues on a consultancy basis for that firm. Fees are negotiated between the parties.

Independent auditors (*commissaires aux comptes*) check that a company's accounts present a true and fair picture of its activities for the period in question and accurately show its financial situation, including its assets and liabilities. Companies above a certain size (in terms of their turnover, balance sheet or number of employees), which changes regularly, are generally required to have one independent auditor. Fees are negotiated between the auditor and the company's shareholders, to whom they report. They often rely on the work carried out by the firm's certified public accountant.

- You will pay income tax as well as the social charges.
- You are responsible for compensating yourself for any holiday you take.
- Although you won't have access to many of the benefits that are enjoyed by salaried employees, you can write off business-related expenses such as business lunches, equipment, and additional health insurance payments made to a *mutuelle* (see p.229). In addition, you may be able to write off your rent (or a portion of it) if you work from home.
- Sick leave and maternity leave are very poorly covered, although new laws are slowly changing this.
- If your business fails, you will not receive unemployment benefits (although there is insurance for failed businesses).
- You will be responsible for your own professional development, such as paying for training courses.

Travailleurs indépendants pay income tax on their net income. Value added tax (TVA; see p.127) must be added to all your bills. TVA on your expenses is deductible from TVA billed and you must pay the difference to the tax authorities. If you are billing less than €27,000 for the year, you may be exempt from TVA but you will not be able to make deductions.

Self-employed people must decide the type of business structure they want; they usually opt for sole proprietorship (*entreprise individuelle*); see pp.79–82.

If a British freelancer works for a British company while living in France, he or she could keep their British bank account and arrange for their income to be paid into that account. The UK and France have reciprocal tax agreements (see p.145), so the income will be taxed by one country, in this case the UK. But if the freelancer wants to enjoy the benefits of the French social security system he or she has to pay French income taxes.

Even if your company does not require a formal audit (and most small companies do not), it is foolish for a number of reasons to attempt to prepare your own accounts for taxation purposes. First of all, the French system is alien to British, Irish or American eyes, and secondly the rules change regularly and to a significant degree. Additionally, the precise and correct interpretation of the rules (or sometimes the understanding of just how far those rules can be pushed) can save you a great deal of money. Even if you're using one of the simplified accounting schemes that are described on pp.150–51, you should retain an accountant for at least the first and possibly the second year of trading – your bill will be modest because the scheme is simple so the accountant will not have much to do.

Accountants in France are not permitted to advertise. The best way of appointing one is from personal recommendation. Your lawyer or businesspeople in your town may be able to help, or your Chamber of Commerce may be able to assist unofficially. If all else fails, they are listed in the *Pages Jaunes* (*Yellow Pages*), **www.pagesjaunes.fr**. If you live in a small town or village, you may find there is only one local accountant anyway, but the advantage of this is that employing him or her helps you become part of the community.

Having said that, you will need an accountant who speaks English. It is hard enough for lawyers to explain legal concepts in a way 'normal' people can understand – trying to explain the detailed provisions of accountancy rules in faltering English or convey them to someone who speaks little French is well nigh impossible. Unfortunately, relatively few accountants outside the main cities speak good English.

Another issue is that Brits setting up a business in France tend to want their accountant to explain the problem *and* the solution, if only so they can avoid having to pay their fee for resolving the same issue the following year. In general, except when it comes to major strategic decisions, the French do not expect this – they hand the matter to their accountant and he or she presents them with the solution as a *fait accompli*. Therefore, if you want to take an active part in the decision-making process, it is a good idea to make this clear to your accountant at the outset.

If you really don't want to employ a professional accountant, at the very least have your books prepared by the authorised administration centre set up by the Industry Association (*centre de gestion agréé*) that exists for each industrial or commercial sector. You are well advised to join the latter (for a modest annual fee) and adhere to its rules and recommendations, if only because doing so will in many cases result in a 20% reduction in your tax bill because of a special incentive scheme introduced by the government to curb tax evasion.

Book-keeping

Many people have had experience of British book-keeping and think about doing their own book-keeping in France, with the aid of computer packages. Whether this is a good idea depends, first, on how flexible you are, as you will have to forget much of what you have learned when doing book-keeping in the UK. Though the underlying principles of debit and credit remain the same, and though there are similarities in the French and British concepts of the balance sheet and profit and loss account, there are also many differences. French book-keeping is much more structured and subject to rigid rules. Paradoxically, the less you know about British book-keeping, the easier it probably is to convert to the French system.

The time spent learning the French system and then making the relevant entries may be better spent doing other things, in which case you might be better off employing a part-time book-keeper. Your French may not be up to bookkeeping in French, anyway, so your books will have to be translated into French by an accountant at some stage. If, like most businesses, you end up using both a book-keeper and an accountant, you may find that the two come from the same office, particularly if you live in a rural area. If your accountant doesn't offer book-keeping, he or she will be able to recommend someone.

Your ability to communicate with your book-keeper is, if anything, even more important than your ability to communicate with your accountant, as they will often require clarification about a particular item of expenditure.

Taxes in your Country of Origin

In the section that follows, it is assumed that you have left your home country and are now operating, as a business, solely in France. The main exception to this is someone who has simply set up as a representative of a foreign company in France. As explained on pp.96–100, the activities of that office remain taxable in the country where the 'mother' enterprise is based unless you fail to comply strictly with the French rules, in which case your enterprise is deemed to have become a branch of your overseas business and therefore subject to full French taxation. (This is an example of the French phenomenon known as the requalification of facts – *requalification des faits*.)

Liability to French Taxes

Any business in France is liable for French tax on its earnings in France. This rule applies to all types of 'permanent establishment' (*see* below), whether branches, subsidiaries or independent businesses. In addition, French businesses (but not branches of foreign businesses) pay tax in France on their worldwide profits, though they will be allowed to set off any tax already paid on those profits in another country in which the business is conducted. For instance, if you set up a business in France and then decide to set up a branch of it in, for example, the UK or Dubai, the income from those branches will be taxed in France. The British tax paid would be deducted from your French tax bill in respect of that income, but as there is no tax in Dubai you would pay tax on the full amount of that income in France. If a branch of a foreign business is not a separate legal entity producing its own financial statements (which it should be), its earnings from activities in France are reconstituted using the financial statements of the foreign company.

A '**permanent establishment**' is a fixed place through which business is wholly or partly carried out. This could be a branch office, a factory, a workshop, a building site or installation project lasting more than 12 months, or even your own home if that is where your business is based. There are special considerations when it comes to e-commerce (*see* pp.64–5). A person, other than an independent agent, who is acting on behalf of a British company in France and usually exercises in France an authority to conclude contracts in the name of this company is deemed to be a permanent establishment of the company in France – in other words, it is quite possible for a person to be considered a permanent establishment under the terms of the law.

An **'independent' agent** with a French telephone line for professional use should, in principle, be taxed personally on his or her commissions received in France. If, however, they are not truly legally independent and/or carry out most of their work for one company based outside France, they will, most likely, be treated as being a permanent establishment of the foreign company for which they are, notionally, the agent but in fact its full representative in France. In other words, if you are doing business in France from premises in France and are not a simple representative office of a foreign company (see pp.96–100), you will pay tax (and, just as importantly, social charges) in France. People struggle to find ways round this essentially simple concept, but you do so at your peril.

Using the shield of an overseas company is a tempting way to escape the considerable expense and ongoing red tape involved with setting up and running a French business, but it usually won't work. You may get away with it for a while, but if the authorities review your situation, they will declare you to be a French business and subject to the full panoply of French rules, including those relating to tax and social charges. EU law only allows for trading from overseas in specific and very limited situations. You can only **avoid French tax and social charges** if all of the following conditions are fulfilled:

- Your French activity is secondary to your overseas one.
- You do not have a 'permanent establishment' in France.
- You employ no one on French territory, except, possibly, one person in a purely representative capacity.
- You conclude no contracts on French territory.
- Your activities in France cannot be deemed 'continual'. (This occurs in some surprising cases. For example, if you order a book from Amazon UK from France, French TVA appears on the bill, because Amazon is deemed to carry out 'continual' business in France, even when orders for British books are processed through its UK-based website.

If there were no rules to combat 'delocalisation' (artificially basing a company in location A but doing business in location B), any sane person would base their business in Cyprus or Ireland, where there are virtually no corporate taxes. These rules exist by virtue of the EU treaty and bilateral treaties between France and other countries, most notably the UK. Political inertia in terms of enforcing the law is waning, and you can face up to three years in prison and a €45,000 fine on top of the payment of the taxes due, social charges and penalties

Tax Rates

- **Standard rate: 33.33%**
- **Reduced rate: 19%.** This applies in a limited number of cases, such as capital gains on non-voting shares, shares in venture capital funds or companies and patent royalties.

- Small businesses rate: 15% on the first €38,112 in profits, with the standard tax rate in force on remaining profits. 'Small businesses' are companies in which at least 75% of the equity is owned directly or indirectly by individuals or by companies that meet the same conditions, and that report annual sales of less than €7,630,000.

Companies pay an additional levy of 3% of the tax paid, which brings the standard tax rate up to 34.33% for the vast majority. An additional social security levy is applied to high-earning companies (where the income taxed at the standard rate is greater than €2,289,000). The additional levy is 3.3% of the tax payment, after subtracting €763,000. It does not pay to grow too big in France!

Calculating your Liability

Income comprises all the proceeds from activities, sales or provision of services, and generally capital gains on trading assets. Deductible expenses include:

- **Depreciation and amortisation (excluding goodwill).**
- **Provisions.**
- **Rent for buildings and equipment.**
- **Wages.**
- **Social security charges.**
- **Goods purchased.**
- **Energy consumption.**
- **Advertising.**
- **Financial expenses.**

There are limits on some deductions to prevent abuse. For example, the depreciation allowance and deductible lease payments on company cars are capped at €18,300 including VAT, to prevent Bentleys from being written off as a business expense. Management expenses, sales commissions, interest charges and royalties paid to associated companies are deductible if they correspond to actual services rendered and the amounts invoiced are in line with market prices.

Depreciation

France's depreciation rules are particularly favourable. Fixed assets are depreciated according to the straight-line method over their likely useful life. Production assets (e.g. manufacturing equipment) that were purchased new benefit from 'acceleration multiples' ranging from 1.25 to 2.25 applied to the straight-line depreciation rates, depending on the normal useful life of the assets concerned. This gives you much bigger write-offs than in the UK. Equipment and tools used for scientific and technical research, which was purchased or produced after 1 January 2004, can be depreciated using an 'accelerated diminishing balance' method. The acceleration multiples in this case range from 1.5 to 2.5. Software, energy conservation equipment, renewable energy production equipment, noise abatement equipment and non-polluting vehicles (running on electricity, natural gas or LPG) can be written off over 12 months. Finally, fixed assets that have been financed by capital grants, regional development grants or agricultural development grants can be depreciated on the basis of their cost price, plus half of the grant amount.

Write-offs

Provisions for reduction in the value of assets are allowed if they can be justified and if they relate to clearly identified claims, inventories, securities or tangible assets. Allowable provisions include conditions for risks, for doubtful work in progress, for price increases, for holiday pay liabilities, and so on.

Groups of Companies

France's tax rules are particularly favourable for groups of companies, who can offset income and losses from their consolidated French businesses and eliminate inter-company transactions for tax purposes. This option is available if the French subsidiaries in the consolidated group are at least 95% owned by a French parent company. Groups must choose this option for a five-year period and must announce their choice before the first day of the financial year of the first of the consolidated companies.

Tax Incentives

The French enjoy very generous tax benefits and credits. Only a few specialist accountants are expert in this field. If you're thinking of running a standard small business, this might not matter, but if you're looking to do something innovative, it is well worth paying for specialist advice.

Depressed Regions

A variety of quite complex tax incentives have been introduced to help companies invest in France's depressed regions or engage in other activities encouraged by the state. *See* the section on grant aid on pp.110–15.

Research and Training

France is very keen on research, and tax credits are granted for expenditure on research and training by manufacturing, trading and agricultural companies, which can then be applied against their corporate income tax. If they don't owe any tax, they receive a cash reimbursement of the tax credit after three years. Eligible research expenditures are spending on basic research, applied research and experimental development. The tax credit amount is capped at €8 million per company per year. Eligible research spending includes:

- **Staff costs (gross wages) for researchers and research technicians working directly and exclusively on research.**

- Depreciation allowances for plant and equipment used directly for research operations.
- An allowance for overhead expenses set at:
  – 75% of eligible staff costs.
  – 100% of staff costs relating to employees holding doctorates, for their first 12 months on the payroll.
  – Patent filing and maintenance costs.
  – An amortisation allowance for patents acquired for research purposes.
  – 50% of standardisation costs.
  – Spending on research operations contracted out to approved organisations.
  – Spending on patent-defence and technology-watch (the cap on eligible spending in each of these categories is now €60,000).
  – Funding provided to public research bodies, universities and technical centres, which now counts double towards the tax credit.

These are tremendous allowances that also give rise to the possibility of some creative accounting. Sometimes it only requires a change in a person's title to make their job into a research or development job.

Work–Life Balance Tax Credit

Since 2004, companies have been able to obtain a tax credit equal to 25% of their spending to enable employees with children to achieve a better balance between work and family life. The eligible spending includes funds for daycare centres, training for employees on parental leave, and the compensation of employees on maternity, paternity or parental leave. The tax credit is capped at €500,000 per company per year. It can be applied against the company's corporate income tax for the year in which the spending was incurred. If the credit is greater than the tax due for the year in question, the difference is reimbursed.

Cinema Tax Credit

Since 2004, cinema production companies that pay corporate income tax have been able to obtain a tax credit for certain production expenditures specified by law. The credit is available to companies that act as assistant producers and for operations carried out in France in the production of feature-length films. It is calculated for each financial year and is equal to 20% of eligible expenditure. The total tax credits for a single film are capped at €500,000 for a fiction or documentary feature and €750,000 for an animated feature.

The credit can be applied against the company's corporate income tax for the year in which the spending was incurred. If the tax credit is greater than the tax due for the year in question, the difference is reimbursed.

Training Credits

This measure was created for small and medium-sized enterprises that incur vocational training expenses in excess of the legal requirement or that provide internships. The tax credit is equal to 35% of the positive or negative difference between training expenditure in excess of the legal requirement for the current year and the excess amount for the previous year; and to €450 for each intern in excess of the number of interns in the previous year. It is capped at €150,000. If the credit is greater than the tax due, the excess amount is immediately reimbursed.

The 'One-Man' Venture Capital Company (SUIR) Exemption

This entity is a special legal structure owned by a single individual. It provides tax benefits commensurate with the high risk of investing in new companies. Such companies must be founded for the sole purpose of buying founders' shares for cash or contributing to capital increases in unlisted manufacturing, trading and craft companies located in the EU and liable to corporate income tax. Investments must be in 'new' companies that are majority-owned by individuals or by other companies themselves majority-owned by individuals. The 'one-man' venture capital company must own 5–20% of the shares in these companies. The tax benefits come in the form of two exemptions: a corporate income tax exemption for the first 10 years of the venture capital company's existence; and an exemption from personal income tax for the original shareholder on income distributed by the venture capital company, including capital gains on the disposal of shares in target companies.

Temporary Corporate Income Tax Exemption

New companies in certain areas may be eligible for a temporary, and diminishing, corporate tax exemption. This for 100% of the income for the first 24 months. After that, tax is levied on quarter of the income in the next 12 months, half the income in the following period, and three quarters of income in the period after that. The tax-exempt income is limited to €225,000 in any 36-month period.

It is restricted to companies not more than 50% owned by other companies. The eligible companies may also be exempt from business tax and property tax for two years, if the local community has decided to take such a measure.

Innovative New Companies (JEI)

This exemption is aimed at new companies with research spending accounting for at least 15% of total expenses. It provides for a partial exemption from corporate tax, business tax and property tax over eight years up to a limit of €100,000 in any 36-month period. The wages of such companies' research staff are exempt from the employers' social security charges for eight years.

This is for small and medium-sized enterprises owned mainly by individuals, or companies that meet the same criteria. Sales of shares in such companies are exempt from capital gains tax if the seller has held them for three or more years.

Tax on Real Estate Owned by a Foreign Company (*Taxe sur les Immeubles ... des Personnes Morales*)

In practice, this is an issue mainly for real estate owned via a company based in a tax haven. Amounting to 3% of the value of the real estate held without deductions for mortgages or other debts, it applies to all companies except property developers and dealers. It's based on the market value of the property (not the lower cadastral value) and is payable unless:

- The real estate is less than 50% of the company's assets in France.

- The company's registered office is in a country with which France has a taxation treaty for the suppression of tax evasion and the company makes an annual declaration of its real estate holdings and the identity of its shareholders.

- The company's effective seat of management is in France or in a country with which France has a double taxation treaty and the company agrees to disclose its land holdings and the identity of its shareholders on request or make such a declaration every year.

- It is a publicly quoted company.

- It is a state or international organisation such as the Red Cross.

- It is a non-profit-making company and can justify its ownership of the property on the basis of social, charitable, educational or cultural activities.

If the real estate is owned by a chain of companies, the test is applied all the way up the chain. British companies do not have to pay, but those in tax havens such as the Channel Islands and Isle of Man do.

Taxes on the Repatriated Profits of Overseas Companies

Overseas companies' profits are usually repatriated in three forms: as transfers or distributions of net profit from branches and subsidiaries; as interest on loans and advances from the foreign parent company; and as royalties or management fees. There is no French tax (except withholding tax; *see* below) on interest, royalties or management fees.

The amounts invoiced must be justified and in line with the prices for arm's-length transactions between independent companies. The French authorities are entitled to proof that transfer prices are in line with true market prices.

If the parent company is in a country that does not have a tax treaty with France, there is a **withholding tax**. The rates are: 25% on dividends, branch profits and royalties, and 15% on interest payments. Tax treaties between France and many countries significantly reduce withholding tax rates. For example, there is no withholding tax on dividends or branch income paid to EU parent companies or the head office of European companies. The tax treaty between France and the USA sets the withholding tax rate on dividends, branch profits and management fees at 5%. The withholding tax rate rises to 15% for dividends paid to individuals who are residents in the USA and own fewer than 10% of the shares in the French company in question.

Tax Treatment of Losses

From 1 January 2004, losses have been able to be carried forward indefinitely. There is also an arrangement for deducting the current year's losses from income in previous years – this 'carry back' system makes it possible to deduct the current year's loss from any income in the three previous years. This results in a claim on the treasury for the repayment of taxes already paid for those earlier years.

Long-term capital losses on the disposal of fixed assets can be offset against capital gains of the same type over 10 years.

Taxation of Holding Companies

When holding companies located in France and owning equity in French and foreign companies redistribute dividends from companies in which they own more than 5% of the equity to their foreign shareholders, there is no tax if it parent company is in an EU member state. If it isn't, the only tax liability is the withholding tax at the rate determined by the relevant tax treaty. However, holding companies that are more than two-thirds foreign-owned enjoy special exemptions and deductions not available to companies under French ownership.

Customs Duties

Goods move freely inside the EU, and customs duties are only charged once on non-EU imports, even if they are sent from one member state to another after import. Goods entering France for re-export to another EU member state may enter France with no VAT charge – VAT is paid in the country where the goods are consumed. A special arrangement suspends VAT payments for goods in transit that will be placed under the Union's system of customs duty relief or in a bonded warehouse. This is to delay payment of VAT until a later stage. The New Computerised Transit System (NCTS), which manages the transit arrangements, has been compulsory since 1 April 2004.

Companies are not required to complete any administrative formalities for the movement of most merchandise between countries in the EU. They must merely file an exchange of goods declaration (Intrastat) on intra-community trade for statistical purposes. Any company that receives merchandise worth more than €100,000 per year from another member state or exports the same amount to other member states must file an Intrastat form each month. The form provides information about types of products, countries of origin and destination, values and weights.

Imports and exports of merchandise between member states of the EC and other (non-EU) countries require a customs declaration, which must be filed using the Single Administrative Document (SAD).

Business Tax (*Taxe Professionnelle*)

Business tax is levied on behalf of local communities and calculated each year according to the location(s) of the company's premises. It is the local community's largest source of tax income.

A plan to reform the business tax is currently under consideration. In the meantime, capital goods acquired by companies give rise to a business tax deduction. The tax base is *currently* calculated on the following values: the rental value of the premises used by the company for its business; and 16% of the value of the fixed assets that the company uses for its business. Tax is then levied on 84% of the sum of these two values at a rate that local communities set each year.

In certain areas, local communities (municipalities, *départements*, regions and intermunicipal authorities with their own tax systems) have the right to grant temporary business tax exemptions to companies that set up or expand their business or take over troubled establishments. The exemption may be total or partial and it is limited to five years.

If your sole activity is letting *gîtes* (see p.54) or providing B&B accommodation (see p.56), you may be exempt from this tax. The policy varies from place to place. There are also certain general exemptions, including artists and writers, artisans who are sole traders, artisans who have apprentices, certain journalists, certain schools and training establishments, and certain activities linked to religion.

Local Property Taxes

Other local taxes include the property tax (*taxe foncière*) that owners pay on buildings and land, and the housing tax (*taxe d'habitation*) that owners or tenants occupying residential property pay. These are based on the rental value of the properties, which is assessed by the government. They are low, see p.147.

A local tax is levied on the completed construction of new buildings in some *communes*. It is raised on a tax base of 1–5% of the theoretical value of the building calculated in accordance with the scale and on a per square metre basis. Half the taxes are payable within 18 months of construction, the rest within 36 months of the end of construction. There are certain exemptions.

Payroll Tax

This is paid by businesses that do not collect VAT. It is not paid by Micro enterprises (see pp.52 and 80). The basis of the calculation for tax is the total salary bill, as used to calculate social security contributions but ignoring some benefits in kind. For people earning an annual salary below €6,675, the tax is 4.25%; between €6,675 and €13,337 it is 8.5%; and above €13,337 it is 9.35%. The company then aggregates the tax due in respect of all of its employees and pays it in January.

Apprentice Tax

This is more a training levy than a tax, paid by all businesses that pay corporate tax and all commercial businesses, industrial businesses and artisans who pay tax by way of personal income tax. The liberal professions (*see* p.81) are exempt, as are those who employ a certain number of apprentices. The tax is 0.5% of your gross salary bill as it is used to calculate social security contributions.

Professional Training Tax

This catches companies that don't pay apprentice tax, as well as those that do. Allow 0.15% of your salary bill if you do not pay apprentice tax, 0.10% if you do. You can recycle some of this tax into your own training scheme.

Home Construction Tax

The most French tax of all, this speaks volumes about the French social model. Employers are expected to encourage their employees to buy houses by making subsidised loans, which are likely to be tax deductible. If you don't, or your contributions are less than the amount of this tax, you have to pay – the tax is 0.45% of your salary bill calculated on the same basis as for professional training tax.

Car Tax

This is different from the tax drivers pay to keep their car on the road. If a company owns a car or cars less than 10 years old it must pay tax calculated on the basis of its official tax horsepower. For a car of less than 7hp it is €1,130 a year, for a larger car €2,440. If you use the car for company business, you can set certain specified running costs off against your general tax liabilities. This mainly catches people who use company cars for private mileage.

Personal Taxes

Overall, France is a high tax society, and lots of French people (probably around 30%) don't pay the taxes that they owe. Around 50% of foreign residents suffer from this selective amnesia, too. As mentioned on p.129, the penalties are severe, and the rules are applied more strictly year on year. The ideal situation is to address tax issues and find out about the legitimate tax-saving devices before you go to France.

By law, individuals are responsible for acquiring their tax return form, completing it, and filing it and paying the appropriate amount of tax by the deadline. It is submitted to your local tax centre (*centre des impôts*) or, in the case of non-residents (*see* p.144), to the central tax centre for non-residents in Paris. There is a complex timetable for submitting the various types of return. Simple failure to file normally results in a surcharge of 10–20% of the tax payable; more serious failures result in escalating penalties up to and including the criminal.

If you're a French resident, you may also have to fill in a tax return if you possess any 'obvious signs of wealth' – this is to get round the problem of people turning up at their tax hearing in their Ferrari or speedboat and claiming to have no income. These 'signs' include main and holiday homes, cars, yachts, planes and domestic staff, each of which is given a notional income value by the tax inspector, who will then assess your tax on the resulting total (*revenu forfaitaire*) even if you declare you have no income at all.

Tax on income for the year 1 January 2005 to 31 December 2005 is declared and paid in 2006. You can pay in three equal instalments (31 January, 30 April and 30 September) or by monthly instalments over 10 months from 8 January to 8 October. In both cases, the tax paid on account is paid on the basis of the tax paid in the previous year, with a final adjustment to reflect your liability this year.

If the tax due is less than €500, you'll receive a payment from the tax office of the difference between your tax liability and the rebate level, called the *décote*. For those seeking redress against the tax office, it is part of the administration and therefore subject to the remedies provided by administrative law (*see* p.27).

Tax Planning

The earlier this is done the better, in order to benefit from the many possibilities for tax planning for someone moving to France. The first consideration is that of timing your departure from the UK to get the best out of the British tax system – think, in particular, about when to make any capital gain if you are selling your business or other assets in the UK. Arrange your affairs so that there is a gap between leaving the UK (for tax purposes) and becoming resident in France – this gap can be used to make all sorts of beneficial changes to the structure of your finances.

Tax Credits

The complicated tax credits system includes credits for mortgage interest in a small number of cases where mortgages were taken out before 1 January 1998, renovation of your main home, a small number of life assurance premiums, charitable donations, certain childminding expenses, 50% of a sum paid to employ a home help (to a maximum), 25% of the cost of residential care if you are over 70 (to a maximum), and allowances for children in school (€60–180 per child). Seek tax advice if you want to make a claim.

Tax Residency

If you have a foot in two countries or are moving to France permanently, you need to consider the tax systems in both countries with a view to minimising your tax obligations in each. It's not just a question of paying the least tax in, say, France – the best choice there could be very damaging to your position in the UK, while the most tax-efficient way of dealing with your affairs in the UK could raise problems in France. You need to find a compromise that allows you to enjoy the major advantages available in both countries without incurring any of the biggest drawbacks.

Your decision depends on your priorities. Some people are keen to screw the last halfpenny of advantage out of their situation; others recognise they will have to pay some tax but want to moderate their bill; and still others want a simple structure they understand and can manage without assistance in the years ahead.

The biggest single factor in determining how you will be treated by the tax authorities in any country is whether you are resident there for tax purposes. This concept of **tax residence** (*domicile fiscal*) causes a great deal of confusion. It has nothing to do with whether you've registered as a resident in a country or obtained a residence permit or card (though a person who has a card will usually be tax resident). Nor does it have anything to do with whether you have a home (residence) in that country (although a person who is tax resident will normally have a home there). Nor is it much to do with your intentions.

Tax residence is a question of fact. The law lays down certain tests, and if you fall into the categories stipulated you will be considered tax resident whatever you want or intended. It is your responsibility to make your tax declarations each year, and the tax office will make the decision as to whether you fall into the category of resident. If you disagree, you can appeal through the courts. The basis on which decisions are made tends to be regulated by international law and to be pretty consistent from country to country.

In the UK, there are two tests that help determine where you pay tax, which assess your domicile and your residence. Your **domicile** is your 'real' home, where you have your roots; for most people it's the place where they were born. Under English law, residence is divided into 'simple residence' and 'ordinary residence'. A person will generally be treated as a simple **resident** if they spend 183 or more days a year in the UK. A visitor will also be treated as simple resident if they come to the UK regularly and spend significant time here; if they spend, on average over a period of four or more years, more than three months a year here, they will be treated as tax resident.

A person continues to be **ordinarily resident** in the UK, even after they have stopped being resident here, if they spend an average of 91 or more days a year here over any four-year period – they don't want you to escape too easily! Many people worry they will be classified as ordinarily resident if they keep accommodation available for their use in the UK, but this unfair rule was abolished in 1993.

Double Taxation Treaties

Double taxation treaties may be similar in concept but can differ in detail depending on the two countries. They need to be read in the light of your personal circumstances.

The main effects of the French–British treaty with regard to residents are:

- Any income from letting property in the UK will normally be outside the scope of French taxation and will be taxed in the UK.

- Pensions received from the UK – except for government pensions – will be taxed in France but not in the UK. Government pensions will continue to be taxed in the UK only and do not count as your income for tax purposes.

- You won't normally be required to pay British capital gains tax on gains made after you settle in France, except in relation to real estate in the UK.

- If you're taxed on a gift made outside France, the tax paid will usually be offset against the gift tax due in France. The same goes for tax on an inheritance outside France.

Tax residence in France is defined by one of more of the following:

- If your main home/long-term home/family base is in France (this is known as your *foyer fiscal*).

- If you spend more than 183 days in France (not necessarily consecutive) in any tax year (1 Jan–31 Dec) and do not have a *foyer fiscal* elsewhere.

- If you spend less than 184 days in France but do not have a home elsewhere or your principal residence is in France.

- If your centre of economic interests is in France (where you have your main investments or business or other sources of income and, usually, where you spend much of your money).

- If you work in France, except where that work is ancillary to work elsewhere.

- If your family is resident in France, unless you show you are not resident.

Hence, you can be tax resident in more than one country under the respective rules of those countries – for example, if you spend 230 days a year in France and 135 days in the UK. In this case, the reciprocal **double taxation treaty** (see box, above) signed by the UK and France comes into play; its 'tie breakers' and other provisions allow the authorities to decide if there is any requirement to pay tax twice and in which country any particular category of tax should be paid.

Taxes Payable in the UK

The significance of the residence rules discussed above is that you continue to be liable for some British taxes for as long as you are either ordinarily resident or domiciled in the UK. As a thumbnail sketch, once you have left the UK to live in France:

- You will continue to have to pay British tax on any capital gains you make anywhere in the world for as long as you are ordinarily resident and domiciled in the UK.
- You will continue to be liable to British inheritance tax on all of your assets anywhere in the world for as long as you remain domiciled in the UK. This will be subject to double taxation relief (see p.145). More complex rules apply in certain circumstances.
- You will always pay British income tax (Schedule A) on income arising from land and buildings in the UK, wherever your domicile, residence or ordinary residence.
- You will pay UK income tax (Schedule D) on: income from 'self-employed' trades or professions carried out in the UK if income arises there (Cases I and II); income from interest, annuities or other annual payments from the UK (Case III) if income arises in the UK and you are ordinarily resident there; income from investments and businesses outside the UK (Cases IV and V) if you are UK-domiciled and resident or ordinarily resident in the UK; all income from government pensions (fire brigade, police, army, civil service, etc.); and sundry profits not otherwise taxable (Case VI) arising out of land or building in the UK.
- You will pay income tax on any income earned from salaried employment in the UK (Schedule E) only in respect of any earnings from duties performed in the UK, unless you are resident and ordinarily resident in the UK, in which case you usually pay tax in the UK on your worldwide earnings.

If you're only buying a property to let and will remain primarily resident in the UK, your tax position in the UK will not change much. You have to declare any income from your French property as part of your UK tax declaration, and the calculation of tax due on that will be made in accordance with UK rules, which will result in a different taxable sum than is used by the French authorities. The British tax office will give you full credit for the taxes already paid in France. If you sell the property, you must disclose the profit made to the British authorities, who will again give you full credit for the French tax paid. Similarly, on your death your assets in France must be disclosed on the UK probate tax declaration but your heir will be given full credit for sums paid in France.

French Taxes Payable by Both Residents and Non-Residents

Local Taxes

The ***taxe d'habitation*** is charged on residential properties you use yourself (or have available for your use). It is paid by the person who occupied the property on 1 January, including the tenant if you let the property. Raised and spent by the *mairie* of the area where you live, this tax is calculated on the basis of the notional rental value of your property, which is assessed by the land registry (*cadastre*). You must send notification of any improvements or changes to the property to the latter within 90 days, and you can appeal against their decision, but the sums involved are usually so small it is not worthwhile. Various deductions are available to those on very low incomes or with dependants.

The **taxe foncière** is paid by the owner of the property, irrespective of who occupies it. If you sell the property part-way through the year, the notary will inform the buyer of the share they have to pay to the seller. It's divided into tax on the buildings (*taxe foncière bâtie*), which includes property that is habitable whether or not it is occupied, and tax on any non-agricultural land (*taxe foncière non bâtie*). New houses are exempt for two years after construction (in some cases 10 or 15 years) if you apply for the exemption within 90 days of completion. In some areas rubbish collection (*ordures*) is taxed separately.

The combined total of these taxes is low – perhaps £100 for a small cottage and £400 for a larger house. If the home is a second home, you should inform the authorities that you want a reduction for not using as many services. A demand for payment is sent each year; failure to pay by the specified date (which varies from place to place) incurs a 10% penalty.

Taxe professionnelle is a tax on business activity levied and spent locally. Though it's paid by most businesses and self-employed people, there is a long list of exceptions, including artisans, taxi drivers, artists, authors, teachers, people letting part of their home as holiday accommodation and, in some cases, people letting *gîtes*. It's calculated by taking the cadastral (rateable) value of the premises owned by the business, 16% of the value of its equipment and other fixed assets as shown in its accounts, the amount it pays for leasing equipment and, depending on the size of the business, a percentage of its payroll costs or turnover. There are certain allowances to set against this sum, leaving a net taxable amount, which is taxed at the rate applicable in that area. It cannot amount to more than 4% of the profit of the business.

Wealth Tax

Both residents and non-residents will also pay French wealth tax (*impôt de solidarité sur la fortune*) on their assets in France, including real estate (land and buildings), furniture, cars and boats, shares in French companies, debts due to them in France, and any shares in a non-French company owning mainly real estate in France. They can deduct from their taxable assets any debts they owe in France or that are secured against the asset. Among the long list of items exempt from wealth tax are antiques and works of art, and shares in companies of which one owns less than 10%. The market value of one's home may be discounted by 20% for wealth tax purposes. Your tax return must be filed (if you are British) by 16 July, accompanied by payment, with assets valued as at 1 January.

Other Taxes

For information on the *taxe sur les immeubles détenus par certaines personnes morales*, see p.139.

Apart from VAT (TAV; see p.127), a major generator of tax for the French, there are a miscellany of other taxes and levies on various aspects of life in France, from alcohol to pornography. Some are national and others local; taken individually they are not usually a great burden.

Other French Taxes Payable by Non-Residents

In general, a person who is non-resident for tax purposes has few contacts with the French tax system and they are fairly painless. As a non-resident you will generally only pay **income tax** on:

- **Income generated from land and buildings in France.** If you own a building in France and let it, it is the French government that collects the first wedge of tax from you. Some non-residents have to pay a tax based on a purely notional or theoretical income based on three times the rental value of any property they own or rent in France but not when there is a double taxation treaty in place, as there is between France and the UK (see p.145).
- **Income from French securities and capital invested in France.**
- **Income from business activities in France.**
- **Earned income if you are employed or self-employed in France**

For each category of income, there are various deductible allowances; see the following section on taxation for residents for more details. For most non-residents, tax is at a minimum rate of 25% of their taxable income. Any tax of less than €300 is not collected.

If you sell real estate in France, you will pay **capital gains tax** at 33.33% of the gain after various small allowances, the costs of acquisition and sale, the cost of repairs and improvements, the cost of tax advice and an indexation allowance to increase the notional purchase price to eliminate the effects of inflation. The resultant taxable gain is reduced by 5% for each year that you have owned the property except for the first two years. The gain is collected by a withholding tax of 33.33% taken at the time of the sale; to recover any balance due to you, you need to submit a tax return. This will usually require a little tax advice. You may be exempt from this tax if you have been tax resident in France at some stage for more than a year; again, if this applies to you, seek advice.

You will also pay capital gains tax on shares in unquoted companies that have more than 50% of their assets comprised of land and buildings in France; on holdings in French companies where you and your family have owned more than 25% of the shares; and on holdings in any fiscally transparent professional companies of which you are an active member.

Inheritance tax (*droits de succession*) is paid in France on the value of any assets in the country as at the date of your death, including real estate (land and buildings), shares in French companies, and shares in a non-French company owning mainly real estate in France. Depending on your tax residence, this potential liability may be modified by your country's double taxation treaty with France – for UK residents, only the real estate in France will be taxable in France. All the assets have to be declared to the British tax office, but, again, double taxation relief will apply so you will not pay the same tax twice.

Tax is paid on the value of the gift at the date of death, which is declared by the person who inherits but is subject to challenge by the authorities. Rates depend on the relationship between the deceased and the person inheriting, and certain people are entitled to reductions on the tax payable, including war invalids and those with three or more children alive at the time of the inheritance. The tax is paid by the person who inherits, not as in the UK by the estate as a whole, and is due at the time of registering the inheritance, though it can, in most cases, be paid over five years (accruing interest at the current statutory rate).

Other French Taxes Payable by Residents

As a tax resident, you will generally pay tax in France on your worldwide income. What follows is a brief summary of an hugely complicated situation.

New Residents

New residents are liable to tax on their worldwide income and gains from the date they arrive in France; until then they only pay French tax on their income if it is derived from assets in France. The most important thing to understand about taking up residence in France (and abandoning British tax residence) is that it gives you superb opportunities for tax planning, in particular for restructuring your affairs to minimise what can otherwise be penal rates of taxation in France. To do this you need good advice at an early stage.

Ordinary Income

Income tax (*impôt sur le revenu*) comprises only a very small part of the French state's revenue because, over the years, it has introduced more and more 'social contributions' (*see* p.125), which, though effectively a type of income tax, are not classified as such for political purposes.

In France, income is divided, as in the UK, into various categories, some of which are taxed at source. Some of the latter involve full payment of the tax due and are thus not included in your tax return; if that is your only income, you normally need not file a tax return. Tax paid at source on other income is simply a payment on account of whatever might ultimately be due in the light of your personal tax rate. Some types of income bear tax at a flat rate, unrelated to your normal tax rate. Some income is not taxed at source and will bear tax when declared to the tax authorities on your tax return.

If your gross income before deductions is less than €7,250, you pay no tax; if you are over 65, the level rises to €7,920. In addition to the specific deductions referred to in the various categories that follow, there are some general **deductions from your gross income** before tax is calculated. These are: maintenance payments (in cash or kind), payments to a parent, payments to a needy adult child, payments to an adult child under a court order, payments under a court order to a minor child of a divorced parent where the child lives with the other parent, or reasonable voluntary payments to such a child, maintenance payments under a court order to one's wife/husband, losses under certain tax incentive schemes, and certain investments in French cinema.

The **total taxable income** is the total income of the household (note that unmarried couples count as separate households, which is, generally, a disadvantage), less the various deductions from gross and net income. **From the net income, there are various possible deductions**: about £1,000 if you are an invalid (80% disabled); between £500 and £1,000 if you are over 65 (doubled if husband and wife are both over 65); and about £350 for each of your children and their children if they are married and either under 21, under 25 and still a student, or in military service, when they can be 'brought back into your family' for tax purposes.

To avoid large families with working children paying too much tax, the French have introduced the concepts of the ***quotient familial*** and the ***part*** or adjusted family unit, whereby some family members are treated as having more 'weight', for tax purposes, than others. The tax is calculated in tranches – you calculate the tax that is payable on each complete slice, then the tax at the highest applicable rate on any excess. It's an incredibly complex system for which you'll need specific tax advice.

Other Categories of Income

Property income (*revenus fonciers*) is basically any income from land or buildings except furnished lettings, which are treated as commercial income. The main examples of such income are income from unfurnished lettings and from letting unwanted land to a neighbour. From your income, you can deduct most normal expenses relating to the property, including repair, maintenance, improvement (but not rebuilding or enlargement), management costs, insurance, property tax, mortgage interest and a depreciation allowance. If your income from letting is less than about £3,000 per year, you can choose to pay tax on the full amount received less 33%, as a general allowance for expenses. This will save you having to keep full records and can be worth looking at if you do not have any mortgage interest to set against income. If you have UK rental income, under the double taxation treaty – and despite the general rule – that income will be taxed in the UK rather than in France.

Any income from a profession or business not subject to company tax, including income from letting furnished property, is taxed as **industrial and commercial income** (*bénéfices industriels et commerciaux*). There are various ways in which you can be assessed to tax. If your business has a turnover of less than about €15,000 a year, you normally pay tax on a simplified scheme whereby you are taxed on 50% of your turnover without further deductions. This scheme, called the **Micro BIC**, greatly simplifies your book-keeping and administration but does have some disadvantages (*see* pp.52 and 80). Alternatively, if you have a turnover of less than about €75,000 per year, you and your tax inspector can discuss your business every two years and agree a sum to be paid by way of tax for each of the next two years; this scheme, the *régime du forfait*, will generally reflect the amount such a business would be expected to earn. Businesses with an annual turnover of less than about €750,000 (if selling goods or providing accommodation) or €200,000 (if engaged in any other activity) usually pay their tax on a simplified version of the normal tax regime, the *régime du réel simplifié*, by which accounting and reporting requirements are relaxed. Or you can choose to be taxed on the full normal basis, as larger businesses are.

There are several schemes for calculating and paying tax on **company directors' pay** (*rémuneration des dirigeants de sociétés*); generally, directors of fiscally transparent companies pay tax in their own right as partners in the business, whereas directors of companies that are assessed for company tax are taxed as employees of that company. There are also various schemes, all of them generous, for taxing **agricultural income** (*bénéfices agricoles*), depending on the turnover of the farm.

Non-commercial profits (*bénéfices non-commerciaux*) are those of lawyers, doctors, architects and so on; as in the case of other businesses, there are several regimes under which tax can be imposed.

Pension income is subject to an initial reduction of 10% before allowances, except in the case of the French state pension, which is tax exempt, and of annuity pensions (*rentes viagères*), only part of which are taxed, dependent on age.

Investment income (*revenus des capitaux*) covers shares, bonds and so on. Dividends from French companies are accompanied by a tax credit (*avoir fiscal*), which is added to the actual dividend for the purposes of calculating tax due. Dividends from overseas companies are added to other income to assess the overall level of tax payable. Bank interest, interest from various types of savings accounts and income from French life assurance policies is either tax free or taxed at source at fixed rates, which vary.

Short-term **capital gains** (usually those made over less than two years) on both real and personal (that is, immovable and moveable) property are added to the overall income for the year in question and thus assessed for tax. Long-term gains are taxed in various ways, depending on the type of gain and whether it has been made by an individual or a business. You will be taxed on your world-wide gains. Tax on short-term gains is paid as part of your income tax; tax on long-term gains can be paid by instalments over five years.

In terms of gains by private individuals, several gains are exempt, including, most importantly, the gain on your main residence or any other residential property held for more than 22 years. Otherwise, gains on property and land are taxed by calculating the difference between sale price and cost, less various allowances (*see* the section on taxes for non-residents, p.148). If you are selling a second home that you have owned for more than five years, part of the gain may be tax free, depending on your circumstances. If you make a loss selling your real estate, you cannot set this off against other gains or claim a tax refund. For long-term gains on real estate, 20% of the amount of the gain is added to the taxpayer's income for income tax purposes in the year of the gain. The tax payable is five times the increase of tax resulting from this step.

Bonds and securities where you own less than 25% of the company are taxed on the difference between purchase and sale price. Losses can be set against other gains under this category. The rules concerning **shareholdings** in a company, whether French or foreign, can be complex. Gains are taxable if the total sale price of the shares exceeds €15,000. They are taxed at 16% plus the social charges (11%) and healthcare charges (8%). No relief is given for inflation. There is no differentiation between long-term and short-term gains. Gains on the shares of property-holding companies are taxed in the same way as gains on the property itself, provided you own more than 50% of the company shares.

Gains on cars and furniture are not taxed. Gains on other **moveable assets** are taxed only if the sale proceeds of that asset exceed €5,000. Short-term gains – gains on assets held for less than one year – are taxed as part of your ordinary income. There is no adjustment for inflation. Gains on assets held for more than one year are generally granted an allowance for relief against the effect of inflation and there are various other asset-specific allowances that might apply. There is no relief for losses.

Note that once you become resident in France, you have to pay capital gains tax on the gains that arose on assets you held a long time before you became resident, even if those assets might have been capital gains tax-free in the country from which you came. Because the gain is usually added to your income and is subject to social security and healthcare costs, the taxes can be significant. There are generally ways of avoiding this problem, quite legally, provided you get good advice before you move to France.

Subject to the provisions of double taxation treaties, **inheritance tax** (*droits de succession*) is paid on your worldwide assets as at the date of your death. All of the assets have to be declared for the purposes of UK taxation, but the double taxation treaty ensures you don't pay the same tax twice. The long list of exemptions includes the proceeds of most life policies, certain items given to the state, and some rented housing. If you leave your estate in France to the government or one of various educational institutions or charities, the gift is tax-free. Otherwise, some gifts on inheritance are partly tax exempt. Tax is paid on the value of the gift at the date of death; this is declared by the person who inherits but subject to challenge by the tax authorities.

Taxes on gifts (*droits de donations*) are paid on gifts made of any assets anywhere in the world. Certain assets – the same as on inheritance – are exempt, as are gifts made informally by delivery of the asset into the hands of the recipient, unless the recipient chooses to disclose the gift to the tax office.

Any sum received tax free by way of gift within the 10 years preceding the death of the donor will reduce any tax-free entitlement on that death. The taxable value is stated by the parties but subject to intervention from the tax authorities, and the tax rates are as for inheritance tax. The tax is payable by the recipient of the gift at the time the gift is received.

If you're thinking of buying a French home in the name of your children, this could create a gift tax problem. You may be able to avoid it by making the gift of the cash to buy the property in the UK, which would then be subject to the British 'seven-year rule' whereby, if the donor survives that long, the gift will be tax free.

Non-Taxable Income

Among the long list of bits and pieces of income that are not subject to income tax, the most important are income from various French savings schemes, provided the money is left in them, typically for four to eight years; a reasonable amount of rent earned from letting part of your own home to a permanent tenant; and rent (up to about €1,000 per year) from using your home as a B&B (*see* pp.56–7).

Immigration and Work Permits

The French immigration system is rather more warm and welcoming than an American citizen might expect, because France is looking to encourage foreign businesses to set up there. If you have a bit of money and aren't going to be dependent on the French welfare system, your application for permission to settle in France and start a business should be successful, after the usual paper trail. Dealing with the immigration authorities can be a pain, because the people you actually come into contact with are relatively low-paid, low-grade officials who speak little or no English and take any opportunity to send you away in the hope that when you come back your problem will land on someone else's desk. If your form isn't fully completed and accompanied by all necessary documents, it will simply be rejected. If you don't turn up to an appointment (you won't get a reminder), your application will be rejected wholesale.

When dealing with the French immigration system, you would be well advised to take along a specialist lawyer familiar with French immigration issues relating to your country; there are a good number of these, most of them based in Paris.

EU Citizens

If you're a citizen of one of the EEA (European Economic Area) states (Austria, Belgium, Cyprus, the Czech Republic, Denmark, Estonia, Finland, France,

Germany, Greece, Hungary, Iceland, Ireland, Italy, Latvia, Liechtenstein, Lithuania, Luxembourg, Malta, the Netherlands, Norway, Poland, Portugal, Slovakia, Slovenia, Spain, Sweden and the UK), or of Switzerland, you do not need a visa to live in France (note that British citizens native of the Channel Islands and the Isle of Man are not regarded as EU citizens), and you are free to live and work in another EEA country on the same conditions as that state's own citizens.

Rather confusingly (since it contradicts the above in some cases), citizens of the countries that joined the EU in 2004 – Cyprus, the Czech Republic, Estonia, Hungary, Latvia, Lithuania, Malta, Poland, Slovakia and Slovenia – may be subject to transitional arrangements that restrict their right to work and set up in business in France. Until at least 2006, and possibly until 2009, they may need to comply with many of the formalities associated with non-EU citizens, including obtaining a residence permit (unless you can live from income or savings from outside France). This is comprehensively dealt with at **www.europa.eu.int**.

Non-EU Citizens

Anyone from outside the EU wishing to stay in France for longer than three months must have an appropriate visa issued by the French consulate covering the area of the country where they live before moving. If you come from a country that has a visa waiver programme with France, including the USA, note that you cannot convert a visa waiver (issued for short-term tourist or business visits) into a full visa once you are there. Similarly, if you come on a short-stay visa hoping to get a residence permit, you will probably find yourself having to fly home to apply for a visa. Visa application forms can be downloaded from the French Embassy website in your country. They are simple to fill in, but it's a good idea to have them looked over – or even completed – by a immigration lawyer, since accidentally saying the wrong thing or using a word that means different things in French and English can cause you problems later.

Non-EU nationals are not allowed to take up employment in France, even temporary or unpaid work, unless they have obtained an *autorisation de travail* (work permit) before arriving; see **Working in France**, pp.170–71. If you intend to work in France as an employee, your employer should already have asked for a work permit, which you need to present with your visa application. If you intend be self-employed (*travailleur indépendant*), you must say so on your visa application form.

Obtaining a *Carte de Séjour*

Non-EU citizens staying in France for more than three months must apply for a residence permit after arriving with their visa. You need to produce:

- **a valid passport.**
- **a birth or marriage certificate.**

- proof of accommodation (*see* below).
- proof that you pay contributions to the French social security scheme or other proof of medical insurance (*see* below).
- three passport photos.
- a contract of employment if you are employed.
- the necessary authorisations from the Chamber of Commerce if you are self-employed.
- proof that you receive a state pension (from France or your home country) if you are retired.
- proof that you are registered with a French university if you are a student.
- evidence of means of support (*moyens d'existence*), e.g bank statements.

Proof of accommodation can take the form of a property purchase or rental contract, or, for those in private accommodation, a letter signed by the owner (or a legal representative) confirming that he or she is providing accommodation (*justificatif d'hébergement*). This attestation must include an undertaking to take financial responsibility for the foreigner for the length of his or her stay and must be authorised, at a cost of €15, by the local town hall or other relevant administrative body. Proof of accommodation isn't required in certain cases, for instance when a foreigner is on a cultural exchange or is visiting France for urgent medical treatment or to attend to a seriously ill relative.

The proof of medical insurance will be a certificate provided by a recognised insurer against medical expenses, hospitalisation and any other 'assistance' required as a result of treatment undergone in France, including repatriation. If you have obtained permission to work in France, you'll be covered by the public healthcare system and don't need to take out private insurance, though you may still want to take out a complementary insurance (*mutuelle; see* p.229) to cover the part that is not refunded or to provide cover beyond what the public refunds. In other cases, you have the option to pay contributions to the public system through the CMU scheme (*see* p.229) instead of taking out private insurance. If you are self-employed, the certificate will be from the entity that insures you (*see* below); again, you may also want to take out a *mutuelle*.

In terms of procedure, the necessary documents must be presented at a *préfecture* or *sous-préfecture* in your *département*. Depending on where you are applying, you will probably be given a date to return. This is often long after your original visa and entry stamp have expired, but don't worry – the receipt for your application and appointment document is justification for your continued presence in France. It will be vastly easier and less stressful if your paperwork is checked by a specialist lawyer before presentation and if you are accompanied to the interview by the lawyer or someone who speaks good French.

Permission to stay can be refused if the necessary documents aren't provided or don't include the required information, or if any condition is not fulfilled. You can appeal to the *préfet*, who will make a decision within two months. If your application isn't rejected, you will be called to undergo a simple medical examination, which involves a chest X-ray but no AIDS test. When collecting your residence permit from the Préfecture, you have to pay €220 (€55 for students) for special tax stamps (you can't use the ordinary tax stamps, or *timbres fiscaux*, sold in *tabac* stores).

There are two types of residence permit (*titre de séjour*). The **carte de séjour temporaire** (temporary residence permit) is valid for a maximum of one year and can be renewed within the last two months of its validity if your situation entitles you to remain in France (many people do this year after year, until nudged by an official into applying for a permanent permit). Your right to work is restricted to the activities mentioned on the card. The **carte de résident** ('permanent' residence permit), valid for 10 years, is available to those who have lived in France for five years continuously and legally, on certain conditions – they must provide evidence of their intention to remain in France for a considerable time and of their integration into French society, which requires a 'sufficient' knowledge of French and of the principles governing the Republic (the local mayor may be asked to confirm that such integration has taken place); they may be asked to proof their means of support; and they may be asked to prove the status (including the tax situation) of any professional activity. A *carte de résident* is renewable automatically unless you've committed a serious offence, and gives you the right to exercise the profession or business activity of your choice, subject to your having the necessary qualifications.

Cartes de résident can also be issued to the spouse and children under 18 of a cardholder provided they have been granted permission to stay in France in order to keep the family together (*au titre du regroupement familial*) for at least two years; and to a foreigner who has a child who has been living in France for at least two years and holds a temporary residence permit. Foreigners who are admitted to France to keep a family together are automatically entitled to a temporary residence permit after three months.

Citizenship

Having a *carte de résident* is nothing to do with becoming a citizen of France – a bit like a US Green Card, it merely allows you to stay there indefinitely. If you want to apply for citizenship, France permits dual citizenship, which means that you do not need to give up your original citizenship unless your own government requires it.

Spouses, children and parents of citizens enjoy the same right to live and work in France as the person on whom they depend, no matter what their nationality, but unless they are citizens of the EU, EEA or Switzerland they must apply for a visa before travelling to France and a residence permit once they are there.

Professional and Other Qualifications

In principle, qualifications obtained in one EU country ought to be recognised in another, and you should be able to go to France to work or set up in business as you please. The French, as founder members, have felt able to go a little slowly down this road, wary of opening their commerce and industry to competition, whether from Polish plumbers or *avocats anglais*, to the extent that the European Commission has had to issue them with some not-so-gentle reminders of their obligations and the possibility of fines. Hence, the recognition of qualifications in France is an area where the law may say one thing but practice may well require the surmounting of strange obstacles.

All this said, the situation is immeasurably better today than it was five years ago, and this whole sorry area may have been cleared up by a fresh directive that was in the pipeline as this book went to press. This directive applies to all EU member state nationals, whether employed or self-employed, who are required to carry out their activities under the conditions laid down in the host state. The proposal distinguishes between the 'free provision of services' and the 'freedom of establishment'.

Provision of Services

A person is a 'service provider' if he or she carries out a professional activity in a member state for no more than 16 weeks a year. In principle, if they are legally established in that state, they may provide services on a temporary and occasional basis under their original professional title without having to apply for recognition of their qualifications. If they provide services for more than 16 weeks, they must provide evidence of two years' professional experience if the profession is not regulated in the state. If it is regulated, they must register in compliance with the local procedure. The host member state may ask the administrative authorities in the member state of origin for proof of the nationality of the service provider and of his or her lawful pursuit of that activity. The service provider is exempted from any authorisation by, or registration with, a professional or social security body, but is required to inform the contact in the host member state if he or she travels to provide such services.

This amended proposal tightens up the conditions that need to be met by service providers in the health sector by introducing a requirement for *pro forma* registration with the competent professional association of the host state. In addition, the host state may demand that the service provider informs the competent body there before moving.

Service providers must provide potential customers with information that is easy to read and understand, given that the profession might not perhaps be regulated in the host state. They must allow give the consumer proof that they are insured against any challenge to their professional liability.

Establishment

The 'freedom of establishment' is the framework by which a professional enjoys the effective freedom to establish themselves in another EU member state to conduct a professional activity there securely.

There are three systems of recognition:

- The general system for the recognition of professional qualifications applies to all professions not expressly referred to elsewhere in the proposal and to situations that do not meet the specific conditions underlying the other recognition schemes. It is based on the principle of mutual recognition, and if there are substantial differences between the training acquired by the migrant and the training required in the host state, an adaptation period or aptitude test may be required.

- The system of automatic recognition of qualifications attested by professional experience applies to the industrial, craft and commercial activities listed in the proposal. In this case, the competent authority in the host state allows access to this profession and the pursuit of it on the same basis as nationals if the applicant holds a training qualification obtained in a member state that attests to a level of training at least equivalent to the level immediately below that required in the host state. Other elements taken into consideration are the number of years of professional experience, and the form of experience (i.e. employed or self-employed).

- The system of automatic recognition of qualifications for specific professions on the basis of co-ordination of minimum training conditions covers the following professions: doctors, general nurses, dental practitioners, veterinary surgeons, midwives, pharmacists and architects. For further information on the medical professions, see pp.70–73.

The proposal distinguishes five levels of professional qualifications:

- Attestation of competence, which corresponds to general primary or secondary education, demonstrating that the holder has acquired general knowledge, or which is issued by a competent authority in the home member state on the basis of a very short training course.

- A certificate corresponding to training at secondary level, of a professional nature or general in character, supplemented by a professional course.

- A diploma certifying the successful completion of a training course corresponding to training at post-secondary level lasting at least one year, or professional training comparable in terms of responsibilities and functions.

- A diploma certifying the successful completion of an intermediate training course corresponding to a course of training at higher or university level and lasting at least three years and less than four.

- A diploma certifying the successful completion of a higher training course corresponding to training at higher education level and of a minimum duration of four years.

Occasionally, other types of training can be treated as the equivalent of one of the five levels. If the training is one year shorter than that required by the host state or if it covers substantially different matters, or if the profession comprises one or more regulated professional activities that do not exist in the corresponding profession in the home state, the host state can recognise the qualifications subject to the applicant's completing a compensation measure, consisting of an adaptation period of a maximum of three years or an aptitude test. In principle, the applicant must be offered the choice between the two, unless there are very good reasons for doing otherwise. Host states are also allowed to ask applicants to provide proof of language proficiency.

Member state nationals can use the titles conferred on them both by their state of origin and host state, though if a profession is regulated in the host state by an association or organisation, they need to become a member in order to use the new title.

For details on the qualifications of specific professions, *see* 'Common Ideas: Pros and Cons', pp.35–75.

Getting Your Qualifications Recognised

Applications have to be submitted to the competent authority in the host state, accompanied by certain documents and certificates (as listed in the proposal). The authority has one month to acknowledge receipt of an application and to draw attention to any missing documents, and three months to make a decision from the date on which the application was received in full. Reasons have to be given for any rejection, and a rejection, or a failure to take a decision by the deadline, can be contested in the national courts.

The proposal requires that member states designate contact points to provide the public with information as to the recognition of professional qualifications and to help them enforce their rights, particularly through contact with the relevant authorities.

Legal Advice for Businesses

The specialists in France.

Download or ask for our **FREE** information pack.

John Howell & Co
Solicitors & International Lawyers

The Old Glass Works,
22 Endell Street,
Covent Garden,
London, WC2H 9AD

tel: 020 7420 0400
fax: 020 7836 3626
web: www.europelaw.com
email: info@europelaw.com

"Cost effective **solutions** to our clients' legal problems"

FREE Seminars
We present seminars all over the country - many free. Please check our website or phone for confirmation of dates and times.

Regulated by the Law Society of England and Wales

Working in France

Business Practices 162
Finding a Job 164
Job-hunting **165**
The Curriculum Vitae and Covering Letter **169**
Interviews **169**
Terms and Conditions of Employment 170
Employment Contracts **170**
Terms of Employment **171**
Dismissal and Redundancy **172**
Benefits **172**
Pensions and Retirement 174

Those who come to France with the aim of setting up in business may need to find a job to keep them going until the enterprise takes off. Alternatively, their partner may want to get a job, or need to get one in order to support the family. Those who do this become French for all practical purposes, and contributing members of an energised and proudly productive society.

There are no bureaucratic obstacles preventing an EU national from looking for work in France for up to three months, and once you do find a job you will pay social security and be on the way to settling permanently and enjoying state benefits. Non-EU citizens are forced to jump through more hoops and usually must arrange employment before moving to France. They also must arrive *with* the visa to work, which can be difficult to arrange. For more detail on these areas, see **Red Tape**, pp.153–60.

But whether you're from the EU or elsewhere, finding employment in France will be a battle. Your French is unlikely to be good enough. Your lack of knowledge of the way the system works makes you, in many ways, inferior to a 16-year-old office junior. And you will have trouble fitting in – especially in smaller enterprises, French people employ French people, often ones already known to them or their existing employees. They would have to have a good reason to employ a foreigner. So, in practice, you will only get an 'ordinary' job in France if you have skills that are in short supply or if your employer is trying to develop a market in the country that you come from.

There are two main exceptions to this rule. First, if you work for a large, often multinational, company, you will frequently find that their culture is pan-European or even global, and your boss in France is as likely to to be Dutch or German as French. Secondly, there are lots of fairly low-grade, often seasonal (and often 'illegal' jobs) in tourist areas, where you act as the interface between the French business and its English-speaking clientele.

Business Practices

The dos and don'ts of doing business in France do not differ drastically from what you're accustomed to in the UK, but in the former, affairs are executed with more elegance, which you will notice in the formal language used and the respect paid to colleagues. The French also place much emphasis on non-verbal communication and first impressions, on the basis that a firm handshake, direct eye contact and body gestures are often more revealing than words.

Introductions

It is important to know how to present yourself, your company and your ideas in a proper way. When setting up a business meeting, remember that no matter how many e-mails and telephone calls you exchange, nothing will be more vital than the first one-on-one encounter. The French, especially in urban settings, are very conscious of how people dress and will notice things such as unpolished shoes or shirts that need ironing. Both women and men are well groomed, and women usually wear heels and light make-up. Another way to make a good first impression is to have an elegantly printed business card ready in your breast pocket or purse. Start with a handshake at the first meeting (in some offices, employees shake hands every day even if they have been working together for 20 years). Successive meetings, depending on your work environment, can be sparked with a cheek-to-cheek kiss known as *la bise*.

It goes without saying that you should greet all new acquaintances using the formal *vouvoiement* form until the person you are addressing says it is alright to use the informal address – to *tutoyer* them. In many businesses, work colleagues never switch to the informal *tu,* while in others – especially when young people work together – conversations start off in the informal tense. It is better to err on the side of being too formal.

Meetings

Conference-room conversation often doesn't cut to the chase as you'd expect, and instead becomes an opportunity for participants to expand on thoughts and opinions. To be part of the forum of ideas, prepare with research and charts and displays when necessary. Don't necessarily expect a course of action to be ironed out at the end of the meeting. Business decisions may be finalised in the future or at a second meeting.

Never plan business meetings for the week of 15 August, when going to the office is almost considered a criminal offence. In fact, cross August off your business planner. Scheduling meetings around Christmas isn't a good idea either, and avoid the smaller holidays sprinkled throughout the year (*see* **References**, 'National and Local Holidays', pp.246–7).

Making the Call

The French are a chatty bunch, but not when the telephone is involved. Because local calls can be expensive, people generally do not spend hours on endless conversation. They would prefer to meet in person and that is, of course, the driving force that keeps France's lively café culture in business.

If calling someone for the first time, include a title: '*Bonjour, Monsieur*' for a man and '*Bonjour, Madame*' for a woman. Avoid simply saying '*Bonjour*'. Then introduce yourself with your name and work title. For example, '*Jean-Paul Sartre, philosophe existentialiste et écrivain à l'appareil*' (it's Jean-Paul Sartre, existentialist philosopher and writer here). To end a telephone conversation, include the title once again: '*Au revoir, Madame*' or '*Au revoir, Monsieur*'.

In general, business hours are from 8.30 or 9am to 7pm. Lunch can last up to two hours (or more if you live in the hottest areas of the country). In Paris, punctuality is taken very seriously. Don't get tempted into believing that the rules are more relaxed the further south you go.

If you have agreed to a business lunch, remember it is a time for eating as much as it is for negotiating. It is intended as an opportunity to get to know each other and, as a result, conversation that touches on family life or personal preferences can be expected. Getting down to the 'meat' of your business, especially where money matters are concerned, may be considered abrupt. Business lunches are usually not a quick affair. Instead, they can last hours, giving you and your guests the chance to enjoy a full meal, and wine is always welcome. The person who organised the encounter should be the one footing the bill.

The Corporate Hierarchy

The lines dividing categories of workers in France may be more firmly etched than you are used to, especially in a corporate setting, and fraternising with superiors or people below you on the corporate ladder may raise some eyebrows. Generally, socialising outside the office is done by employees of equal status and is virtually unheard of between bosses and their underlings. Sometimes little cliques form. Other Europeans have complained of barriers being raised, and of limited communication, between different levels of management. This is further aggravated by the importance given to ex-students of France's top business and engineering schools, to the detriment of employees who have not had this privilege. This may lead to a feeling of frustration among foreigners, who are unsure of where they stand in the corporate hierarchy.

For more advice on business dos and don'ts, see **www.workinfrance.com**.

Finding a Job

France's labour force is 26 million people strong – a figure that equates to roughly 40% of its population. Of these, about 20 million people currently earn a wage or salary. Roughly 3% of the workforce are farmers or agricultural workers; about 6% are self-employed non-professionals such as carpenters, plumbers, instructors and shopkeepers; 11% are managers or 'professionals'; 18% are intermediate workers, i.e. in temporary jobs; 25% are white-collar workers; and 23% are manual labourers. The remaining slice of the pie represents the jobless (some 2.6 million people) and those who have never worked.

The high rate of unemployment means it is often not easy for a non-French person to secure a job in France, whether in the public or private sector, which is one of the reasons so many people set up on their own. Few jobs come up, and people holding good jobs do not give them up easily, especially to foreigners.

That said, the EU has increased the mobility of its nationals seeking jobs in other EU countries, so it is now easier to look for a job in France. Your biggest selling point is your ability to speak and write English fluently, which makes you attractive to businesses, especially ones involved in finance, media, technology or foreign markets. It is assumed that you will be able to understand software, Internet pages, manuals and other work-related literature better than most. Your second asset is having a bicultural outlook, or European perspective. You may be able to bring a new attitude and valuable new ideas to the French workplace. How successfully you can use that to your advantage depends on your ability to speak French – a solid command of the French language is paramount to most jobs. See pp.176–8 for advice on learning the language.

Job-hunting

If you don't have any leads through university contacts, personal friends or former colleagues, you will be faced with starting your job search from scratch. British newspapers are a good place to start, especially publications that speak to a European audience, such as the *Guardian*, the *Independent*, *The Times*, the *Economist* and the *Financial Times*. All of these carry job advertisements from a range of other European countries. Two American publications, the *Wall Street Journal* and the *International Herald Tribune*, also print job listings. National French newspapers such as *Le Figaro*, *Le Monde* and the weekly *L'Express* carry advertisements in French and are commonly available on British news stands, especially in London.

Temporary Work

If you're just looking for a little casual work to tide you over while your business takes off, you'll be glad to know that seasonal jobs, usually linked to the natural cycles of agriculture, are in plentiful supply in France.

Each September, for instance, vineyard managers start their mad scramble to find temporary workers to pick wine grapes. Burgundy alone, the land of pinot noir and chardonnay, needs 7,400 pairs of helping hands; the prestigious Bordeaux region needs 9,000; and the land of bubbly, Champagne, calls for 4,500. Roussillon, the Rhône and Alsace also have a high demand for autumn labour. In addition, apple-pickers are needed in Limousin, Pays de la Loire and the Var. All you need is an ID card (or passport) and a copy of your insurance card. You must be over 18 and an EU citizen. People holding a French work permit may also be employed. The harvest starts in late August or early September and usually lasts seven to 10 days. Depending on the region, payment is usually set at the minimum wage per hour for eight hours a day, but you're almost certain to be given a few bottles with your cheque.

Other seasonal possibilities include work in a bar or restaurant that is particularly busy in the summer season, for instance those in seaside resorts.

Working Illegally

'The temptation to buck the system and hire illegal workers is there and usually works out fine – unless you get caught,' warns Mike Meade, editor of the *Riviera Reporter*, the most popular English-language magazine in the south of France, who has lived in France for 32 years. 'I've seen dozens – perhaps even hundreds – of people caught, fined and even arrested for working in the black economy.'

Even more terrifying are the stories he has collected of people who have hired illegal workers (many of them English people who have not set themselves up properly to do business in France) and are ruined now because of it.

'A few years ago, an incident came to my attention of an English couple in their 70s who invested their savings in a house in Vence. They had taken on a young Englishman to do some gardening and the lad accidentally chopped off his thumb while pruning their trees with a chainsaw. Ambulance, hospital, surgery... and the bill. Despite having a resident's permit, the young man had not set himself up as a registered gardener in France, nor had the couple declared him as a domestic employee. The authorities automatically considered him an *ipso facto* employee of the household, who should have checked his legal status. The elderly couple faced €500,000 in fines and medical bills. Their dream retirement villa was seized and sold at auction and they were ruined.'

There are more stories. In one, the undeclared chef at a dinner party set fire to the kitchen and himself. The insurance company would not pay because he was not supposed to be cooking for money. In another, an illegal British 'painter' set up scaffolding on a countryman's house. His scaffolding fell on to his 'client's' new Mercedes. No insurance claim could be put in and the man lost his car – thankfully the painter did not fall too, or he might have lost his house.

'France is an expensive place to be in business. You can't hope to survive if your competitor is not playing on a level field. You wouldn't let a perfect stranger fill up his supermarket trolley on your credit card, so why should you pay taxes for roads, hospitals, schools and public services that hangers-on benefit from at your expense?' explains Mike. 'The bottom line is, hiring workers in the black is fine until an accident happens, or there is a random tax control or work inspection. It's unlikely, but crazy things happen.'

The *Riviera Reporter* website (**www.riviera-reporter.com**) includes an online discussion forum. Mike Meade takes the time to answers many of the e-mails personally and has provided an invaluable resource with the dos and don'ts of living and working in the south.

There are also lots of online resources; good Internet sites for Britons looking for work in France are: **www.overseasjobs.com**, **www.careermosaic.com**, **www.jobware.net** and **www.monster.com** (with a whole section on France). If your French is up to par, log on to **www.apr-job.com**, **www.emploi.com**, **www.emailjob.com** or **www.paruvendu.fr**. If you are already in France, explore local resources available to expats. In Paris, **www.parisfranceguide.com** has classified ads, as does **www.parisvoice.com**. In Monaco, Nice and the Var, Riviera Radio (**www.rivieraradio.mc** or tune to 106.3 Monaco or 106.5 France) has an on-air 'Works for Me' programme in which all kinds of positions are advertised. You could become a bilingual assistant in an office in Monte-Carlo or be hired as a chef on a yacht off St-Tropez. The *Riviera Reporter* (**www.riviera-reporter.com**) also has an excellent database of jobs. The site **www.french-news.com** has a 'small ads' section with some job listings all over the country.

Another alternative is to go to an agency. The concept of a private employment agency doesn't exist in France because the government holds a monopoly on matching jobless with jobs. The state-run agency that fulfils this function is the **Agence Nationale pour l'Emploi (ANPE)** at **www.anpe.fr**. As a result, human resources multinationals such as Manpower (**www.manpower.fr**), which has 1,050 branches in France, are only allowed to focus on temporary work, not full-time contracted employment. Employment through these agencies (and many of the ones listed below) will only result in a contract of no more than 18 months, unless the employer negotiates with you otherwise.

You might be better off accessing the **European Employment Services (EURES)** network from national job centres, which allows you to find out about job vacancies in other member states. Its website, http://europa.eu.int/eures,

Volunteering

As well as fulfilling an altruistic need that many people feel at one time or another, volunteer work abroad can be a stepping stone for establishing a long-term life in another country, allowing people a more direct and immediate entrée into the language and culture in question while providing them with some valuable work experience.

There are dozens of French and international organisations that oversee volunteer programmes. Some are linked to religious groups, others are non-denominational. Some receive public funding or are affiliated with local universities. They operate in diverse sectors, but the main ones are art restoration and archaeology, environmental and animal rights issues, human rights, social services, and working with people with disabilities.

In rare cases, volunteers receive a small allowance. More realistically, you will be asked to pay a registration fee, ranging from €20 for two weeks to €150 for a month, to cover food, lodging, transport and insurance. Many groups operate in summer only. Two good resources, with bulletin boards and 'want ads' from a variety of organisations, are **www.responsibletravel.com** and **www.volunteerabroad.com**.

If you decide to look for volunteer work outside such organisations, the opportunities are limitless. You could volunteer to work in a vineyard during the harvest, or work with a local church to collect clothing for the poor. Or you could put your English-language skills to use at a local school, library or learning centre.

answers questions about benefits, contracts, transfers and other European work issues as well as listing employment opportunities. If you're not interested in contacting an agency, you could try networking through the various institutes that cater to trade and business between France

Teaching English in France

If you want to teach in France, a TEFL qualification will net you the best jobs and, probably, the best pay. However, many people simply turn up in France and put an ad on the supermarket noticeboard or in the newsagent's window offering *cours d'anglais*. In big cities there seems to be an inexhaustible supply of people wanting to learn English or improve their existing language skills, and *ad hoc* teachers can generally build up quite a client base via contacts and contacts of contacts. Many such teachers fail to register themselves as a business and don't pay social security or tax, which is illegal.

Others contact one of the many schools specialising in teaching the English language, which have a constant turnover of staff and therefore frequent (often very low-paid) vacancies. If you are offered employment by such an establishment, check that you are being recruited legally, are registered as an employee, and are paying social security. More lucratively, you might be able to get a short-term contract teaching English to company employees on their premises, as a *travailleur indépendant* (see pp.130–31).

Obtaining a job as a teacher of, for example, maths or another mainstream subject in the state system as a qualified teacher requires you to take competitive exams, such as the CAPES or Agrégation, which are open to EU nationals. It's this hurdle that results in most foreign teachers in France working as teachers of English, though this is much more straightforward for a British or Irish citizen, since it's very hard to get a visa to work as a salaried teacher when so many other English-speaking teachers from within the EU are available.

Americans should contact the Cultural Services at the French Embassy in the USA (e-mail **assistant.washington-amba@diplomatie.fr**), which offers 1,000–1,700 teaching assistant positions in French primary and secondary schools and *instituts universitaires de formation des maîtres* (IUFMs) in all regions of France and the DOM-TOMS (overseas territories) to US citizens or Green Card holders aged 20–34 who are pursuing or have obtained a college degree and are proficient in French (including students without a major or minor in French but who have studied the language for about three semesters). Successful applicants spend six to nine months in France and earn a monthly stipend of €890 for teaching about 12 hours of English conversation classes a week.

Finally, you can set up your own business as a teacher; no special formalities are involved. Even then, it's a competitive and poorly paid choice, unless you break into a major corporate market. Experienced teachers (or simply the more confident) ask for €25–30 per hour. As a career, though, it's generally pleasant, and you get to meet plenty of French people and learn a lot about life in France.

and England (embassies and consulates will not help you find a job). One obvious solution is to order a copy of the business directory of companies operating in France. The **Chambre de Commerce Française de Grande-Bretagne** in London (**www.ccfgb.co.uk**) publishes pamphlets and directories to help you understand the business scene, as does its equivalent in France, the **Franco-British Chamber of Commerce** (**www.francobritishchamber.com**).

The Curriculum Vitae and Covering Letter

The CV is a marketing tool to make an employer interested in you. It should be concise (a page, except in certain fields such as higher education or entertainment) and direct. Shorter CVs are easier to send as file attachments if you are applying from abroad. Make sure to have a native French-speaker check it over.

British and French CVs differ only slightly in length and content. Most French CVs are listed in reverse chronological order, with the most recent activity first (*le CV chronologique*), or grouped thematically (*le CV fonctionnel*). You should include a passport photo and personal information such as age and marital status, which you might not include on your British CV. It should be one page only. Contact information should include your e-mail address and a phone number with the international code.

The rules governing the content of a good covering letter (*demande d'emploi* or *lettre de candidature*) are almost precisely the same as anywhere else in the world. The letter should be short and should state your purpose and give a general thumbnail overview of your qualifications and background. They are generally hand-written because up to 80% of French employers use graphology (handwriting analysis) in the application process (so if you e-mail a covering letter, you may be asked to submit back-up writing samples). Larousse publishes an excellent book on business letter-writing: *Larousse Lettres d'Affaires*.

The two main types of letters are a *lettre de réponse à une annonce* (in response to a published advertisement) or a *lettre de candidature spontanée* (an 'on spec' letter to ask about possible openings).

For a sample CV and covering letter, *see* pp.275–8.

Interviews

The French take interviews seriously. If you have been invited to one, it means your candidacy is important to the selection team and your qualifications have caught their eye. The actual interview can be a formal event – either a one-on-one encounter or an interview in front of a panel of people. That means that you should use every means in your power to make a good impression from the moment you walk through the door. The importance of dressing well, using eye contact and conveying confidence cannot be exaggerated.

If your interview is in French (and hopefully you have not stated that your French is fluent on your CV if that is not the case), you will be expected to use the formal *vous* form of addressing your peers and should use appropriate titles. A *Monsieur* or *Madame* alone, without the name, is the correct form of address. You should offer a firm handshake at the start and end of the interview. If your French is not great, there's no harm in explaining that you're working on improving it and you look forward to continue doing so in the future. Another good hint is to read the French newspapers for a few days or weeks prior to the interview so you can offer opinions and comments on other topics should you be given the chance.

You may have to wait a while before an offer is made. In general, the French don't negotiate offers (salaries) with the same intensity we do. Often when an offer is made, it is immediately accepted, though there is nothing wrong with taking a few days to mull an offer over and, perhaps, come back with a counter-offer (in fact, it may win you points for professionalism and determination). The types of work contracts, terms of employment and salaries are discussed in detail below.

Terms and Conditions of Employment

Employment Contracts

There are three basic kinds of *contrat de travail*: the temporary contract, the fixed-term contract (*contrat à durée déterminée* or CDD) and the permanent contract (*contrat à durée indéterminée* or CDI). In the case of the **temporary contract**, the employee is usually hired and paid by a temping agency (*see* p.167), whose role is to recruit or replace an employee on a temporary basis in the event of a momentary increase in work (for example in the weeks before the Christmas season) or seasonal work. Temporary contracts may be renewed once, as long as the duration of employment does not exceed 18 months.

A **fixed-term contract** must state in writing the duration of the contract (for example, 'one-year contract'). The probationary period, or 'trial time', of a contract of less than six months may not exceed two weeks; for a contract of more than six months, it may not exceed one month. The maximum duration of a CDD contract is two years, after which a second CDD contract (or a permanent contract) can be offered. **Permanent contracts** provide enormous job security and a wide range of benefits. Basically, there is no 'end' to the contract. Both parties sign it, and it stipulates the date of employment, the social security information (healthcare) and other benefits. The length of the probationary period can last from one to three months.

If you are **not an EU citizen**, you must first obtain authorisation from the French Ministry of Labour to work in France, as a prerequisite for the issue of a visa by the French consulate in your country. You won't get the visa until you have been cleared to work by the French government. If the Ministry of Labour approves your contract, it is forwarded to the Office des Migrations Internationales (OMI), then to the French embassy or consulate you have been dealing with. It is the embassy or consulate's job to notify you when to proceed with the visa process. Once the visa is obtained, you may enter France and apply for a *carte de séjour* at the local police station (Préfecture). This is covered in detail in **Red Tape**, pp.154–5.

Terms of Employment

Once you start working in France, you will receive a payslip (*bulletin de salaire*) with your salary. This document keeps track of wages paid that month, social security contributions made on behalf of the employee, the amount deducted for taxes and the number of holiday days left.

The following are the basic conditions for employment as established by the French Labour Code (*code du travail*).

Wages and Salaries

Your salary (*salaire*) is calculated according to your work category (what kind of contract you have). The main categories are manual workers, office employees and managers, and each has its own fixed salary grade. Manyfirst-time employees earn the minimum wage, called the SMIC or *salaire minimum interprofessionnel de croissance*, and can expect a rise pegged to the cost-of-living index, which is reviewed every six months. When the cost of living increases by 2% or more, the SMIC is adjusted. If a worker falls into a category protected by a national labour union, work contracts are renewed every few years. Collective bargaining (*conventions collectives de travail*) establishes new wage scales each time contracts are renewed. Most salaries are paid monthly.

According to the APEC research centre, the median starting salary in France is €26,000–29,000 per year. In general, French salaries are among the highest in Europe – especially for managerial positions – but they may still be lower than what you are used to in England.

Working Hours

Though the *code du travail* has now established a 35-hour working week, there is some built-in flexibility. For example, if a company needs more workers in the busiest weeks prior to Christmas, it can increase the hours worked per week, as long as they are decreased in less busy times. Companies can increase the number of hours worked per week through collective bargaining and by agreeing to pay employees overtime or giving them more time off.

Dismissal and Redundancy

An employee can be fired only if the employer can prove 'just cause' or a 'justified motive'. Just cause (*faute grave*) means the employee is found guilty of a major offence (*cause réelle et sérieuse*), such as stealing or unexplained absenteeism. This is difficult to prove and even harder to execute because it involves an official summons and a hearing. Justified motives include corporate downsizing (*pour faute du salarié ou pour raison économique*); firings on this basis must include advance notice and are usually negotiated with labour unions, making them difficult to carry out.

If an employee is fired unlawfully, they can claim their job and salary back with compensation for back wages. If an employee is fired because of downsizing, they will be the first one back on the payroll should the company have an opening in the future.

Whether or not an employee resigns or is fired (except in cases of serious misconduct), they get a severance payment (*indemnité de licenciement*), which usually comes to 10% of their average salary during their last three months for each year in service. Payment must also be made if there is outstanding paid holiday (*indemnité compensatrice de congés payés*). Employees can leave their jobs at any time without justification as long as they notify the employer in writing by registered letter. Those who have lost a contracted position are paid unemployment benefits.

If you have any questions regarding the French Labour Code, or the terms of employment, there are two excellent legal pages available on the Internet, **www.journal-officiel.gouv.fr** and the English-language **www.paris-law.com**.

Benefits

Holidays

Workers are entitled to five weeks' paid holiday (*congés payés*) a year, plus 11 public holidays (*jours fériés*) spread throughout the year. (For a list of the 11 national holidays and their descriptions, *see* **References**, 'National and Local Holidays', pp.246–7.) The general calculation is as follows: you must work one month (24 work days) to be entitled to two and a half days of holiday.

Bonuses

Most companies in France pay employees an extra month's salary, known as the 13th month's pay (*13ème mois*). This bonus payment comes in December in time for the Christmas shopping season. If you don't work the entire year, the 13th month's pay is calculated to reflect the time you did work. A few companies also offer a 14th month's pay in July (in general, only banks and finance companies). In addition, senior employees may receive bonuses, of anything from 10 to

25% of their annual salary, that may or may not be linked to the company's financial performance (as with profit-sharing schemes – *participation des salariés aux résultats de l'entreprise*). An employee can be invited to participate in a company savings plan or stock options. Salespeople are often given commissions of 3–6% of sales.

Different forms of bonuses are becoming common. Employee 'packages' may include a car, phone, laptop, expenses and professional training. Bonus 'benefits' offered could include favourable interest rates to finance a car or mortgage.

Health Insurance

All employees, including foreigners working for French companies and the self-employed, must contribute to France's social security fund (*see* p.125), which covers healthcare. The amount you contribute depends on your income but can be as much as a fifth or a quarter of your gross pay. Your employer also contributes a large amount on your behalf.

Some companies offer supplementary health insurances, called the *mutuelle*, to cover a portion of the medical expenses or hospitalisation charges not covered by social security. Some companies also offer private health insurance as part of a larger package of benefits.

For more information on healthcare, *see* **Living in France**, pp.228–32.

Maternity and Paternity Leave

A new mother is entitled to 16 weeks' paid maternity leave (*congé de maternité*) if she is covered by social security – generally six weeks before giving birth and 10 weeks after. She gets up to 26 weeks if she is having her third child. She earns her full salary during this time and can take additional time off with a doctor's note. Maternity leave is granted to all women no matter how long they have been employed, and a mother is guaranteed her job back after the leave at the same salary or higher. New fathers in France receive 11 consecutive days of leave at full pay. Both parents can take up to three years of unpaid parental leave (*congé parental*) and expect to come back to the same job and salary (with the mandatory increases that may have occurred in the meantime). All of these rights apply to parents with adopted children.

Sickness Leave and Disability

Employees unable to work due to an illness are compensated according to the number of years of service. An employee with more than 10 years in service is entitled to two months of full salary, then two months at 75% salary, and two months at half-salary. An employee with between one and five years in service is entitled to one month of full salary, one month at 75%, and one month at half-salary. If they are still sick after that time, they may be considered disabled.

If an accident occurs in the workplace, injured employees receive full salary for the first three months. If they are permanently injured, they receive a pension. Many of the *mutuelle*, or health insurance supplements, include both temporary and permanent disability coverage on top of the *sécurité sociale* benefits.

If there is a death in the family or some other reason for an employee to need additional time off from work, employees can ask for a special leave of absence (*congé special*).

Pensions and Retirement

France is taking controversial steps to raise the retirement (*retraite*) age to 65, in line with many other European countries. At the moment, both men and women can retire at the age of 60 after working in the private sector for 40 years and in the public sector for 37½ years. Early retirement applies to particularly burdensome professions.

A retiree earns a pension of about half their average salary for the last 20 years of employment. Proposed pension reform has led to massive protests in Paris and other big cities, and this very sensitive subject is constantly under scrutiny.

Living in France

Learning French 176
Finding a Home 178
Buying a Property 179
Renting a Property 209
Home Utilities 210
Mobile Phones 214
The Internet 215
Television and Satellite 216
Postal Services 216
Money and Banking 217
Shopping 218
Transport 220
Crime and the Police 226
Taking Your Pet 227
Health and Emergencies 228
Social Services and Welfare Benefits 230
Retirement, Pensions and Death 232
Education 233

You're finally ready to make the move. This chapter details step-by-step the things you need to do – and not do – to make your experience as comfortable and rewarding as possible. Information is included on a wide range of topics, from how to install broadband for a faster Internet service to enrolling your children in school. Of all the things we recommend for a productive life in France, first and foremost is to learn the language (*see* below).

Although you're unlikely to suffer from serious bouts of culture shock, other expats have identified various phases of cultural adjustment they experienced when they moved to France. First is excitement and enthusiasm. You'll love studying the dozens of cheeses in the supermarket or tuning your radio to the latest French music. The next stage is disbelief, frustration and loss. After a few years, or just months in some cases, you start to question why you came to France in the first place. In the third stage, you make a renewed effort to learn French culture from a new and balanced perspective. The fourth and last stage is acclimatisation and belonging. Your cultural transition is complete.

Learning French

If you can't speak French, learn it. If you don't, you'll never become integrated into French culture and accepted by your community, either on a personal or a business level, and will find yourself scraping around on the margins, serving only English-speaking customers, which increases your risk of failure. It's also worth considering that if you begin learning while you are still exploring the prospects for a new business, it will motivate you.

On the whole, foreigners who don't speak French find themselves stuck running illegal 'businesses' providing low-paid services to other foreigners, such as hairdressing, gardening and odd jobs, computer maintenance, and dog-walking. We do have clients who run successful businesses in France whose command of the French language, even after 10 years there, is best described as modest, but these are few and far between – you need a very good product or service that is otherwise unavailable, bucketloads of charm, or a great deal of luck (or all three). But even in such cases, the business would do much better if they were run by people who spoke French, and the foreigners would be happier in themselves because they could have conversations with their neighbours, read the newspapers, watch TV, and argue about fares with taxi drivers.

Methods of learning range from the traditional and now slightly unpopular grammar and vocabulary system to 'point and name', 20 words a day, word association and many more. With the wonders of modern technology, you can learn not only from books and tapes but also from CDs, CD-ROMs and DVDs. Which method suits you depend on your own preferences and lifestyle; shop around, and don't start off with preconceptions as to which will suit you best.

Getting Up to Scratch

If you're looking for a language course and require an officially recognised fluency certificate at the end of it, there are various options. The **DELF** (*diplôme d'études en langue française*) and **DALF** (*diplôme approfondi de langue française*), the most recognised exams to test fluency skills, are sponsored by the French Ministry of Education. The DELF has six levels of competency; after you pass the first four, you receive a degree, and, following successful completion of the last two, you receive an advanced diploma.

Another alternative is to study for one of the prestigious diplomas offered by the **Alliance Française** (**www.alliancefr.org**). These are designed for students of all levels whose native language is not French. The diplomas are recognised internationally (in the 130 countries where the Alliance Française operates) and are based on European Council recommendations as outlined by the ALTE (Association of Language Testers in Europe). Alliance Française is also a testing centre for DELF and DALF certificates. Its exams have different levels, including CEFP 1 (*certificat d'études françaises*), CEFP 2, the DL (*diplôme de langue française*), DS (*diplôme supérieur d'études françaises*) and the DHEF (*diplôme de hautes études françaises*). The DL and the DS are the most common, and the DHEF is recommended for teachers of French. These are 'pass or fail' exams.

Other language certificates are organised by the Chamber of Commerce and Industry in Paris and test a candidate's ability to use the language of a specific professional realm. Candidates must participate in a three-month preparatory course to qualify for the exam.

'Unofficial' ways of learning can be very effective – once you get to a certain point, TV is a great way of improving your vocabulary and sentence structure (tip: documentaries are normally spoken at a slightly slower pace than dramas or news programmes), as is watching films on DVD, with a creative use of subtitles (watch in French with English subtitles, in French with French subtitles, or even in English with French subtitles).

Try to read a newspaper every day, and from time to time read something connected with your business, whether it be a trade journal, an Internet newsletter or the specialist pages of an ordinary newspaper. Carry a small dictionary in your handbag or briefcase and always look up words you don't understand. Join a conversation class and take every opportunity to speak French – manufacture opportunities, even. Practise words and phrases before going into a shop and make sure you use them. It also helps to learn along with other people, for mutual encouragement and a sense of solidarity.

The fastest and most effective way to learn French is to take a language course. There are intensive courses that last a few months, with classes five days a week, or more relaxed courses in which you might study one day a week over many months. The telephone directory and the Internet are full of advertisements (check **www.pagesjaunes.fr**). If you absolutely need to learn French to deal with clients and suppliers, try to find time to take a course in business French. If you can't, set yourself realistic goals – try to study a little every day, and try to speak to your customers and suppliers in French at least part of the time, however much they try to speak to you in English, because they'll respect you for it and your business will benefit.

Alternatively, sign on for private one-on-one lessons (the going rate is about €30 an hour) or become involved in a language exchange, swapping an hour of English with an hour of French conversation. Or you could arrange for a wine-tasting or cooking session at home with other Francophiles.

Above all, don't try to do too much too quickly and try to have fun learning – don't be depressed when the going is slow but rejoice when you exceed your objectives or expectations. Most importantly, stick with it.

For more on the French language, see **Getting to Know France**, 'French and Dialects', p.18).

Finding a Home

Making a home in France is by far the most important component of life abroad. In many respects, it *is* your life abroad. Thankfully, there are more resources available now than ever to help turn your dreams of life in France into bricks and mortar. It is relatively easy to set up a home in France, thanks to the Internet, increased financing options, banks that operate internationally, property prices that hold good over the long term, a wide range of properties on the market, bilingual estate agents, more published reference sources (such as Cadogan's comprehensive *Buying a Property: France*) and, most importantly, a growing and vibrant expatriate community. Many thousands of Britons have successfully made a home in France and have paved the way for your own transition abroad.

The most pressing consideration is where you will make your home. Choosing the location that is right for you is paramount, but your business idea is likely to dictate the shortlist of options unless you are looking for a place from which to carry on a freelance career.

Moving Times

It's often said that moving home is one of life's most stressful events, so you would assume that the stress doubles when you're moving to a new country. However, moving to continental Europe doesn't need to be any more complicated than moving within the UK – the trick is to use a member of the **British Association of Removers (www.bar.co.uk, t** (01923) 699480) with experience in relocating people to the continent (and in some cases, to certain specific destinations). The firm you choose will be able to advise you on any documentation and entry requirements regarding your possessions.

Buying a Property

Buying and selling property in France is different from the system in England; the many superficial similarities can lull you into a false sense of familiarity and over-confidence. But the most important thing to remember is that buying a home in France is just as safe as buying a home in Cardiff, provided that you take the right professional advice and precautions when doing so.

Town or Country?

Deciding where to live in France is not just a matter of deciding which French region you like best. As well as depending to a large extent on what kind of business you're intending to set up, it entails deep thought and on-the-ground research about other significant factors, such as proximity to shops, schools for your children, businesses, doctors, transport and community. You might stumble across your dream home on a remote hilltop in Provence drenched in golden sunlight and surrounded by lavender fields, but when you realise the nearest shop selling foreign newspapers is 50km away, that idyllic vision may lose its lustre. Many city-dwellers make the mistake of buying homes based purely on aesthetic impact, and once the sun sets what they thought was 'quaint isolation' becomes *Friday the 13th* terror – they lie in bed with their eyes wide open listening to the deafening sounds of nature: screeching owls, the human-like wails of felines on heat and the pitter-patter of rats scurrying on tile roofs. After a night, they're ready to move back to the city.

There are other practical issues. The first is shopping. Country homes are usually only serviced by a small collection of food shops with erratic opening hours, selling basics such as bread, sugar, cold meats, tinned goods and cleaning detergents, plus a produce market that's open in the mornings only. If you can't live without a full-blown shopping centre, you're better off at least near to a city or big town. And if you do brave country life, make sure you have a large vehicle, as your shopping expeditions will be as momentous as when Noah filled his ark. Besides food shopping, you may also have to think about access to gardening materials and DIY equipment, as well as services available nearby – if your water heater has a habit of breaking down, getting a service representative to travel kilometres over dirt roads might be more trying than braving ice-cold showers.

Choosing a location also means identifying the nearest hospital and accessibility to doctors, especially if you are getting on a bit or have children or an elderly relative. Transport is another concern. If you often travel for work, you'll need to be close to an airport, major motorways or a train station. You'll need to know if there are schools in your area for your children. If your preference is an English-language education, this will further limit your choices. Thought should be given to whether you want to live near a gym, swimming pool or golf club. Again, most of these things are easier to find closer to urban centres. Some country areas in France are completely desolate.

Research

These days, house-hunting usually starts in front of the computer with a search of properties listed on the Internet. Plug in a few key words such as 'property', 'buying', 'house' and 'France', and your search engine is likely to throw thousands of weblinks back at you. But don't discount the traditional media. In the UK, *World of Property* and *International Homes* are two publications with ample listings in France. More specific to France are *French Property News*, *Focus on France* and *Living in France* magazine, all available in the UK.

France is exceedingly well represented at property shows in the UK, and often an entire trade show will be focused on the country. There, you can meet estate agents, lawyers for consultation and financial advisers who can explain the intricacies of mortgages. Seminars are organised, and the exhibition gives you a chance to rummage through thousands of photos and pamphlets. *French Property News* (**www.french-property-news.com**), *Homes Overseas* and *World of Property* organise shows. For information on when the next trade show will take place, see **www.internationalpropertyshow.com**.

Estate Agents

The vast majority of foreigners who buy property in France do so with the help of an estate agent, but opinions on them are polarised. Some estate agents are the subject of frequent complaints and have been tagged with every insult imaginable, from greedy to dishonest. Others are praised for their ability to supply the buyer with a wealth of information and knowledge about a particular property. As a result, it is very important that you choose well and establish a strong rapport with your agent. But keep one thought firmly in the back of your mind: the estate agent represents the seller's interests, not yours.

In a sense, the Internet is your fiercest ally because it provides a system of checks and balances. You can preview properties from home, forming impressions – whether positive or negative – with a few clicks of the mouse. Ironically, the Internet makes the estate agent's job both easier and more difficult: easier because it connects sellers to agents, and agents to buyers; more difficult because the estate agent can no longer rely on haughty adjectives printed in a black and white advertisement to attract customers. A picture is worth a thousand words.

There are two main groups of estate agents, French and foreign, and there are pros and cons in using each. Some buyers swear by French estate agents, especially ones based very close to the property in question, because they have a deeper understanding of the practical issues – planning regulations, possible problems and the neighbourhood. Many estate agents are also close friends or relatives of the people surrounding your target property (or even of its owner), which guarantees an 'insider's' approach. Having a French agent to represent you might remove some of the seller's temptation to overcharge.

On the other hand, a foreign estate agent – and many are British – can speak your language and therefore better understand your needs; for example, a foreign estate agent has probably dealt more extensively with buyers who want to restore a property or with people transferring large sums of money from abroad. Choosing between the two groups might ultimately be decided by your fluency in French. The importance of good communication between agent and buyer cannot be exaggerated.

A French agent (*agent immobilier*) must be professionally qualified and must hold a *carte professionnelle* to practise (*see* p.39). Most have indemnity insurance and a fidelity bond (*pièce de garantie*). The agent's licence is usually framed on display in his/her office. In order to sell property, they must be licensed and must have written permission from the owner (*mandat*). Many agents operate illegally without these, including some Britons selling to Britons or Germans selling to Germans. You will be told to avoid their services, but the truth is that many are excellent at what they do.

There are also a growing number of estate agents based in the UK, who are technically not licensed to sell in France but who do so anyway. They often work in association with French agents, generally covering a wider area than a single French agent would. Most charge a fee or a commission of the sale. They are a convenient alternative for those buying from the UK.

Other buyers, particularly those with a good command of French, opt to buy property directly from the seller (*de particulier à particulier*). There is nothing wrong with this; in fact, many buyers prefer it. Un-agented property is common in France, although foreigners usually have a hard time finding it because they instinctively gravitate towards the agencies. Some 20% of property in France is sold by a notary public (*notaire*) acting as an estate agent. It may seem strange that the person charged with the transfer of ownership on behalf of both the buyer and seller would be representing the property (imagine a solicitor selling a property), but it is considered normal in France.

When you make an appointment to visit a property, take along a notepad, a digital camera and a map. Take notes and pictures of rooms you might like to restore, bathroom fixtures you might like to move and gardens you'd like to plan. These will come in handy when you come back for a second visit. Most experts recommend not seeing more than four properties per day; after that, the details concerning the first house will be indistinguishable from those of the last. After you've seen a batch of possibilities, find a good restaurant, relax over a glass of wine and discuss. When you've reached an initial decision, make an appointment with a contractor to check plumbing, roofs, floors and humidity as soon as possible.

Basic Questions

- **Have you worked out a budget, and do you need to secure a loan?**
- **Do you plan to remodel? If so, factor this into your budget.**

- How much should you offer? If you feel a property is overpriced, don't be afraid of offering 20–30% below the asking price to start with. Factors such as a sitting tenant, a leaking roof, warped or unlevel floors, termites or damp in walls should be used as 'negotiating chips' in your favour. If it is priced at what you think it is worth, make an offer slightly below the asking price. If it is underpriced, ask no more questions and buy.
- Are there outstanding property taxes on the property?
- Are there any utilities connected to the property?
- Does the property have the relevant building licences? If a window has been enlarged, or an extra room added, make sure it has been recorded on the property deed.
- What is the water situation? Some country properties have shared wells. Check that all relevant neighbours have given their consent for water use.
- Have you checked the planning regulations? If you plan to turn a barn into a residence, make sure planning permission is available.
- Are any major public works projects (railways, motorways, bridges) being planned for your area?
- Is there a sitting tenant in the property? If there is you may have an impossible time kicking them out, even if they simply decide to stop paying rent.

Auctions (*Ventes aux Enchères*)

Property in France can be bought at auction, just as in Britain. Some auctions are voluntary, others are by court order. The relatively rare **voluntary auctions** are run by notaries (*marché immobilier des notaires*) and feature properties that have 'stuck' in the market, properties the sellers think will sell best at auction, and properties that have been inherited and that the heirs wish to dispose of quickly. One attraction of such auctions for the seller is that their share of the auctioneers' fees (usually 1% of the price) is lower than the average level of estate agents' fees (say, 5%).

Other auctions are **judicial auctions** (*ventes judiciaires*). In a judicial auction you'll find properties sold as a result of mortgage repossession, unpaid debts, disputes between joint owners, in connection with the administration of the estate of someone who has died or by virtue of some other court order.

Prices can be very attractive. A few years ago, during the last recession, there were some incredible bargains, with prices listed at 30% of 'value'. Today, there is still the possibility of a good deal because, particularly in many judicial auctions, the process is intended first and foremost to recover someone's debt. Once that and the considerable costs have been covered, there is little reason to press for a higher price.

Buying a property at auction is not at all simple for someone who does not live in the area, and it is vitally important that you have taken all the normal preparatory steps – including seeing a lawyer – before you embark on the process. The **procedure** leading up to the auction is basically the same whether the auction is a judicial auction or a notarial auction.

First, you must know the auction is taking place. They are usually advertised six to eight weeks in advance. Auctions ordered by the court will be advertised by order of the court in the local press. Notices will also be posted in the area.

Secondly, you must find out what is in the auction. Brief details of the property to be sold will be listed, including the *commune*'s land/rating registry (*cadastre*) reference, the arrangements for viewing, the notary dealing with the sale, the reserve price and the deposit that must be lodged so you can bid. These details are only a start. The place could be derelict or next door to a nuclear power station – you will need to inspect it personally and decide whether it's of interest, which is a time-consuming and potentially costly process. You might have to inspect 20 properties to find three you like, and then you might be outbid on all three. An alternative to personal inspection is to get someone to do it for you. This is not as satisfactory, but a local estate agent will, for a fee of about £200, go to look at the property and give you a description of it.

Thirdly, you need to check the legal situation of the property before the date of the auction. Most of the steps needed in an ordinary purchase will be required. Fourthly, many properties on sale by auction are not in good condition, so you will need to get estimates for the cost of repairs or improvements to verify that the price you bid is not so high as to make the project non-viable. Fifthly, you must appoint a notary or local lawyer (*avocat*) to act on your behalf – at a judicial auction, individuals can't turn up and bid as they can in the UK. Even at an ordinary notarial auction you would be brave or foolish not to be represented. The lawyer will explain precisely what needs to be done at a particular auction. You must establish the **maximum price** you want to offer and pay the lawyer a **bidding deposit** – a refundable fee levied by the auctioneer to allow you to enter a bid. You must also give your personal details (marital status, occupation, nationality, passport number, etc.) and a **deposit** of 10% of the price you're offering, less the bidding deposit. The full deposit is paid when your bid is accepted.

You do not need to attend the auction. The lawyer can act on your behalf but will probably require a power of attorney for that purpose. His or her fee can be substantial, so get an estimate in advance. Still, an auction (especially a judicial auction) is a most interesting event, so you might want to attend anyway. The traditional auction, gradually disappearing, is the 'candle' auction (*vente à la chandelle*). The sale is *à la bougie* or *aux trois feux*. This picturesque, if confusing affair sells the property in the time it takes for three candles to burn out.

If you win, your deposit will be taken. You then wait 10 days to verify that you have the property. The results of the auction can be challenged during that period by anyone prepared to bid 10% above the sale price (*surenchère*). He or she might, for example, be the dispossessed owner of the property that has been sold for a pittance by the bank that repossessed it. If the auction is challenged, it will be repeated. It can only be challenged once, and a challenge is a rare event.

Although prices at an auction can be very attractive, bear in mind that you face costs over and above those of a normal purchase, which are likely to raise the overall costs of buying from the average 8–9% to perhaps 17–20% of the price paid. The extra costs include the fees paid to your lawyers for dealing with the auction, extra land registry fees for publishing the result, and the charges related to the auction itself.

On the other hand, many people are entitled to automatic mortgage finance of 60% of the price paid if they buy at a notarial auction. Check with your lawyer whether this applies to you.

What Preparation Should You Make?

See a Lawyer

It is a good idea to see a lawyer before you start your property search. There are preliminary issues that are best discussed during the period of relative calm before you find your dream house rather than after, when you are under pressure to sign important documents. These issues include:

- **Who should own the property? Bear in mind French inheritance rules and the French and British tax consequences of ownership (see pp.192–4).**
- **Whether to consider mortgage finance, and if so in which country.**
- **What to do about converting the money you pay into euros.**

A British lawyer who specialises in foreign property purchases will be able to help you best. Your normal British solicitor will know little or nothing of the issues of French law, and a French lawyer is likely to know little or nothing about the British tax system or the way the transaction should be arranged. A good lawyer may also be able to recommend estate agents, architects, surveyors and other contacts.

Decide on Ownership

Who should be the owner of your new home? Because of French inheritance rules – which do not allow you to leave your property as you please – and the French and British tax systems, getting ownership wrong can be a very expensive mistake. It can lead to the wrong people being entitled to inherit the property (a problem for people with children from more than one relationship), as well as unnecessary taxes during your lifetime and upon your death. See 'Who Should Own the Property?', pp.192–4.

Get an Offer of Mortgage/Finance

These days, with very low interest rates, more and more people borrow at least part of the money they need to buy their home in France. Often, a loan makes good business and investment sense. If you want to borrow money to part-finance your purchase, get clearance *before* you start looking at property. Whether you want to borrow on your British property or on the overseas property, your lawyer should be able to put you in touch with suitable lenders.

Think about How You Will Pay a Deposit

Once your offer has been accepted, you will be required to put down a preliminary deposit of 5 or 10% of the price of the property. Some estate agencies, particularly those operating from Britain, will ask you to take a banker's draft for the amount of the deposit. This is not a good idea, though it is ideal for the estate agent and the seller. The most simple and effective way of paying the deposit is with a British cheque for the sterling equivalent of the euros needed.

An increasingly popular option, however, is to leave your deposit with your British lawyer. When you find the right property and the estate agent asks you to sign a contract, you explain that your lawyer has the money. That way, you sign the contract as soon as the lawyer has approved it, and he or she transfers the funds into the *notaire*'s bank account by electronic transfer. A lawyer should be able to check a contract faxed to them while you wait and be able to tell you whether the terms appear reasonable. This system takes a lot of pressure off you and makes it hard for the agent to persuade you to sign a document that may have far-reaching consequences without getting it checked first. From the *notaire*'s point of view, the system ensures he or she will receive the funds within a couple of days rather than the two or three weeks it can take for your British cheque to clear. However, bear in mind that this preliminary check by the lawyer is limited. They will not have seen proof of title or planning consents, inspected the documentation relating to the construction of a new building, or been able to carry out checks on the property.

Building from Scratch or Renovating a Property

Prepare a huge reserve of elbow grease if you plan to build or restore a property, and think twice if you're not keen on DIY or if your bank account is close to imploding. But if you're a creative and enthusiastic home restorer, there's no shortage of property, available in all stages of decay, poised to become your next pet project.

Building a new home costs about €800 per square metre for finished work (unfinished work, which is just walls and plumbing but not decorative details such as carpeting or tiling, is about half that). Restoring an old home also costs €800 per square metre for finished work. That means it costs roughly the same amount to build from scratch as it does to renovate. In most cases, renovation costs are greater in the long term because demolition expenses must also be factored in. The only way to bring down renovation costs is to do most of the work yourself. You will face steep prices if you need to install electricity cables, water, septic tanks, air-conditioning, broadband wiring, wells or swimming pools, or hook up to utilities if they are far away. Remember that an old country house rarely has these amenities. DIY materials are readily available in France but can be very expensive (this is exacerbated by VAT), although you can find junkyards and salvage dealers selling antique bathtubs, masonry and ironwork. Many foreigners drive over with loads of building supplies, such as paint, that may cost less elsewhere.

French labour is highly specialised and extremely good. Many builders consider themselves artisans and take great pride in carrying out the trade that was passed on to them by their fathers, though bad apples do exist. The VAT tax should always be included in estimates (*devis*) and should reflect the tax paid on building labour and material. (Keep receipts so the costs can be set against the perceived gain on the resale of the property for French capital gains tax. The VAT charged for home improvements and renovations is 5.5%, that charged on materials is 19.6%. If you approve an estimate, you are usually asked to pay a deposit of 10–25% before work starts and follow up with monthly payments or some other payment scheme. Never give too much money up-front, and check the price of materials to make sure you're not being overcharged.

It is always a good idea to establish a completion date with your builder, too. As with anywhere else, there are stories of builders taking deposit money and then disappearing, or builders who get halfway through the project then vanish, leaving you roofless or waterless.

Property Inspection

Whatever property you're thinking of buying, have it inspected before you commit yourself to the purchase. Foolishly, very few buyers do this.

A new property will be covered by a two-year guarantee (*garantie biennale*) starting from the date of handover (*réception des travaux*) and covering defects to equipment on the property. The property also benefits from a guarantee against major structural defects that lasts for 10 years (*garantie décennale*).

Property more than 10 years old (and, arguably, younger property too) should be inspected by a surveyor. Most surveys can be completed within seven to 10 days. Whichever type you opt for, its quality will depend in part on your input. Agree clearly and in writing on things you want covered. If you don't speak French (and the surveyor doesn't speak good English), ask someone to intervene on your behalf – your British lawyer is probably the best bet. Some matters you may wish to include are listed in the checklist on p.188. Ask your surveyor what is covered under the standard fee and get an estimate for anything extra.

Types of Survey

Estate Agent's Valuation and 'Survey'

It may be possible to arrange for another local estate agent to give the property a quick 'once over' in order to get his opinion on the price and possible problem areas. This falls short of a real survey and is likely to cost about £200.

Mortgage Lender's Survey

This is no substitute for a proper survey. Many lenders do not ask for one and, when they do, it is peremptory. Basically, the bank needs to make sure the property is indeed worth the money it will be lending to you.

French Builder

If you plan to demolish and rebuild much of the property, you could ask a builder to submit a report. A qualified builder (*maître d'œuvres*) will be able to comment on the asking price and the state of the property. Make sure you ask for a binding written estimate (*devis*) for any building work proposed. Getting several quotes is also a good idea to help you shop around for the best prices.

French Surveyor

Surveyors don't make up a single professional category as they do in England. Instead, different surveyors offer varying services, which can lead to some confusion. Your best bet is to seek advice from your notary, estate agent or lawyer regarding a surveyor who can address your specific issues.

*Architect (*Architecte*)*

An architect's survey will, as you might expect, focus on issues of design and construction, although it should also cover all of the basic subjects needed in a survey. The people to contact for a list of local architects are the Association of Architects, the architects' professional body (**www.architectes.org**); it has 26 regional councils, protected by the Ministry of Culture. Costs depend on the size and complexity of the house; allow £500–1,500 for an average house.

Valuer/Surveyor (Expert Immobilier)

The report from an expert surveyor will focus on measurement and valuation, but it will also cover the essential issues relating to the structure of the property. For a list of experts, contact the Chambre des Experts Immobiliers (**www.experts-fnaim.org**). Surveyors produce two types of report. The more common is the *expertise* – what amounts to the initial observations of a trained eye, containing little in the way of testing. The second is the structural report (*bilan de santé*), which involves testing the home's foundations and other hard-to-access parts of the property. As with architects, costs vary depending on the size and complexity of the house. They also vary to reflect the depth of report requested. Allow £200–500 for a basic report on an average house and £500–1,500 for a more complex survey.

Whichever type of report and whether it is from an architect or a surveyor, you will find that it differs from the survey you would expect from an English expert. Many people find it a little 'thin', with too much focus on issues that are not a primary concern. It will, hardly surprisingly, be in French, therefore you must have it translated unless you speak very good French and have access to a technical dictionary. An alternative to a full translation is to ask your lawyer to summarize the report in a letter and translate only areas of particular concern. Alternatively, a growing number of French surveyors and architects have geared themselves to the non-French market and can produce a survey that reflects the ones you are accustomed to. Some are also happy to supply the report in both English and French for no extra cost. A number of savvy British surveyors have also seen the gap in the market and set themselves up in France to provide British-style structural surveys. If you do opt to go with a British surveyor in France, probe them on their knowledge of French building codes and regulations, as the rules in France differ greatly from the ones in the UK. Prices are generally slightly more expensive with a foreign surveyor, but the final report will be in English. Check that the UK surveyor has indemnity insurance covering the provision of the report in France.

Checklist – Things You Should Ask Your Surveyor to Do

- **An electrical condition and continuity check – kitchen and bathroom wiring should be connected to ground and a trip-switch.**
- **A plumbing check, including assessment of drains to where they join mains sewers or a septic tank.**
- **A septic tank check.**
- **A rot check in roofing and dry wall.**
- **A check on cement for signs of cracks or movement.**
- **A check on the adequacy of foundations.**
- **A check against roofing leaks.**
- **A check of underfloor areas, where access cannot easily be obtained.**
- **A check on heating and air-conditioning.**
- **A check on pools and all pool-related equipment.**
- **A wood-boring insect check (roughly half of France's buildings are infested with termites).**

Contracts 'Subject to Survey'

These are most unusual in France, and though legally there is nothing to stop a French preliminary contract (*compromis de vente*) containing a clause (*clause suspensive*) stating that the sale is conditional on a satisfactory survey being obtained, it's unlikely to meet with the approval of the seller, their agent or their notary unless the transaction is unusual – if, for example, it's a castle or property of historic value with many precious assets. In an ordinary case, the seller is likely to tell you to do your own survey. This does expose you to some risk: the seller could sell to someone else before you get the results of the survey. One way to avoid this is to draft a reservation contract in which the property is taken off the market for a couple of weeks. Or, you could settle on a 'gentleman's agreement' in which the seller promises to wait for the results of your survey.

Raising Finance

If you decide to take out a mortgage, you can, in most cases, mortgage either your existing British or your new French property. There are advantages and disadvantages to both. Many people buying property in France look closely at fixed-rate mortgages so they know their commitment over, say, the next five, 10 or 15 years.

Mortgaging your UK Property

There is is fierce competition to lend money in the UK, with the result that there are some excellent deals available, whether you choose to borrow at a variable rate, at a fixed rate or on one of the hybrid schemes now on offer. Read the weekend papers or the specialist mortgage press, or consult a mortgage broker to learn about the latest deals. A mortgage broker would be able to provide you with the most detailed information. A British mortgage is generally the better option for people who need to borrow relatively small sums and who will be repaying it out of British income, e.g. for a holiday home.

French Mortgages

A French mortgage taken specifically for your French property will either be from a French bank (or other lending institution) or from a British bank that is registered and does business in France.

The basic concept of a mortgage is the same in France as it is in Britain. It is (usually) a loan secured against land or buildings. Just like anywhere else, if you don't keep up the payments the bank will repossess your property. In France, if they do this they will sell it by judicial auction (*see* pp.182–4) and you are likely to see it sold for a pittance and recover little if anything for the equity you built up in the property.

French mortgages are governed by the **Loi Scrivener**, which creates a complex administrative regime for the granting of mortgages and gives some significant elements of consumer protection. Key elements of the *loi* (which applies only to commercial mortgages of residential property) are:

- That if the purchase is subject to a mortgage, the contract is automatically subject to a get-out clause (*clause suspensive*) stipulating that one month of time is established for the buyer to secure a loan. If the loan is refused during that time, the contract is null and void and the buyer's deposit returned. The buyer must make every effort to obtain a mortgage and, if they don't, will lose the protection of the law. This clause needs to be drafted most carefully to ensure your protection.

- That every offer of a mortgage must be in writing and contain full details of the loan including its total cost, interest charges, mechanisms for varying the interest rate and what ancillary steps the borrower must take to get the loan (such as taking out a life policy). It must also disclose any penalties for early repayment and must state that it is valid for acceptance for 30 days.

- That the loan offer cannot be accepted for a 'cooling off period' of 10 days from receipt and no money can be paid to the lender until that time.
- That the contract be completed within four months of acceptance of the loan.
- That there are restrictions on the ability to impose penalties for early repayment of the loan.

The Main Differences Between British and French Mortgages

- French mortgages are almost always created on a repayment basis. That means the loan and the interest on it are both gradually repaid by equal instalments over the period of the mortgage.
- The formalities involved in submitting an application, signing the contract subject to a mortgage and completing the transaction are more complex and stricter than in the UK.
- Most French mortgages are granted for 15 years, not 25 as in England. In fact the period can be anything between two and (in rare cases) 25 years. Normally, the mortgage must be repaid by the borrower's 70th (sometimes 65th) birthday.
- The maximum loan is generally 80% of the value of the property, but 75 or 66% is more common. Valuations by banks tend to be conservative – they are thinking about what they might get for the property on a forced sale in the case of repossession. As a planning guide, you should borrow no more than two-thirds of the price you are paying. The rate of interest you pay is likely to be lower if you borrow a lower percentage of value and for a shorter period.
- Fixed-rate loans – with the rate fixed for the duration of the loan – are more common than in the UK. They are very competitively priced.
- The calculation of the amount the bank will lend is different in France. In addition, each bank employs its own calculation. A bank is not allowed to lend you more than an amount that corresponds to 30% of your net disposable income per month.
- There is usually a minimum loan (say €30,000), and some banks will not lend on a property of less than a certain value.
- Stage payments on new property are dealt with differently.
- The paperwork is different in France: there is (usually) no separate mortgage deed, with the existence of the mortgage mentioned in your purchase deed (*acte de vente*) instead.

Applying for a French Mortgage

The information required will vary from bank to bank. It also depends on whether you are employed or self-employed. Applications can receive preliminary approval (subject to a survey of the property, confirmation of good title and confirmation of the information supplied by you) within a few days. A formal letter of offer takes a couple of weeks to issue after the bank has received the necessary information from you.

The documents needed to apply for a French mortgage are:
- **Copy of passport of all applicants.**
- **Application fee.**
- **Completed application form.**
- **Proof of outgoings such as rent or mortgage.**
- **Copy of last three months' bank statements.**
- **Cash flow forecast for any anticipated rental income.**
- **Employed people: proof of income (usually three months' pay slips or a letter from your employer on official paper).**
- **Self-employed people: Audited accounts for last three years.**
- **Self-employed people: Last year's tax return and proof of payment of tax.**

Allow at least four weeks from the date of your application to receive your written offer. You then generally have 30 days to accept it; after that it is void. Remember that you cannot officially accept the offer before the initial 10-day 'reflection period' has expired.

Payments for New Property
In France, one normally takes title to the land at an early stage and then makes payments as the development progresses. You need to tell your bank that you want to draw down the mortgage to make the stage payments. Usually you pay off the amount you are providing yourself and then take money from the bank as and when it is due. During this period (*période d'anticipation*) before the handover of the house, you will only be borrowing part of the agreed loan and usually paying only interest on the loan amount. Once the property has been signed over to you (and thus the full loan has been taken), normal monthly payments begin.

Property Needing Restoration
Not all banks will finance fixer-upper property. If you have enough money to buy a property but need a mortgage to renovate it, you *must* apply for the mortgage before buying the property, because it is difficult to find a lender.

The Cost of Taking Out a Mortgage
Additional charges include an arrangement fee of 1% of the amount borrowed, a 'valuation' fee of about £150–200 and notaries'/land registry fees of 2.5% of the amount borrowed. So taking out a French mortgage is not cheap. These charges are on top of the normal expenses incurred when buying a property, which normally amount to about 8–9% of the price of the property. You will probably be required to take out life insurance for the amount of the loan,

though you may be allowed to use a suitable existing policy. You may be required to undergo a medical. You will be required to insure the property and produce proof of insurance, but you would probably have done this anyway.

The offer may be subject to early repayment penalties. These must be explained in the offer and cannot exceed the penalties laid down by law. Early repayment penalties are of particular concern in the case of fixed-rate mortgages.

The Exchange Rate Risk

If the funds to repay the mortgage are coming from your sterling earnings, the amount you pay will be affected by fluctuations in exchange rates between sterling and the euro. Do not underestimate these variations.

Other Loans

There are alternatives to a mortgage. If you have paid off your British mortgage and your British home is on sale, yours may be the following scenario: let's say you found your dream home in France and have £180,000 of the £200,000 needed for the new house available from savings and pension lump sums. The balance will be paid from the sale of your British home, but you are not sure that that will take place before you are committed to the purchase of the house in France in a few weeks' time. It is probably unnecessarily complicated to mortgage the British home for such a short period, and indeed, it could be impossible to do so if the bank knows you are selling. In this case, you could ask your bank for a short-term loan or overdraft.

Who Should Own the Property?

Naming the correct owner on your property deed will save thousands of pounds in tax and expenses during your lifetime and upon your death. Because, in France, you do not have the freedom British people do to distribute your assets as you please among your heirs, the wrong choice of owner can result in the wrong people being entitled to inherit the property when you die. This is a problem especially for people in second marriages, unmarried couples, and people with children from previous marriages.

Sole Ownership

In some cases it makes sense to put the property in the name of one person only. If your husband runs a high-risk business, or if he is 90 and you are 22, you should put it in your name. If you intend to let the property and need the income to be yours for tax purposes, sole ownership is worth considering.

Joint Ownership

If two people are buying together they normally buy in both their names. There are two ways of doing this: separate ownership (*en indivision*) or in a loose equivalent to an English 'joint tenancy' called *en tontine*. The choice you make is of great importance.

If you buy **en indivision** then half is yours and half is theirs. On your death, and subject to the owners' *régime matrimonial* (*see* p.197), your half will be disposed of in accordance with French law. You may not be able to give it to the people you want to. If you buy **en tontine**, your half will pass to your co-owner automatically on your death. In this way, you bypass French inheritance laws.

There are further complications. A person who owns *en indivision* (even if they own by virtue of inheritance) can usually insist on the sale of the property. So if your stepchildren inherit from your husband (as is likely under French law), they could insist on the sale of your home. A person who owns *en tontine* cannot usually insist on the sale of the property during the lifetime of the co-owner. Creditors of the co-owner cannot claim the asset. But ownership *en tontine* can lead to more inheritance tax being due.

If you decide to buy *en indivision*, it could make sense to split the ownership other than 50/50. If, for example, you have three children and your wife has two, in order to secure each of those children an equal share on your death you might buy 60% in your name and 40% in your wife's name. You might also think of giving the property to your children (or other preferred beneficiaries) but reserving your and your co-owner's right to use the property (*usufruit*). On your death, your rights would cease but your second wife or partner, who still has a life interest, would be able to use the property. Only on their death would the property pass in full to your heirs. This device can protect your right to use the property and save large amounts of inheritance tax (particularly if you're young, or the property is valuable). There are various drawbacks, however, not least the fact that after the gift you no longer own the property. If you wish to sell it, you need the agreement of your heirs, who will be entitled to the proceeds of the sale.

Adding Your Children to the Title

If you give your children the money to buy part of the property and put them on the title before your death, they will save a lot of inheritance tax. On your death you will only own (say) one-fifth of the property rather than one half. Only that fraction will be taxable. You may be able to reduce the tax liability so much, it actually becomes a 'tax-free inheritance'. Your children must be over 18. Of course, there are drawbacks: if they fall out with you, they can insist on the sale of the property and receive their share of proceeds.

Putting the Property in the Name of Your Children Only

If you put the property in the name of your children (possibly reserving the right for yourself to live there as explained above), there will be little or no inheritance tax and no legal expenses for dealing with an inheritance. This may sound attractive, but remember that you have lost control. If your children divorce, their husband/wife can claim a share. If they die before you without children of their own, you will inherit the property back and face inheritance tax for the privilege of doing so.

Limited Company

Some people opt to own a property via a limited company. In this case, they own the shares in a company, not a house in France. If they sell the house, they do so by selling the shares in the company rather than by transferring the ownership of the property. This can save the roughly 9% acquisition costs that the new owner would otherwise have to pay and, arguably, they can charge a bit more for the property when they sell it. When they die, they do not own 'immovables' (*immeubles*; land and buildings) in France and therefore avoid inheritance laws, which (as far as foreigners are concerned) usually only apply to land and buildings.

UK Company

Purchasing through a UK company usually does not make sense for a holiday home or investment property. In other cases, being able to pay for a property with UK company money (without drawing from the company and paying British tax on the dividend) is attractive.

Offshore (Tax Haven) Company

This has most of the advantages and disadvantages as ownership by other types of company, with the added disincentive that you pay a special tax of 3% of the property value every year. This is to compensate French coffers for the inheritance and transfer taxes they won't receive when the company owners sell or die. For a person who is (or intends to be) resident in France for tax purposes, there are more disadvantages. If they own more than 10% of an offshore company, they have to pay tax in France on their share of its income and assets.

This tax treatment has more or less killed off ownership via such companies.

The Process of Buying a Property in France

Buying property in France is as safe as buying property in the UK. Before we explain the buying process in detail, here is a nutshell version of the steps you will take before becoming a home owner in France.

If you and the owner agree on a price you make an offer (*offre d'achat* and then *promesse de vente*) and sign a document or sales agreement (*compromis de vente*). It is accompanied by a down payment (*indemnité d'immobilisation*) of up to 10% of the negotiated price. A 2001 law establishes a mandatory seven-day cooling-off period at this stage (*période de rétractation de sept jours*), during which either party can pull out. Otherwise, the *compromis de vente* determines the final date by which the transfer of ownership will take place (usually three months hence). A *notaire* will prepare this document as well as the next one (*acte authentique de vente*). The *acte authentique de vente* is the final deed and marks the official change in ownership, which is cemented by the signing (*acte final*). Then your property will be registered with the land registry (*cadastre*).

Choosing a Lawyer

Some estate agents will tell you that you do not need to use a lawyer – that the services of the local notary public (see below) will suffice. It is quite true that the average French person would not use the services of an independent lawyer when buying a house unless there was something complex about the transaction or about their own circumstances. For a foreigner, however, this is generally not good enough. There are many issues with which you will need guidance that the notary will not provide. Furthermore, many French notaries will know nothing about British law and will be unable to help with vital issues such as who should own the property in order to make the most of British *and* French tax and inheritance rules.

*The Notary Public (*Notaire*)*

The notary is a type of lawyer specific to France (*see* pp.26–7). He or she is in part a public official but also a businessperson who makes a living from the fees they charge. There are about 8,000 notaries in France. Notaries also exist in the UK, but they are seldom used in day-to-day transactions.

Under French law, only deeds of sale (*actes de vente*) approved and witnessed by a notary can be registered at the land registry (*bureau des hypothèques*). Although it is technically possible to transfer legal ownership of property by a private agreement not witnessed by the notary, and although that agreement will be fully binding on the people who made it, it will not be binding on third parties – people who want to make a claim against the property or banks wanting to lend money on the strength of the property – who must rely on the details of ownership as recorded at the land registry. If you are not registered, you are at risk. Practically speaking, all sales of real estate in France are witnessed by a notary. The notary also carries out checks on property sold and has duties as a tax collector and a validator of documents presented for registration. His or her fee is fixed by law; it's normally 1–1.5% of the price, though there are often extra fees added on top of this.

The notary is appointed by the seller, but the buyer can insist on appointing their own notary, in which case the two notaries share the same fee. In simple transactions this is seldom necessary and it can cause delays and complications. It is only worth considering if the notary is also acting for the seller as estate agent, in which case you may be more comfortable with independent scrutiny. Remember, 20% of property in France is sold by the *notaire*.

Despite the notary's many hats, he or she must remain strictly neutral during the whole property-buying process. The notary is like a referee between buyer and seller and the French government. It is their job to confirm that all paperwork complies with the law and is accepted by the land registry.

Many French notaries, particularly in rural areas, don't speak English – or not well enough to advise on complex issues. Very few know about British law or tax, or other consequences in the UK of your plans to buy a house in France. In any case, the buyer seldom meets the notary before the signing, so there is little opportunity to seek detailed advice. It is very unusual for notaries to offer comprehensive advice or explanations, least of all in writing, to buyers.

The Price

This is freely agreed on between the parties. Depending on the current economic climate, there may be ample or very little room for negotiating a reduction in the asking price. You will have more luck haggling down a price in undiscovered France, or if the property needs repair. In addition, the more expensive a property, the more chance you have of negotiating a better deal.

In every area there are properties that have stuck on the market, usually because they are overpriced and/or in a poor location. Find out when the property was placed on the market by asking to see the agent's sale authority (*mandat*). Negotiating a reduction is always worth a try, but if your advances are rejected bear in mind that this is not mere posturing but reflects a genuine confidence that the price asked is achievable. Also remember that once a formal offer is accepted, it is binding on both of you, so the price cannot be reduced. The best strategy is to start a little low and test the water.

How Much Should Be Declared in the Deed of Sale?

In the past, it was common practice in France (and other southern European countries) to under-declare the price paid for a property on the deed of sale (*acte de vente*). This was because taxes and notaries' fees due are calculated on the basis of the price declared. Lower price, less taxes for the buyer and less capital gains tax for the seller. This no longer happens as frequently. In rural areas you may still come under pressure to under-declare, but it is rare. Under-declaration is foolish – in the worst case, the state can forcibly buy the property for the declared price plus 10%; in the best, fines and penalties are charged. Also, unless your future buyer also agrees to under-declare, you will be liable for higher captal gains tax than you have actually made.

Nevertheless, you can legitimately reduce the price declared and reduce tax owed. For example, if your purchase includes furniture (or, in the case of a holiday home, a boat or a car), there is no need to declare the value of those items – you can draw up a separate contract for the 'extras' and save some money in taxes.

Where Must the Money Be Paid?

The price, with the taxes and fees due, is usually paid by the buyer into the notary's bank account and then passed on to the seller, the tax office, and so on as applicable. This is the best and safest way to handle the transaction. Any money paid to the notary is bonded, which is a guarantee of safety. Avoid arrangements, usually part of an under-declaration, in which part of the money is handed over in cash in brown-paper parcels. Apart from being illegal it is dangerous at a practical level to carry all that cash around.

General Enquiries and Special Enquiries

Certain enquiries are made routinely in the course of the purchase of a property. These include a check on the planning situation of the property. This *note de renseignement d'urbanisme* will reveal the position of the property, although it will not tell you about its neighbours nor will it reveal general public works plans for the area. If you want to know whether the authorities plan to put a prison outside your village or run a TGV line through your back garden, you need to do further research. There are various organisations you can approach but, just as in the UK, there is no single point of contact for such enquiries. If you are concerned about what might happen in the area, your best bet is to make an appointment with the local town hall (*mairie*) and ask authorities what public works projects they have in store. They can access a central database in Paris for works that have already been given a green light. For long-term projects you would need a crystal ball.

Normal enquiries include confirmation that the seller is the registered owner of the property and that it is sold (if this has been agreed) free of mortgages or other charges. For further enquiries, you need to know your plans for the property. Do you intend to let it? If so, would this be on a commercial basis? Do you intend to use it for business purposes? Do you want to enlarge or modify the exterior of the property? Do you intend to make interior structural alterations? Once your have answered those questions, your lawyer will instruct you on the additional enquiries necessary. Or, in the case of new construction or modifications, your builder or architect will guide you through the questions that may arise in your case.

Your Civil State (*Etat Civil*) and Other Personal Details

This is something you will not have thought about. When preparing documents in France, you will be asked to specify your civil state (*état civil*), which includes all your personal information: your full name and address but also, potentially, your occupation, nationality, passport number, maiden name and sometimes the names of your parents, date and place of birth, date and place of marriage and, most importantly, your *régime matrimonial*.

A *régime matrimonial* is something we do not have in the UK. In France, when you marry you specify the *régime matrimonial* that applies to your relationship. There are two main options: a regime of common ownership of assets (***communauté de biens***) or a regime of separate ownership of assets (***séparation de biens***). Under the first, all assets acquired during the marriage, even if put into just one party's name, belong to both. Under the second, each spouse is entitled to own assets in his or her name, and the other spouse has no automatic claim to them. Marriage under English law is closer to *séparation de biens*. The notary, when specifying your matrimonial regime, should state that you are married under English law and, in the absence of a French marriage contract, do not have a regime but that your situation is similar to a regime of *séparation de* *biens*. The correct working in French is: *'mariés sous le régime anglais équivalent au régime français de la séparation de biens à defaut de contrat de marriage préalable à leur union célébrée le* [DATE] *à* [PLACE]*'*.

This is no idle point. The declaration in your *acte de vente* is a public declaration, and it will be hard in later years to go against what you have declared. If you say you are married in *communauté de biens*, even if the money came from only one of you, the asset will be treated as belonging to both. This can have undesirable tax and inheritance consequences.

If appropriate, you will also declare if you are single, separated, divorced, widowed, etc. The authorities are entitled to ask for proof of this in the form of birth, marriage or death certificates. Official translations into French may be required. Often the notary will take a more relaxed approach and ask only for the key elements of your *état civil*. Make sure your *état civil* paperwork is in order before you make the appointment to sign the final sales deed to avoid delays.

The Community of Owners (*Copropriété*)

This device is common in continental Europe but most unusual in the UK. The basic idea is that a group of people own land or buildings together. Each has exclusive use of part of the property but shares the common spaces (garden, corridors, pool) in a joint-ownership arrangement. Houses on their own plots with no shared facilities will not be a member of a *copropriété*. In a *copropriété*, the buyer of a house owns their house outright – as the English would say, 'freehold' or more accurately 'commonhold' – but shares the use of the remaining areas as part of a community of owners (*en copropriété*). Most commonly, these areas include a shared pool or the lift shafts, corridors, roof, foundations, entrance areas, parking zones, etc. in the case of apartment buildings. Members of the *copropriété* are each responsible for their own homes, but collectively they agree on the maintenance needs and budgeting. They are responsible for paying their share of those common expenses, as stipulated in their title.

The *règlement de copropriété* establishes how the *copropriété* is managed and stipulate how expenses are calculated. (This is usually done according to the size of each apartment, with a larger financial responsibility going to any commercial area included in the *copropriété*.) The ruling body of any *copropriété* is the general meeting of members (*syndicat des copropriétaires*). General meetings are scheduled at least once a year to approve expenses and deal with other business. You must be given two weeks' notice before a meeting is scheduled so you can add items to the agenda. Voting is, for most issues, done by simple majority. If you can't attend you can appoint a proxy to vote on your behalf. The *règlement* may be amended or added upon, but your basic rights will always be protected. Day-to-day management is usually delegated to an administrator (*syndic*). The *copropriété* provides for routine work and sets aside money for major repairs. If they do not – or if the amount set aside is inadequate – the general meeting can authorise a supplemental levy to raise the cash needed.

The rules set by the *copropriété* are intended to improve the quality of life of residents. They could, for example, put bans on noise (no radios by the pool), prohibit the use of the pool after 10pm, forbid the hanging of washing on balconies, etc. More importantly, they could ban pets, commercial activity in the building, or short-term holiday letting. Make sure you know what the rules are. Also make sure you understand what monetary contributions will be expected of you before you agree to a *copropriété* ownership.

Initial Contracts

Most sales start with a **preliminary contract**. The type of contract depends on whether you are buying a finished or an unfinished property. Since 2001, a law establishes a mandatory seven-day cooling-off period called the *période de rétractation de sept jours*, during which either party can pull out of the preliminary sales agreement. If one party pulls out, the buyer's deposit must be refunded. If you decide to pull out, you must do so by register/receipt mail. Strict compliance with the rules and timetable for cancellation is essential.

Generally, the preliminary contract is prepared by the estate agent – who is professionally qualified to do so – or by the notary. Estate agents often operate on standard formats and it is important these contracts are not accepted as final. They almost always need to be modified – sometimes extensively. Some contracts penned by estate agents who are not familiar with the needs of foreign buyers contain extra clauses that are potentially harmful. More likely, they will omit one or more of the 'get-out clauses' (*clauses suspensives*) essential for cancelling the contract should you need to do so.

If You are Buying a Finished Property

- **Offer to buy (*offre d'achat*)**: This is, technically, not a contract. It is a formal written offer from the potential buyer to the seller stating that you wish to buy the stated property for a stated price and will complete the transaction within a stated period. It is normally accompanied by a **deposit** to the estate agent (if they are licensed to hold the seller's money) or to the notary dealing with the transaction. The deposit is not fixed but usually ranges from 2 to 5% of the price offered as a show of good faith, although a larger deposit will be expected soon. Although this document binds you (you and the seller are legally bound to proceed with the transaction), it is not an absolute guarantee that the seller will sell you the property. Its main use is in situations where the property is offered through a variety of estate agents and the seller wants to wait a week or two to see what offers come in before making up their mind. Generally we do not like *offres*. We prefer the idea of making a verbal agreement on price and moving directly to the sales agreement (*compromis de vente*).

- **Promise to sell (*promesse de vente*)**: This is a written document in which the seller offers to sell a stated property at a stated price to a stated person at any time within a stated period of up to six months. It is the mirror image of the *offre d'achat*, except that it is penned by the seller. The seller usually requires that any person taking up his offer pay a **deposit** (*indemnité d'immobilisation*). The amount of the deposit is not fixed by law, but is usually 5 or 10% of the price of the property. Once he or she has received the deposit, the seller must reserve the property for you until the end of the period specified in the contract. This is similar to an English option contract. You are not obliged to buy the property but risk losing your deposit if you pull out too late. Remember that the 2001 law gives you seven days to walk away from the agreement and keep your deposit.

The *promesse* should contain more special 'get-out clauses' (*clauses suspensives*) stipulating the circumstances in which the buyer is entitled to the refund of their deposit. These might include not being able to obtain a mortgage, discovering that the property is infested with termites, finding that the property cannot be used for a certain purpose, etc. The drafting of these clauses is of vital importance.

• **Sales agreement (*compromis de vente*)**: This is also known as a joint promise of sale (*promesse synallagmatique de vente*) and, in most parts of France, it is the most common type of sales contract. It commits both parties. The seller must sell a stated property at a stated price to a stated person according to the terms set out in the contract. The buyer must buy.

This is the most important of the three documents, and you must be satisfied that it contains all the points needed for your protection. Under French law, you technically become the owner of the property when you sign this document (even though you still need to sign a deed of sale, *acte de vente*, and register your ownership to be safe as far as third parties are concerned).

The contract must contain the safety clauses necessary to ensure that, for example, if all is not well with the title to the property, you are released from your obligations and get your money back. These include clauses about mortgages you may be applying for (the Loi Scrivener clauses; *see* pp.189–90), clauses requiring proof of various planning matters, and clauses determining what should happen if a right of pre-emption is exercised (*see* below). A standard contract (*compromis de vente*) should include the following:

- **The names of the seller and buyer.**
- **A full description of the property, with reference to its land registry details.**
- **Usually, a statement saying that full details of the title will be included in the final deed of sale (*acte de vente*).**
- **A date for the signing of the *acte* – usually 60 days after signing the contract. The delay is caused because there are various documents that must be obtained from the French authorities. In particular, you must wait for confirmation from the SAFER (Sociétés d'Aménagement Foncier et d'Etablissement Rural), the French Rural Development Agency, that it does not intend to exercise its right of pre-emption. You also need to wait for a planning certificate (*certificat d'urbanisme*), which takes eight weeks.**

- A statement establishing when possession will take place – normally, on the date the final deed is signed.
- The price.
- A receipt for any deposit.
- A statement is saying the property is sold subject to any rights that exist over it.
- A statement saying the property must be sold with vacant possession.
- The name of the notary who will prepare the *acte*.
- The name of the person paying the purchase price.
- The name of the estate agent involved, his or her commission, and the name of the person will pay it.
- A statement of the consequences of one or both parties breaking the contract.
- The name of the lawyer overseeing the contract and their contact details.
- A clause for breach of contract.

If the buyer or seller drops out of the contract, various arrangements may be made. A **deposit** (*arrhes*) might be payable by the buyer. For example, if the buyer fails to complete the contract, they will lose the deposit (*arrhes*). If the seller fails to complete, they must return double the deposit paid. Alternatively, the contract may establish a sum of agreed compensation to be paid (*un dédit*). The *dédit* for the buyer could be the loss of their deposit. The *dédit* for the seller could be fixed in the contract. If either party is in breach of the contract, the other can serve notice requiring them to sign the *acte* or pay the *dédit*. There can be an additional penalty clause, although the courts were granted the power to decrease such penalties, making them difficult to enforce.

If the parties fail to comply with their obligations, the ultimate remedy is to seek a court order. This is a last resort as it is costly and time-consuming, and there is no guarantee of the outcome.

If You Are Buying Unfinished Property

- **Full contract**: There are two types of contract in this case. The first is a sale *à terme*. In this case you agree to buy a plot of land and building but pay for it once it has been developed. You take title and pay the money at a later date. This type of contract is rare. The second is *en l'état futur d'achèvement*, more commonly known as 'on plan'. Here, the seller transfers their interest in the land and any existing buildings to the buyer at once. As construction proceeds, the building automatically becomes the property of the buyer. In return, the buyer pays an initial sum representing the value of the asset and further payments, by stages, during the construction process. The contract must guarantee secure completion of the construction in the event, for example, that the seller goes bust.

- **Reservation contract** (*contrat de réservation*): When you buy unfinished property, you will usually be asked to sign a reservation contract. There are various ways this contract may be drafted, but in general:
    - It must be in writing.
    - A copy must be given to the seller before money changes hands.
    - It must contain a full description of the property to be built, including its size and the number of rooms.
    - It must detail central facilities or services to be provided.
    - The price must be specified, as should any extra charges or price variations, such as official cost of construction index increases.
    - The scheme for stage payments must be explained.
    - The deposit or reservation fee (*réservation*) must be recorded. This cannot exceed 5% of the price (if completion of the work will take place within one year of signing the reservation contract) or 2% (if it will take place more than one year but less than two years from the date of signing). If it will be more than two years until work is completed, no deposit may be taken.
    - It must state the circumstances in which the reservation fee is to be returned. These include: if the *acte de vente* is not signed on the date agreed on because of the seller's default, if the final price (even if calculated according to the variation terms) is more than 5%, if any stipulated loan is not obtained, if the property is reduced in size or quality, or if the services promised are not supplied.
    - It must provide for the buyer to receive a draft title deed (*acte de vente*) at least one month before the date for signing.
    - It must contain details of the guarantees to secure a refund of any money paid by the buyer if the seller cannot complete the building.

Your payment scheme will follow pre-established stages – and each payment is due once the architect issues a certificate of completion for foundations and building. There is a limit on stage payments permitted at any point:
- **Foundations** – 35% of total price.
- **Rough construction (walls, plumbing, electricity)** – 75% of total price.
- **Completion of building with finishing work (tiles, carpeting, painting, etc.)** – 95% of total price.

The building is 'complete' when all the elements indispensable to your use of the building are finished. Minor deficiencies or small outstanding jobs are not a failure to complete and therefore not an excuse for delaying final payment. If there are outstanding jobs or defects, they are listed and a timetable is agreed on for rectifying them. The buyer has up to one month to report defects to the seller (and can ask for the seller to fix them). You should have the property inspected by a surveyor or architect before you accept it as completed. The remaining 5% is held back until all of these issues have been cleared. If the defects cost more than 5% to rectify, the seller's liability is not limited to that 5%. The seller must offer compulsory two-year and 10-year guarantees, which represent another good safety net for the buyer.

• **Other documentation**: You will be given a full description of the property, a copy of the community rules (*règlement de copropriété*) if the property shares common facilities, and a copy of any agreements regarding management or letting of the property. Pay particular attention to the property description. If marble floors and wooden kitchen cabinets were promised, make sure they are delivered. All too often, the buyer ends up with cheap tiles and particle board cabinets they never wanted.

Checklist: Signing a Contract

Property in the Course of Construction   **Existing Property**

Are you clear about what you are buying?
Have you taken legal advice about who should be the owner of the property?
Have you taken legal advice about inheritance issues?
Are you clear about the property lines (boundaries)?
Are you clear about access to the property?

Are you sure you can modify/add to the property as you want?
Are you sure you can use the property for what you want?
Is the property connected to water, electricity, gas, etc?
Have you had a survey done?

Have you included 'get-out' clauses for checks not yet made?
Is your mortgage finance arranged or a 'get-out' clause inserted in the contract?
Is the seller clearly identified?
If the seller is not signing in person, have you seen a power of attorney/mandate to authorize the sale?
Are you fully identified?
Is the property fully disclosed with regard to land registry details?
Is the price correct?
Can the price increase and are the extra expenses described fully?

Are the stage payments fully described?   Does contract say when possession will be given?
Do stage payments meet the   Receipt for the deposit paid?
legal restrictions?
Is the completion date agreed upon?
Is the date for signing the *acte* agreed upon?
Does the contract provide for the sale to be free of charges and debts?
Does the contract provide for vacant possession?
Who is the notary?
Is the estate agent's commission dealt with?

What happens if there is a breach of contract?
Are all the necessary special 'get-out' clauses included?
Is the mortgage arranged and ready?

Steps Between Signing the Contract and Signing the Deed of Sale (*Acte de Vente*)

*Power of Attorney (*Procuration; Pouvoir; Mandat*)*

Completion dates on French property transactions are notoriously fluid. You could plan to be present at the contract-signing but suffer a last-minute delay that makes your attendance impossible. If you cannot sign the *acte de vente* in person, you can assign power of attorney to your lawyer or someone else recommended by the notary to do so. This document authorises the person appointed (the *mandataire*) to act in the place of the person granting the power (the *mandant*). You can have someone already in France to act as your *mandataire*, and your lawyer can draw up the documentation necessary.

Getting the Money to France

- **Electronic transfer**: The most practical way of moving your money to France from the UK is to have it sent electronically by SWIFT transfer from a British bank to the recipient's bank in France. This costs about £20–35, depending on your bank. Allow a week for the money to arrive, despite everyone's claims that it will be there within a matter of days. IBAN and BIC numbers (account numbers for all bank accounts, incorporating a code for the identity of the bank and the account number of the individual customer) should be quoted, if possible, on all international currency transfers.

  You can send the money from your bank, via your lawyer's bank or via a specialist currency dealer. For the large sums you are likely to be sending, you should be able to negotiate an exchange rate that is more favourable than the 'tourist rates' published in the newspapers. If you do a lot of business with a particular bank, you're likely to be offered a better rate than a one-off customer.

  You might use a specialist currency dealer to transfer the funds instead of a British bank. Such dealers often offer a better exchange rate than an ordinary bank, but do make sure the dealer you are using is reputable. Your money could be at risk if the dealer is not bonded or otherwise insured.

  Remember to establish before you send the money whether you or the recipient will be absorbing the bank wiring fees. If you need a fixed amount in France, make allowances for the wiring fees, either by sending a bit extra or by asking your British bank to cover the charges. Make sure you have the details of the recipient bank, its customer's name, the account codes and the recipient's reference precisely right. Any error and the payment is likely to return to you as undeliverable – minus the cost of its conversion back into sterling.

- **Banker's drafts**: You can arrange for your British bank to issue a banker's draft (bank-certified cheque) that you can take to France and pay into your bank account. Make sure your bank knows that it will be used overseas and thus issues an international draft. Generally, this is not an ideal way to transfer money. It can take a considerable time – sometimes weeks – before the funds deposited are available. The recipient bank's charges can also be surprisingly high and the exchange rate offered may be uncompetitive, as you are a captive customer. If the draft is lost it can, at best, take months to obtain a replacement and, at worst, be impossible to do.

- **Cash**: This is absolutely not recommended. You need to declare the money on departure from the UK and on arrival in France. The exchange rate offered for cash is usually very uncompetitive and the notary may well refuse to accept it.

- **Exchange control and other restrictions on moving money**: There is no longer exchange control when taking money to or from France if you are a EU national. There are, however, some statistical records you need to fill out that show the flow of funds and state the purpose of the transfer. When you sell your property in France, you will be able to bring the money back to the UK without obstacles.

Fixing the Completion Date

The date stated in the contract for signing the *acte* could, most charitably, be described as flexible or aspirational. More often than not it will move, if only by a day or so. Sometimes, the *certificat d'urbanisme* may not have arrived in time. In other cases, the seller's need to declare French capital gains may cause delays. Or your money to buy the house might get stuck in the banking system for a few extra days. Don't book your travel to France until you are almost sure matters will proceed on a certain day. That may mean a week or two before signing.

The Deed of Sale (*Acte de Vente*)

This must be signed in front of a French notary, either by the parties in person or by someone holding power of attorney. The document itself is, largely, a copy of the preliminary contract with a few new elements.

A typical *acte* might contain the following sections:

- **Name and address of notary** (*Nom et adresse du notaire*).

- **Identification of the parties** (*Identification des parties*): This includes the full details of both buyer and seller (their *états civils*) or details of any persons apperaring under a power of attorney.

- **Designation** (*Désignation*): This is a full description of the property, including land registry details (*cadastre*), plot numbers and restrictions affecting the property. If the property is an apartment this section will detail common parts – i.e. community property – from which you will benefit.

- **Ownership and possession** (*Propriété – jouissance*): This justifies the current claim to ownership and states the date on which the buyer will take possession of the property (usually, the same day the deed is signed). It also confirms that the property is free of tenants (or not, as the case may be) and confirms liability on the part of the seller for all utility bills up to that date.

- **Price** (*Prix*): The price is stated. Methods of payment are stated. A receipt for payment is given.
- **Administrative declaration** (*Déclaration pour l'administration*): This stipulates the nature of the sale and the nature of the taxes payable with regard to the sale.
- **Capital gains tax** (*Plus-value*): This states the seller's liability regarding possible capital gains tax on the sale.
- **Calculation of taxes** (*Calcul des droits*): This section, if present, will calculate all of the duties payable on the sale.
- **Persons present or represented** (*Présences ou représentations*): Details of witnesses present at the sale.
- **Sale** (*Vente*): The sale is confirmed to have taken place.
- **Planning and roads** (*Urbanisme – voirie*): Details of the town planning situation are provided and the *certificat d'urbanisme* is attached.
- **Rights of pre-emption** (*Droits de préemption*): Confirmation that the various (named) people and organisations who might have pre-emptive rights (*see* p.200) have renounced them.
- **History of the property** (*Origine de la propriété*): How the present owner came to own the property – e.g. by inheritance or through sale. Details of the penultimate owner might be given.
- **Ownership and occupation** (*Propriété – occupation*): The date on which the buyer becomes owner and confirmation of vacant possession.
- **Charges and general conditions** (*Charges – conditions générales*): Any charges or burdens registered against the property are listed together with the seller's warranties and guarantees.
- **Loans** (*Prêt*): Details of mortgage finance used to buy the property. This only applies to French mortgages: it is of no concern to the French if you mortgaged your British home to buy the property.
- **Statement of sincerity** (*Affirmation de sincérité*): A statement that both parties confirm the truth of all statements made in the *acte*: the price has been fully disclosed and (usually untrue) the notary has warned the parties of the sanctions that may stem from false declaration. You can set out additional sanctions: the right to raise a supplemental demand for tax not paid plus interest plus penalty. Or, if there is a clear and intentional understatement, the right to buy the property at the price stated plus 10%. This right must generally be exercised within six months.

Formalities

Certain procedures are followed at the signing of the *acte*. The parties are identified by their passports or identity cards. The notary's clerk will go through the content of the *acte* with the parties. This tends to be very superficial and often in limited English. After the clerk, the parties meet the notary. In addition to the buyer and seller, it is possible for the group to include the notary's clerk, the other notary if a second has been appointed, your lawyer, a translator, a representative of the *copropriété*, a representative of your mortgage lender, the estate agent and any sub-agent appointed by the estate agent. Most of these people are there to receive money.

After the *Acte* Has Been Signed

The signing of the *acte* does not conclude the matter. The notary will, from the money you have given him or her, pay your taxes and settle his or her fees. They will also pay off sums due to the estate agent and the *copropriété* (if they are responsible for these), leftover debts and any other extra expenses. Eventually the balance is sent to the seller. The notary is allowed one month to pay the taxes, but should do so much sooner.

Once the taxes have been paid, your title and any mortgage should be presented for **registration** at the land registry. By law, this must be done within a period two months, but it should be done as quickly as possible because there is the danger of someone registering another transaction (such as a debt or judgment) against the property before you. The person who registers first gets priority. After several months have passed, the land registry will issue a **certificate** (*expédition*) confirming that the title has been registered. This is mailed to the notary. The notary will then send you the certificate and various other paperwork related to the purchase with their final bill and a breakdown of how they used your money. Some notaries are very slow at sending out this final paperwork, possibly because they have overcharged slightly to be safe and now owe you a refund.

The Cost of Buying a Property in France

These are the fees and taxes owed by the buyer when acquiring a property in France. They are sometimes known as 'completion expenses' or 'completion or closing costs'. Although exact figures are impossible to predict, what follows is a general guide of expenses you will face.

It is very important to remember that the following fees are calculated on the basis of the price declared in the *acte de vente*. In the past, underdeclaration of the price was common as a way of evading taxes. Today, this rarely happens. The notary is usually charged with making the payments outlined here.

Notary's Fees

These are fixed by law and depend on the type of property bought and its price. As a general guide, calculate 1.3% for properties costing less than €75,000 and 1% for properties costing more than €75,000. If you have asked the notary for additional work or for any advice, there will be additional charges. All of the notary's charges will be subject to VAT of 19.6%.

New Property: VAT (*TVA*) and Land Registration Fees

A 'new' property is one that is less than five years old *and* is being sold for the first time. The taxes and land registry fees usually amount to about 20% of the declared price of the property:

- **VAT (*TVA*)**: This is 19.6% of the declared purchase price of the property. It is normally included in the price of the property quoted to you – make sure that this is the case.
- **Land registry fee** (*Cadastre*): Usually 0.615%.

Resale Property: Taxes and Land Registration Fees

- **Departmental tax** (*Taxe départementale*).
- **Communal tax** (*Taxe communale*): Always 1.2%, no matter what *commune* you live in.
- **Levy for expenses** (*Prélèvement pour frais*): 2.5% of the *taxe départementale*.
- **Land registry fee**: The total of the taxes and land registry fees amounts to 4.89% of the declared price of the property.

Mortgage Costs (if applicable)

If you are taking out a mortgage, there will be additional costs. These typically amount to 3% of the amount borrowed. Most of these charges will be subject to TVA at 19.6%.

Estate Agent's Charges (if payable by the buyer)

If an estate agent has sold the property, their fees (3–5% depending on the location and value of the property) are usually paid by the seller. This can vary by agreement. If a notary has sold the property, their fee will be paid by the buyer. These will be subject to TVA at 19.6%.

Miscellaneous Charges

These include architect's fees, surveyor's fees, British legal fees (typically 1%), first connection to water, electricity, etc. These are subject to French TVA at 19.6% (except your British lawyer's fee).

Home Insurance

Insurance is big business in France – so big, in fact, that two of the largest groups, Groupement d'Assurances Nationales and Assurances Générales de France, are nationalised. There are in excess of 500 insurance companies, who are regulated by a *code des assurances* and overseen by a Commission de Contrôle des Assurances. The main difference between insuring your house in France and Britain is that, in France, you must have third-party coverage by law. How likely it is that your house is going to damage somebody or something is debatable, but this is a legal requirement.

Property Taxes

There are two types of property tax in France: the *taxe foncière* and the *taxe d'habitation*; see **Red Tape**, p.147.

Renting a Property

Ways of finding rental property include hiring an agent, scanning the Internet, and searching local publications or the property section of a local newspaper. The best option, however, is word of mouth.

If you're not renting for a short period (such as a holiday let), most **leases** (*contrats de location* or *baux*) last a fixed time and are renewable. Contracts lasting three months, six months, a year or any other length of time can be negotiated with the owner. To lease in your own name (*bail au nom propre*), you need your passport and proof of financial stability, such as a work contract or bank statements.

You must pay one or two months' rent in advance as a safety **deposit** (*dépôt de garantie*). If the property is in good condition when you leave, the deposit is refunded. Make sure you check **appliances** well (especially the refrigerator and washing machine) before signing the lease, preferably in the presence of the owner. The high calcium content in French water makes dishwashers and washing machines clog easily, and you don't want to have to fix damage done by a previous tenant. Also, make sure the water heater functions well. It's a good idea to make a detailed **inventory** of all the furniture, cutlery, kitchen and bathroom items before you sign the contract. Itemise everything and make a note of its condition, then get the owner to sign the list.

Rent is paid monthly (sometimes quarterly) by direct bank transfer, cheque or cash. You must get a *quittance de loyer* from the landlord as proof of payment. In addition to the monthly rent, you will be expected to pay for **utilities** and other **expenses**. These may include water, gas for heating, telephone service, electricity, cleaning and maintenance of the building, lift expenses and the porter's fee. Maintenance is usually paid quarterly and is calculated by the administrator of the building based on the size of your apartment and the floor it is on (for the lift fee). The tenant is also responsible for the occupancy tax (*taxe d'habitation*). As a rule of thumb, **major repairs** such as wiring, plumbing and blinds are the owner's responsibility; **minor repairs** due to wear and tear are the tenant's.

Most leases call for six months' advance **notice** in writing prior to the **termination of the lease** (sent via registered-return receipt mail). Three months' notice is required on leases of one year, but in most cases leases are for three years. In general, if you help the landlord find a replacement tenant, you can arrange your departure with the owner without waiting.

You can rent apartments either furnished, semi-furnished or unfurnished. **Semi-furnished** apartments usually include major appliances, such as a cooker and refrigerator, and little to no furniture. **Unfurnished** ones are usually bare, with tubes protruding from the walls for you to connect your own kitchen appliances. *Concierges*, or custodians, usually live on the ground floor of an apartment building and sit in a little booth at the entrance. They do light repairs and cleaning, collect mail, sign for packages that don't fit in the postbox (great if you're not often home during the day) and guard the building against strangers during working hours. You should tip them at Christmas.

Home Utilities

France has a refreshingly simple system when it comes to utilities – because many are state-run monopolies, you often don't need to shop around for the cheapest rates but just take what you get and pay your bills on time.

Computer-generated bills come by post and contain a remittance slip for making payments. The bill (*facture*) will contain your personal data, account number (*numéro de compte* or *numéro de contrat*), the amount owed (*montant à régler*) and the due date for payment. If your utilities are paid by direct debit from your bank (*prélèvement automatique*), there is no remittance slip but you will see the amount deducted (*montant prélevé* or *montant facturé*) and the date of the next withdrawal (*prochain relevé*). Remember that many bills are not itemised. A phone bill, for example, might list 18 local calls (*appels locaux*) and 10 calls to a foreign mobile phone (*vers mobiles internationaux*) but won't tell you the numbers dialled. Other bills are calculated by your 'estimated' consumption, which is then adjusted either up or down when the meter (*compteur*) is read. When installing your electricity, water and gas make sure you know where the meter is located so you can keep track of billing. If you leave the house empty for long periods, request that the meters be placed on an outside wall (even if the meter is in your basement a wire can be brought to street level) so that the electricity company can make readings when you are not home. The electricity meter must be read once a year.

To set up new service you should contact each utility and be able to produce documentation such as your passport, lease if you are letting, and bank account details if you intend to pay by direct debit.

Utility Companies

Electricity	Electricité de France	*www.edf.fr*
Gas	Gaz de France	*www.gazdefrance.com*
Water	Générale des Eaux	*www.generale-des-eaux.com*
Telephone	France Télécom	*www.francetelecom.com*

In the majority of cases, EDF (Electricité de France) and GDF (Gaz de France) are billed on the same statement. France's water company, Générale des Eaux, is privatised, so you may be billed by one of its subsidiaries under a different name.

Payment

There are several options for paying, but by far the most convenient is direct debit from your bank account (*prélèvement automatique*), especially for foreigners who travel often. Bills usually come every two months or six months depending on the service. These are the ways of paying:

- **Pay at the utility company**: This is highly inconvenient because it usually means trekking across town at dawn to queue with everybody else.
- **Pay through your bank**: Give your bank information to the utility (called your RIB or *relève d'identité bancaire*) – your name or *nom du titulaire du compte*, your bank's name or *nom de la banque*, the account number or *numéro de compte*, the bank code or *code établissement* and the branch number or *code guichet*) and wash your hands of the affair. The bank will charge you a small fee for this service. The utility company will send you an invoice every two months so you can keep track of the amounts deducted and you will also see them on your bank statement. Make sure you keep a reserve of ample funds in your bank account otherwise the service might be cut off.
- **Internet**: You cannot yet pay your bills on the Internet, although this will probably change soon. You can, however, keep track of your expenses and account online.

If you need to dispute a bill, don't expect an easy ride.

Electricity (Electricité de France)

France generates two-thirds of its power by nuclear reactors, with the rest coming mostly from environment-friendly hydro-electric plants. For this reason, electricity is cheaper than almost anywhere else in Europe and consequently most appliances (such as hobs and ovens) run on electricity. Home heating is often electric.

Contracts can be set up for various levels of power – from three kilowatts to 36 kilowatts. Three, six and nine kilowatts are not very much: you won't be able to vacuum your floors and toast bread at the same time without blowing a fuse. To avoid being left in the dark looking for the circuit box, make sure you know how to reset your system *before* you overload it. Systems lower than nine kilowatts can't support electric heating, which requires at least 12 kilowatts.

There are different tariffs available that carry different pricing schemes according to usage and time of day. The French have juggling these tariffs down to a science. For example, if the cheapest tariffs are at night, they will set heaters and water boilers to run then and reserve enough hot water for the next day. There are two domestic tariffs: blue tariff (*tarif bleu*) divided into *option base* and *option heures creuses*, and *tempo*. In *option base*, night and day rates are priced the same. In *option heures creuses*, you can select your own reduced-rate period. With *tempo* you are encouraged to use electricity when demand is lowest.

French wiring is different from British wiring, so you should not bring an electrician from home to do work here, nor attempt it yourself. Fiddling with incompatible wiring is downright dangerous. Almost all property is connected at 220/240 volts. Any property still connected at 110/120 volts can be converted. Because of old wiring, power outages and surges are frequent. Get a UPS (uninterruptible power supply) and a surge protector to protect your television sets, video recorders and especially computers. Electric plugs are two-pronged, or sometimes have a third 'earth' prong if the wiring is connected to ground as is required in kitchens and bathrooms.

Your EDF bill serves as proof that you have an address in France, and you might find a copy useful when you open a bank account or perform other bureaucratic tasks.

Gas (Gaz de France)

Although gas is available in towns and cities, gas pipes do not extend to many remote rural areas, in which case you buy refillable gas tanks (more expensive in the long run). Bottled propane or butane is found at supermarkets and petrol stations, and you can arrange to have it delivered to your home.

Like electricity, the gas company offers different tariffs and bills you every two months. For all practical purposes, EDF and GDF are one company and are billed together. Some hob and oven units rely on a combination of gas and electricity (gas for the hob and electricity for the oven), and many larger houses and apartment complexes have gas-generated central heating. Household gas from GDF is methane, and burns much hotter than propane or butane.

Water (Générale des Eaux)

Water is supplied by a number of private companies, which fall under the *Générale des Eaux* umbrella. Water is priced per cubic meter and tariffs vary according to reserves, rainfall and how much water is used. For example, if you live in an area with many swimming pools, you will have a higher water tariff. If you share a meter with neighbours, you will be billed in equal parts even if someone else takes 12 showers a day.

When you go on holiday, turn off your water, as much plumbing is old and leaks are frequent. Pipes burst especially frequently in August, when the mass exodus of vacationers influences water pressure. If you live in a rural area, expect water shortages and restrictions on supply, particularly in summer, so think ahead and fill a storage tank, especially if you have a garden.

Here are some other water-related issues to keep in mind:

- **Hot water**: Make sure your tank or boiler is big enough. A small storage tank only holds enough warm water for one quick shower or one dish-washing session.
- **Wells (*Puits*)**: Even if you don't intend to draw drinking or domestic water from a well, they are a useful way of watering your garden or filling your pool (you don't pay for water from wells or natural springs, but you do pay for the electricity to power pumps). Some wells dry in summer; others acquire such a high salt content that they can't be used for irrigation.
- **Septic tanks**: Most rural properties depend on a septic tank for drainage and waste removal. This acts like a filter and treats sewage by breaking it down with bacteria. Modern equipment treats all the waste you produce and discharges it safely. Septic tanks have a natural lifespan and need to be replaced. Generally, they need to be cleaned, or pumped out, every five years. If you are installing a new one, get the right size (a 3,000-litre tank should be fine for a three-bedroom house) – if your tank is too small, you will spend more time and money emptying it.
- **Swimming pools**: If you live in an arid area with frequent water shortages, your town hall might not grant you a permit to build one.

Telephone (France Télécom)

Partially privatised France Télécom has dramatically improved its service and quality in recent years. Because the nation's wiring and infrastructure belongs to France Télécom, it has been able to branch off and add more vital services in a country dependent on the Internet.

Through the company Wanadoo, France Télécom offers broadband lines for faster connection speeds (*see* 'The Internet', pp.215–16). Second phone lines for your fax machine or for your computer modem are also easy to get. Remember slower baud rates may make faxing and dialling up the Internet pricey.

France Télécom also offers a range of services you'll be familiar with, such as call waiting, call forwarding, caller identification and automatic answering services. These will add a bit more to your phone bill. Rates are competitive, though, and you can negotiate different pricing schemes according to your needs. For example, the *tarif général* is for private users who call mostly at weekends, while the *tarif professionnel* favours daytime calls.

Every area has its own phone prefix: for example, Paris is 01, and 02 is for the northwest (*see* p.243). Mobile phones start with 06, and most toll-free numbers start with 0800. All operations concerning your telephone (obtaining a phone line, laying the cables, billing options and payment, special services) can be done through the local France Télécom bureau (Agence Commerciale des Télécommunications), or by dialling **t** 1014. For billing queries call **t** 3000 (a free automated service).

Since 1998, the telephone market has been deregulated and there are two new national operators, CEGETEL and Bouygues, which both compete with France Télécom on long-distance calls only. France Télécom keeps its monopoly on local calls. You can sign a contract with one of these private companies in stores such as FNAC, Darty or Auchan, or ones specialising in telecom equipment.

There are a few other ways to steer clear of France Télécom, including buying one of the pre-paid phonecards (*télécartes*) available at *tabacs*. They come in different denominations (€5–100) and offer attractive rates (as low as 300 minutes of phone time to the UK for €10). The drawback is that you must dial a tiresome series of numbers and secret codes (provided when you purchase the card) to access the system. But you dial into a free number, so you can use the card from a payphone or from your home phone at no cost.

In recent years, more working professionals and busy travellers opt not to install a fixed-line telephone service in their homes (thus avoiding the monthly base charges and taxes) and instead rely exclusively on their mobile phones, although this won't give you Internet access.

Mobile Phones

The three main mobile phone companies, SFR, Orange and Bouygues, offer similar rates and service. To sign up, visit one of the thousands of telecommunication shops throughout the country or a local electronics store.

To apply for a subscription, you need a billing address (and proof of address, such as an EDF bill in your name) and ID, such as your passport. If you opt for a subscription (most provide at least one year of service), the company will often throw in a cellular phone for free or almost free and you will be billed at home. Your mobile phone bill is like any other utility and can be paid via direct debit from your bank account.

The alternative is to buy a phone at full price and recharge it with pay-as-you-go cards (*mobicartes*), or to use your British phone, removing the SIM card (the memory chip that contains your phone number) and buying a French SIM card, which means you will have a French mobile phone number that starts with 06 and will pay French rates, thus avoiding international calling rates from your British SIM. Most foreigners find this method to be the most convenient as there are no bills or contracts involved, though your UK phone may need to be 'unlocked' from its UK network. No address or ID is required for the prepaid cards, which you can buy at any *tabac* or supermarket. Note that when your money runs out, you can no longer make *or receive* calls when you're outside France, because you have to pay to receive as well as make calls abroad, and can only receive calls within France.

As far as the handsets are concerned, you can choose from the same models you will recognise in the UK. GSM is the standard technology, and new 3G phones let you surf the Internet, or take digital photos or short movies and send them to other users. All phones let you send SMS or text messages and have answering machine and address book functions.

The Internet

Almost two decades ago, France invented the Minitel, a small computer that hooked into the phone system to provide information, train timetables and booking services. Though it never had a global scope, it is still used by millions of French people. It's the grandfather of the Internet as we know it, and a symbol of France's determination to stay on the cutting edge of technology.

Partly due to deep affection for the Minitel, the Internet had a slower start In France. But what started as an ember has burst into flame, and French public institutions, universities and small businesses have launched some of the world's most beautifully designed and informative websites. France may have missed out on the 'dotcom' glory years that sparked the rapid rise and fall of so many companies elsewhere, but that may be the very reason why it is so enthusiastic about the Internet today.

The main internet service provider is **Wanadoo**, which is technically a free Internet service provider (ISP) – although you do pay for your time online and this is reflected on your France Télécom bill. Although the fee is only a few euro cents per minute, time does add up very fast. Wanadoo provides free software to connect to the Internet and you will receive an e-mail address with a wanadoo.fr suffix. France Télécom offers special deals to keep connection costs down. You can pay per minute of Internet use, or sign on for a monthly fee that gives you a limited number of hours online per billing cycle. To set up an account, you need a fixed phone line and a contract for France Télécom service.

Far more interesting is Wanadoo's **broadband** service. There are different packages available that offer various speeds – from 128K, 512K and higher (up to 20 times faster than normal Internet connections). Selecting which is right for you depends on how much time you spend surfing and whether you download and upload heavy graphics and music files. Downloading a two-hour feature film, for example, might take a few hours via broadband and a few days via the normal phone line. This is returned to you when you terminate your contract and return the modem.

Broadband means your Internet is always turned on and you pay a flat fee no matter how long you use it. You can use your phone and fax normally even when your computer is logged on. The French phone company and Wanadoo are betting on broadband business to outpace mobile phone profits in the long term and are engaged in an aggressive campaign to attract new subscribers. Unfortunately, it is not available everywhere; Wanadoo can tell you if your town or area is set up for broadband service.

If you decide to stay with your British ISP, make sure it has an access number in France. Also check that it doesn't charge surplus fees when you dial up from abroad. To connect, you might need to check 'ignore dial tone' if your modem has difficulty communicating with French phones.

The most popular search engines are **www.voila.fr** and **www.google.fr**. The French *Yellow Pages* are online at **www.pagesjaunes.fr** and are an incredible resource for people looking for language schools, cookery classes, builders or anything else in their neighbourhood. Site **www.laposte.net** details the functions of the postal system. For Internet vocabulary, *see* p.258.

Television and Satellite

France has a mandatory **television tax** (*redevance*) due each year (your bill comes by post and you pay it from your bank account). Anyone who owns a TV is technically obliged to pay it (unless they are over 64 or are poor). Don't bother bringing your UK television to France because it won't work (unless you aim to use it solely with British video recorders or DVD players for watching films).

Your money gets you five main **terrestrial channels** that many French people avoid at all costs – TF1, France2 and France3, Arte/France 5 and M6. For an additional subscription fee you can buy **Canal Plus** service, with a satellite dish and a decoder box. It specializes in high-quality films and top-level sport. Recent newcomers are **Canal Satellite** and **Télévision Par Satellite**, two new satellite digital TV groups, the former an offshoot of Canal Plus, the latter a conglomeration of all the other networks. Between them they have it covered, from sport to feature films, with foreign-language channels bunched into their bouquets. **Digital TV** was launched a decade ago and has seen its audience numbers rise thanks to multichannel packages and themed programming.

If you are a Sky user, your British card does not authorise you to receive pictures in France because Sky is not licensed to operate outside Britain. However, thousands of holidaymakers and British residents in France happily use their British cards anyway. If you go to a specialised satellite servicer, they will even arrange a card for those who never had one in the UK.

Postal Services

The **post office** (*la poste*) is much more than a place to buy stamps – in many respects, it's a public service station where you can open a sort of bank account, receive welfare payments, and pay some tax bills, as well as sending and receiving mail. Many post offices also have free Internet stations (with free e-mail addresses for clients, ending in laposte.net) and Minitel service. For more information, go to **www.laposte.net**.

The overnight service *Chronopost* is equivalent to UPS or Federal Express. A registered letter is *lettre recommandée simple,* and a registered letter that must be signed for is *recommandée avec accusé de réception*. You can buy pre-stamped envelopes at supermarkets or post offices for domestic and international mail, allowing a slight saving if you use the mail a lot. You can also buy **stamps** at *tabacs*.

Money and Banking

Anybody can open a bank account if they are over 18 and have proof of identity and an address in France (such as an EDF bill; *see* p.212). The type of account you open ultimately depends on whether you're a resident or non-resident. If you're running a business or have multiple sources of income, you may require fairly sophisticated services; otherwise your needs are likely to be very simple. For most foreigners, the only real concerns are finding a bank close to them and with English-speaking staff. France's biggest banks – Banque Nationale de Paris (BNP Paribas), Crédit Lyonnais, Société Générale and Crédit Agricole – fit the bill.

The biggest advantage of French banking is that you can pay your utilities, mobile phone service and broadband Internet bills by direct debit. All the big banking institutions offer Internet banking, which allows clients to keep track of deposits and deductions, and even arrange to wire money online. You can also check your account by phone or Minitel; your bank will send the secret codes for accessing these services to your home address.

If you are choosing between banks, select the one that charges the least for receiving money (French banks charge for absolutely everything). If you choose to use Barclays or another British bank, the services will not differ much from a French bank but you can count on English-speaking tellers.

French banking hours are generally Mon–Fri 9am–4.30pm; most branches close for lunch from noon until 1.30 or 2pm. Some are also open on Saturday mornings, but if so they close the following Monday.

Foreigners can open a normal French account (*compte courant*) with a chequebook (*carnet de chèques*) included, and a debit card (*carte bleue*; CB). The latter

> **Quick Banking Tips**
>
> - Learn to write the date on your French cheque: 5 November 2006 is 5/11/06, not 11/5/06 as in the States.
> - Cross the '7' so that it is not confused with a '1'.
> - Note that, in French, a comma replaces a period and vice versa – i.e, where you write €2,500.00, a French person would write €2.500,00.
> - The blank space at the lower right of your cheque is for your signature.
> - On a cheque, in France you write 'Pay xxx euros to Mr X', not, as in the UK, 'Pay Mr X xxx pounds'.

can be a simple debit card or a combination of debit and credit cards (*carte de retrait* and *carte de crédit*). You can't generally withdraw more than €500 a day, but you can negotiate individual limits with your branch. In France, you have to pay the full balance on a credit card each month, and cannot run up a debt.

Among the various accounts are a chequing account (*compte-chèques*) and a savings account (*compte sur livret*), which pays interest. Your *relevé de compte* is your bank statement, which is sent monthly. You will have no problem sending or receiving wire transfers (*virement*) as long as you can supply the sender with the following information: your bank name, the bank code (*code établissement*), agency code (*code guichet*), your account number (*numéro de compte*) and the key number (*clé*). International transfers may require a SWIFT number, IBAN (international bank account number) and BIC (bank identifier code).

All this information is listed on your statement. Funds wired in different currencies will be converted into euros based on the day's exchange rate. Foreign cheques can be deposited or cashed, although there is usually a fee.

Cheques

Don't even think about writing a cheque on your French account if there are insufficient funds (*un découvert*) – this is a criminal offence. Bounced cheques lead to substantial charges and your bank can force closure of the account. In extreme cases, you will be banned from opening another account for five years.

'Offshore' Accounts

Some people think that by having an offshore bank account they do not have to pay tax in France. This is not the case. The only way to not pay tax is by illegally hiding the existence of the bank account from tax authorities.

Shopping

Not too long ago, France was a staunch promoter of the concept of speciality and boutique shops. To make a meal, shoppers had to visit almost as many shops as ingredients they required: one for bread, one for meat and one for vegetables. The pay-off was a guarantee of quality and a higher standard of service. The drawbacks were inflated prices and inconvenience.

As in so many other countries, this kind of shopping is sadly on its way to extinction. Busy office workers and parents with better things to do than stand in queues opt to shop at the nearest supermarket, where everything is located under one roof. France is the birthplace of a mutant species of supermarket so big it is technically a 'hypermarket'. The Carrefour chain is an excellent example. Employees get around on rollerskates, and shoppers can reach for a new mountain bike or kitchen unit in the aisle after the milk and butter.

Hypermarkets have permanently changed France's consumer landscape by wiping out many corner shops. Where a town may have had three bakeries and two butchers, now it has one of each, and because of the virtual monopoly each holds in its sector, both bread and meat quality has declined. In a sense, one is forced to shop at hypermarkets, and so the vicious circle perpetuates itself.

Shopping Hours

France's employment laws dictate the hours and days a shop can be open for business. But these regulations have been relaxed, giving more autonomy to individual shop owners. You would expect most stores to be closed on Sundays, but that's not always the case – in some towns, a strange phenomenon has developed: because supermarkets are closed on Sundays, local shops open for business and rake in the biggest profits then.

Shops are generally open 9am–7pm and take a lunch break 1–3pm. These hours apply to clothes shops and most food shops. A bakery, for example, will open just as the ovens are hottest, at about 6am. In big towns and cities, shops are known to keep their doors open until 10pm.

You can count on smaller shops to take two to four weeks off in the height of summer, usually in and around the month of August. At the same time, larger shops in tourist areas usually expand their summer opening hours and stay open seven days a week to accommodate the number of holidaymakers. When small shops close in a town or neighbourhood, shop owners usually compare notes. If the butcher across the way from you shuts down in August, the butcher two streets up will stay open and vice versa.

Payment

As you would expect, in smaller shops cash is golden; cheques are accepted sometimes reluctantly, only for minimum payments of €10, €15 or €20 depending on the shop, and only with an ID card or passport. In larger shops, bank cards are the norm. Beware that many international bank debit cards seem to have a hard time communicating with the French system. Problems always seem to happen in dire situations, for example, when you are trying to fill your car with petrol from an automatic dispenser on a deserted road at midnight. French credit cards use the 'chip and PIN' system that is now also in force in the UK, where instead of signing a slip you tap a four-digit number into a machine by the till. There will also be a minimum amount, as for cheques.

Returns

Bringing an item back to the shop after it was purchased was almost unheard of several decades ago. Now it's common practice. Big chain stores have no problem with returns as long as you have a receipt and are making the return within 30 days of the purchase. Smaller shops may need more convincing.

Transport

France's internal air, rail and road networks are superb and, at least by British standards, inexpensive, which is good news not only in terms of getting around but also for those needing to distribute a product or services.

External communications – important to the family and friends you leave behind, your international customers, and to you if you are going to travel abroad to see customers – are good, too, but if you want to travel internationally, you really need to be close to Paris or Nice. Sometimes it can even be cheaper to fly via London.

Public Transport

Using France's excellent network of public transport is one way to go, but although the options are more than adequate and comfortable, the country suffers from debilitating strikes that can bring the whole system to a screeching halt. Industrial action is especially common in spring and autumn, when unions are set to renegotiate their labour contracts – and hits airports, ferry services and the railway at random. Often the strikes are intentionally staged the week before Christmas and can turn travel into a nightmare.

The *Métro*

London, New York and Paris are the holy trinity of underground engineering genius. Some four million people ride the Paris *métro* each day, and their numbers are rising as traffic congestion plagues the surface streets. The network counts more than 300 stations and 15 lines, making it easy to reach all parts of the city. Lille, Lyon, Marseille and Toulouse also have underground services, although they're not nearly as exhaustive as the Paris *métro*.

Buses

City buses are dependable and convenient, and top the list of desirable forms of public transport. The bus service (*autobus*) in Paris, for example, is complementary to the *métro* system; places that one form of transport won't get you to are accessible by the other. You need to stamp your ticket (the same ticket as used in the *métro* is valid for buses) in the machine near the driver. If you are travelling longer distances, you may need to stamp more than one ticket – a plan posted at the bus stop tells you whether one ticket or two is needed for the journey. Service is reduced on Sundays and after 8.30pm.

If you live in the country or a small town, the **regional bus service** (also called *autocars*) is dismal. On some routes, only two buses operate per day, at the hours children need to get to and from school. Night-time service is sketchy at best. You will be obliged to take trains or buy a car, bike or scooter.

Trains

The SNCF (Société Nationale des Chemins de Fer Français), the national rail network, is the largest and most comprehensive in Europe, and a technological masterpiece. It's most famous for its TGVs (*trains à grande vitesse*), which speed along at a mind-boggling 300km/h. TGVs link Paris to major French cities such as Lille, Lyon, Marseille and Bordeaux, as well as Geneva, Brussels, Amsterdam and London (via the Channel Tunnel). The journey from Paris to Marseille by TGV takes about three hours, as opposed to seven by 'normal' train.

Besides the TGV, France has slower trains to other smaller cities. There are local trains and long-distance trains (*trains grandes lignes*). If you live in the south of France, a slower train runs right along the Mediterranean coast linking Menton and Monaco through Nice and Antibes to St-Raphaël, and is handy for towel- and umbrella-toting beachgoers.

Otherwise, if you are travelling to France from abroad, chances are you must pass through Paris. Trains coming from southwest France, Spain and Portugal arrive at the Gare d'Austerlitz. Trains from eastern France, Luxembourg, southern Germany, northern Switzerland, Austria and eastern Europe come in to the Gare de l'Est. The Gare de Lyon services trains from the south of France (Nice and Marseille), Italy and parts of Switzerland. Western France is plugged in to the Gare Montparnasse. Trains originating in northern France, Belgium, northern Germany, the Netherlands and the UK come into the Gare du Nord. Last, trains from northwest France and some from the UK make their final stop at the Gare St-Lazare. All these stations connect into the *métro* system.

The easiest way to buy a train ticket and check timetables and availability is to consult **www.voyages-sncf.com**. You will get an electronic confirmation number after you pay with a credit card, and pick up your ticket at the station before your train leaves. If you are not Internet-savvy, call the SNCF (**t** 08 91 67 68 69) and pick up your ticket at the station (in some areas it can be delivered to your home for a small fee), or simply go to the nearest train station and buy your ticket there.

If you travel by rail often, buy either a rail pass, which gives you discounts of up to 50% if you travel the same route every week. Weekend travel is often available at discounted rates, and fares are reduced for families, the elderly and minors. Remember to validate your ticket in the orange machines before boarding, or you face a fine when the ticket inspector comes along.

Air Travel

Air France (**www.airfrance.fr**) has national flights, but a host of budget airlines have made travel within France often cheaper – and almost always faster – than the train. Some easyJet fares from Nice to Paris, for example, are advertised at €30. The one-way train fare between those two cities is as much as €80 (which is still pretty reasonable by British standards).

For more airline options, go to the French airports site (**www.aeroport.fr**). It's in French, but the airports are listed on the left; the word for airline is *compagnie aérienne*. The site tells you which budget airlines operate from which airport and provides up-to-date timetables. Remember that many airlines add more flights during the summer season.

Cars

The moment you bring your car to France, or buy one there, you cross that invisible line that separates the tourist from the resident; your car becomes a symbol of your willingness to integrate. Getting from point A to point B in France is not only about getting to your destination. It involves fashion-statement automobiles, new standards in etiquette and, unfortunately, a need for speed. Judging from the behaviour on the roads, there is no doubt that France is a hot-blooded Latin country where the lumbering foreigner is either 'flashed' back into the slow lane or risks being mown down. To keep up with traffic, you'll need to make 'adjustments' to the staid road manners you were encouraged to use back home. Or take the bus.

The Rules of the Road

Seatbelts are obligatory in both front and back; the car on the right always has the right of way in an intersection unless otherwise indicated; never pass on the right; if you are 'flashed' it means pull into the slow lane quickly; traffic on the inside of the roundabout has the right of way; try not to overshoot the dashboard-level traffic lights (otherwise you have to back-up and that is embarrassing). You must carry a red breakdown triangle in your boot and are supposed to fix an 'F' sticker to the back of your car if you have French licence plates or a 'GB' if your car is registered in Britain. It is forbidden to use a mobile phone while driving. If any of the above doesn't make sense, buy a copy of the French Highway Code (*Code de la Route*) available at bookshops and magazines kiosks and study it carefully. Otherwise the road is clear.

France is endowed with thousands of kilometres of paved road, much of which is managed by private companies, making it of the highest standard. Repairs and maintenance are impeccable, and the French are justifiably proud of their motorways, which are almost certainly the best in Europe. The biggest drawback is that these *autoroutes* are expensive. One study confirmed that the 50km stretch from Nice to the Italian border was the most expensive piece of roadway, barring bridges and tunnels, in Europe – there are four tolls to pay, or an average of one every 12km. Calais to Nice (about 1,200km) costs about €85. The alternative is to stay on the *routes nationales,* which are often jammed with motorists avoiding tolls on the *autoroutes*. Although you must fork out many euros for the *autoroutes* (in same places you throw coins into an automated basket, so keep spare change handy), they provide an extremely comfortable

Speed Limits

Motorways: 130kph (80mph)
Urban stretches: 110kph (68mph)
Paris ring road (*périphérique*): 80kph (50mph)
Dual carriageways: 110kph (68mph)
Rural built-up areas: 90kph (55mph)
Urban built-up areas: 50kph (31mph)
Motorways when it's raining: 110kph (68mph)
Dual carriageways when it's raining: 100kph (62mph)
Rural built-up areas when it's raining: 80kph (50mph)

drive. You will see rest areas (*aires de repos*) every 15km, with toilets, phones and picnic areas.

Technically, you are not allowed to sleep overnight in an *aire de repos*, although many motorists do. There are also some very cheap motels where, if you arrive late at night, you insert your credit card into an automatic teller machine, tap in how many people you are, *et voilà!* – a room code is supplied. Etap Hotels (**www.etaphotel.com**) generally charge about €35 a night for a basic room with a double bed and a bunk, plus a shower room; they're often located by service stations or in *zones industrielles*.

If you break down or have an accident, there are SOS phones every 2km, as well as in the rest areas.

Driver's Licences

If you hold a driving licence from a **EU member state**, you are *not* obliged to exchange it for a French one when you move unless you commit a driving offence in France, when the French authorities need to take 'points' from your driving record (one for failing to dip your lights, two for driving and talking on your mobile, three for not wearing a seatbelt, six for drink-driving).

Generally, however, long-term residents opt to obtain a French licence, as it simplifies other aspects such as insurance. It is also easier to replace in the case of loss or theft, saving you a trip back home. Also, if you have a British licence, you must inform the DVLA of your change of address, and if you submit your address in France your British licence may become invalid and you will be have to get a French one. If you do exchange your licence, the original is withdrawn.

To exchange your licence, go to the nearest *préfecture* and ask for a *demande d'échange de permis de conduire*. You will be asked for:

- ID, such as your passport.
- proof of address, such as an EDF bill or a lease.
- your original driving licence (you may be asked to provide a translation by a *traducteur expert-juré* if you are a non-EU citizen).

- **two passport-sized photographs.**
- **photocopies of all the above documents.**

If you are **not an EU citizen**, you may be required to exchange your licence; but those with South African and Australian licences do not have to do this. Non-EU licence-carriers (who live in France and have a *carte de séjour*) are allowed to drive in France for one year, at which point their non-EU licence becomes invalid and they are uninsured to drive. They may be able to exchange their licence for a French one provided they do so before the one-year period is up (this depends on the agreement their country has with France); if not, they have to apply for a French licence, which means taking the theoretical and practical driving exams.

The **minimum driving age** is 18; 17-year-old foreign drivers with valid licences cannot drive there (if they do, they face fines and the impounding of their vehicle).

You must carry your licence with you at all times when driving.

Importing a Car

If you have a summer home in France and just visit for a few months each year, there is no reason to import your car officially. If you reside permanently in France, you technically need to register your car within three months; many foreigners are relaxed about the timing, however, since it's almost impossible to prove when you brought the car over in the first place.

If you've paid the **VAT** on your vehicle, you can import your car without incurring additional VAT charges. If you didn't, you need to pay it when you import it. VAT is reduced according to the age of the car, boat or motorcycle. Some savvy foreigners manage to keep their new cars abroad long enough to import them to France as 'used', thus hitting a lower VAT bracket. If you need to pay the VAT on your car, you should do so at the Hôtel/Recette des Impôts where you live.

The next step is to have your car checked to make sure it meets French safety standards. This is called a ***contrôle technique*** (equivalent to a British **MOT**) and amounts to a little sticker that you fix to your windscreen, next to your proof of insurance, proving your car is in good health. Any qualified mechanic can issue it after a complete test of your vehicle (brakes, lights, tyres, steering, suspension, bodywork, seatbelts, mirrors, windscreen wipers and horn). If your car does not conform to these standards, you must make the necessary adjustments, which can be costly. There are also smaller adjustments to make – for example, it is compulsory to place converters on your headlights to ensure that your dipped headlights point to the correct side and won't blind oncoming traffic.

After this, you need a **customs certificate** (*certificat de douane*) that permits you to register the vehicle in France. This is obtained at the local customs office (**Direction des Douanes**) – every town has one. The **DRIRE (Direction Régionale de l'Industrie, de la Recherche et de l'Environnement)** will require the following:

- a customs certificate (*certificat de douane*).
- manufacturers' certificate of construction, which can be obtained at a car dealer (not required for new cars made in the EU).
- completed application for vehicle registration (*demande de certificat d'immatriculation d'un véhicule*), which you can get at your *préfecture*.
- vehicle registration (*titre de circulation*).
- *contrôle technique* proving the car meets French safety standards.
- fee and applicable tax stamp.
- your passport.

Once the DRIRE office has these documents, you get a French **registration certificate** (*certificat d'immatriculation* or ***carte grise***) at the local *préfecture*. The final two digits of the car's registration number reflect the *département* where the car is registered. For example, cars registered in central Paris end in '75'. Once you have your *carte grise*, you are required to order French **licence plates**. Hardware stores and supermarkets can do this; you need one for the front and one for the rear. If you lose your *carte grise*, or if it is stolen, you must ask for a duplicate copy at the *préfecture*, and you will need a police report.

Buying a Car

Depending on the exchange rate, cars in France – even British ones – can be cheaper than in the UK, so it makes sense to buy a new car in France and avoid import hassles. You'll probably also want a car with left-hand drive in the long term. A diesel is a good option since your fuel bill will be about a third less.

If you are interested in a **new car** (note: most French buy French), your local dealer will point you in the right direction in terms of price and financing options. You'll need to apply for a *carte grise* at the *préfecture*, arrange for your licence plates to be made, and get insurance.

If you're buying a **used car**, ask the seller for a *lettre de non-gage* (issued by the *département*) declaring that the vehicle is debt-free (unpaid financing would be passed on to you). Make sure the chassis number matches that listed on the *carte grise* – never buy a car that doesn't have a *carte grise* or one that doesn't match the vehicle, as it will have been stolen. You can also request that the owner write a letter confirming that the car has not been involved in any collisions. Lastly, make sure the *contrôle technique* sticker is current and valid. All cars more than four years old are required to have a *contrôle technique* (*see* left) every two years. Antique or collectors' cars (more than 25 years old) are exempt.

Car Insurance

All cars in France and cars coming into France must at least be insured for third-party risk. If your insurance was issued in another EU country, Switzerland,

Liechtenstein or Norway, your insurance automatically has third-party coverage. If it wasn't, you can buy additional insurance (valid for a set period). If your car is insured in France, you will automatically be give the 'Green Card' or international insurance known in France as the *carte internationale d'assurance automobile*. These are the basic insurance packages you can purchase:

- third party (compulsory).
- third party, fire and theft.
- multi-risk collision (covers damage to your car in an accident when the third party is identified).
- fully comprehensive (covers all accidents even when the third party is not identified).

Insurance premiums are very high in France. If you are in an **accident**, you need to fill out a *constat à l'amiable* or the *constat européen d'accident*, which goes to your insurance company in the event of a claim. The insurance company will arrange for an inspection of the damage.

Proof of insurance must be kept with the car at all times. In addition, an insurance stub is fixed to the windscreen (lower right corner facing the passenger seat). Make sure your stub is valid and current, as this is the first thing a police officer will check. Driving without insurance could lead to imprisonment.

Crime and the Police

After alarming crime statistics were published in 2000, violent crime moved to the forefront of the political agenda and government officials adopted a staunch 'zero-tolerance' policy. As a result, crimes – especially violent crimes – are on the wane. Don't take that as reason to let down your guard, though: pickpocketing rates in Marseille and Paris are high enough to merit a very firm warning, and house burglaries have reached epidemic levels, especially in the area from Marseille to Nice, where many foreigners have summer homes.

Be on guard with your home, your purse and your car. There are basic precautions to take – identical to the ones you'd take back home – to keep criminals and other morally challenged types at bay. You can install iron bars on your windows or fit metal curtains on your doors, which make your home almost impenetrable. You can put in electric alarms or hire a private patrol or guardian, and some owners even install fake security cameras as a deterrent. The best strategy, though, is to know your neighbours and local shopkeepers and stay active in your community. Don't leave obvious signs that your home is empty: a pile of unopened mail or an overgrown garden could attract unwanted attention. The majority of home robberies occur in the summer months.

There are four primary kinds of **police** in France. The Compagnie Républicaine de Sécurité (CRS) is generally the most disliked, since controlling riots and public spectacles is among its primary activities. The Police Nationale, under the control of the Interior Ministry, is responsible for policing Paris and provincial urban jurisdictions with populations of more than 10,000. The jurisdiction is the area around the police station or *commissariat de police*, and the officers often wear white caps. The Gendarmerie Nationale are controlled by the Defence Ministry, wear blue uniforms and patrol rural areas and small towns, either in cars or as paired motorcyclists (*motards*). They look for serious criminal offenders and have national jurisdiction. The last branch is the municipal police (Corps Urbain or Police Municipale) – recognisable by their flat caps – who are hired by the local town hall of medium-sized municipalities and deal with petty crimes and road offences.

In an **emergency**, dial **t** 17 to speak with the police. Be advised that the police can stop you on the road for a random control (*contrôle*), usually to check against drink-driving and to make sure your vehicle registration and insurance is in order. If you are arrested, call your embassy first and ask for a list of English-speaking lawyers. It is inadvisable to sign any statements or paperwork until you have legal representation.

If you are the victim of a robbery, contact the nearest *commissariat de police* or *gendarmerie*. You will be asked to file a report of what was stolen (*déclaration de vol*) that can be used in an insurance claim. You must do so within 24 hours of the robbery – and don't expect a sympathetic shoulder to cry on.

Taking Your Pet

In general, there is no more pet-friendly country on the planet than France, and your four-legged friend will soon learn that a belly-scratch is always a nose-nudge away. Dogs are unofficially tolerated in shops, cafés and even restaurants to a far greater extent in France than in the UK or North America. If only someone would clean up the mess on the streets.

In 2001, Britain's 100-year-old pet quarantine system was supplemented by the Pet Travel Scheme (PETS), in which a cat or dog receives its own British 'Pet Passport', making it much easier to transport them between the UK and France. To qualify for the programme, Felix or Fido must meet these criteria:

- He must be microchipped (a chip is implanted under the skin by a vet).

- He must be vaccinated against rabies. If he is qualifying for PETS for the first time, he must undergo a test to confirm the presence of rabies antibodies in his blood after the vaccination, which sometimes requires a delay of 30 days. Pets that have already qualified for PETS must have documents showing they received their booster vaccinations. Blood samples must be analysed at a DEFRA-approved laboratory. Note that there is a compulsory waiting period after the blood test.

When you are ready to bring your pet back to the UK, you must:
- have it checked for ticks and tapeworms (*echinococcus multilocularis*) 24–48hrs before its journey back to the UK, by a qualified vet.
- sign a declaration stating that it has not been outside any PETS qualifying countries within the previous six months.

Once your pet has lived in France for three months, it is considered 'French' and is subject to French laws governing pets. For example, puppies and kittens are given identifying tattoos on their ears and are registered in a national pet database that issues notifications when annual vaccinations are due. However, a pet that has been microchipped does not need to be tattooed.

If your pet is qualifying for PETS in France, you need to take it (for microchipping) to a veterinary surgeon who holds a *mandat sanitaire* from French authorities. A list of qualifying vets is available at your local town hall (*mairie*).

If you want to bring something more exotic into France, you must check first with the French authorities. Some South American birds and African reptiles, snakes and turtles require special import certificates from the Ministère de l'Agriculture et de la Pêche, which may have a long list of conditions attached to it. In an effort to protect endangered species, many rare animals are simply not allowed to travel across borders.

For more information on bringing your pet to France, consult the UK's **Department for the Environment, Food and Rural Affairs (www.defra.gov.uk)** or the French **Agriculture Ministry (www.agriculture.gouv.fr)**.

Health and Emergencies

France's healthcare system is among the best in the world: waiting times are minimal, treatments are affordable and available to the poor, facilities and equipment are of the highest standards and the services and staff are excellent. Someone will have to deal with the public deficit it is creating, but that's a problem for another day.

If you contribute to the French *sécurité sociale* (*see* p.125), you and your family will receive subsidised or free medical care (visits to specialists, hospitalisation, medicines, maternity care and dental care). You do pay for the services, but the *sécurité sociale* reimburses, either fully or in part, as follows:

- **maternity expenses: 100%**
- **general hospitalisation: 80%**
- **doctors' and dentists' bills: 70%**
- **ambulances, laboratories and opticians: 65%**
- **medical auxiliaries (nurses, chiropodists, etc.): 60%**
- **essential daily medication (such as insulin or heart pills): 100%**

- other medicines: 65%
- minor medicines: 35%

Certain people are exempt from paying any charges, including the disabled and the mentally ill. Those covered under *sécurité sociale* can also take out low-cost private insurance (known as a ***mutuelle***) to cover the 20–30% not covered by *sécurité sociale*. For example, if *sécurité sociale* pays 65% of the cost of your new reading glasses, your *mutuelle* might cover another 20%, leaving you responsible only for 15% of the total cost. Almost every professional trade has its own *mutuelle* for its employees to join. Each *mutuelle* is different – some cover almost all the additional costs and others pay in full for items not completely covered by *sécurité sociale*.

When you register for social security you will be issued with a **carte vitale**, which looks like a credit card but is embedded with a microchip and has your personal information and medical history stored within, makes getting medical reimbursements from *sécurité sociale* very easy – the doctor just swipes your card and the amount due is immediately calculated and eventually credited to you bank account via wire transfer.

Entitlements

- **EU visitors up to 90 days**: To qualify for medical treatment as a tourist from an EU country, you need a new European Health Insurance Card (EHIC), which replaced the E111 form at the end of 2005. Application forms are available from post offices. If you have the card, you're entitled to French medical treatments and must pay the same contribution to charges as a French person. It only covers necessary care (such as breaking a leg or catching a virus) or ongoing care for a serious medical condition such as diabetes. Without it, you're responsible for the full charges and must request a reimbursement when you get back to the UK. EU pensioners enjoy special status that grants them any medical treatment necessary while in another EU country.

- **EU visitors for more than 90 days**: If you are in France permanently, you will either need to contribute to the *sécurité sociale* or apply to be covered by Universal Health Cover (*Couverture Maladie Universelle* or **CMU**), a medical health scheme designed to ensure that everyone (including people on low income, and the unemployed) is covered for basic medical costs. It is not available to people already insured under another scheme.

- **Non-EU visitors**: Non-EU citizens have no automatic entitlements, although some nations have bilateral agreements with France that offer limited benefits. Otherwise, you must take out private insurance.

- **Residents and people entitled to state medical assistance**: Those entitled to state medical care include qualifying workers (workers paying *sécurité sociale* contributions who have worked, generally, 100 hours per month) and retired

> ### Emergencies
>
> As soon as you move to France, compile a list of emergency numbers and the address of the nearest hospital and tape it to your refrigerator door. Check for the numbers in the phone book under *services médicaux*.
>
> In case of a medical emergency, such as a heart attack, call the SAMU (Service d'Aide Médicale d'Urgence) on **t 15**. They will send an ambulance.
>
> For the fire brigade (*pompiers*) call **t 18**.
>
> For the police, look for *commissariat de police* in the phonebook or dial **t 17**.
>
> You will be charged for SAMU services and the ambulance fee but you can deduct these expenses later with your insurance provider.

people from other EU countries and their respective dependants. Workers may also be entitled to sick-leave allowances, similar to British incapacity benefits. Your contributions to the British national insurance scheme are taken into account when calculating your entitlements in France. Thus, you may be entitled in France on the basis of your British contributions alone (ask the DDS for a form E104). If you are a pensioner, ask for form E121, which confirms your status and is your passport to the special benefits to which you are entitled.

- People not entitled are:
    - the economically inactive (those who 'retired' below retirement age).
    - students who are no longer the dependants of an EU worker.
    - non-EU nationals.
    - civil servants covered by special schemes.

For more information for British nationals, see **www.doh.gov.uk**.

Social Services and Welfare Benefits

Healthcare is just one component of the all-embracing *sécurité sociale* system in France that offers welfare benefits such as sickness and maternity benefits, entitlements following an accident at work or occupational diseases, invalidity benefits, old-age pensions, widowers' or other survivors' benefits, death grants, unemployment benefits and family benefits.

Welfare benefits in EU countries are governed by a simple idea: a person exercising his or her right to move from one EU state to another should not lose welfare benefit rights. People covered include:

- employed and self-employed nationals of EU states.
- pensioners who are nationals of EU states.
- civil servants of EU states and members of their families provided they are not covered by an enhanced scheme for civil servants in their own country. This is generally not a problem for UK civil servants.

Note that the EU rules do not cover the economically inactive (people retired early, students, etc.).

EU rules do not replace the national benefits to which you may be entitled. Rather, they co-ordinate varying national schemes and dictate in which of several possible countries a person should make a claim and which country should pay the cost. Apart from the basic principle that you should not lose benefits simply by moving to another EU country, such as France, the other basic principle to keep in mind is you should only be subject to the rules of one country at a time. To make this clearer: the laws of one EU member state cannot – except in the case of unemployment benefits – take away or reduce your entitlement to benefit just because you live in another member state.

If you remain entitled to a British benefit while living in France, payment of that benefit can be made in different ways, depending on the benefit in question. It can be made by authorities in France on behalf of the authorities in the UK, or can be paid to you directly in France from the UK.

How do you decide which rules apply to you? There are two main considerations: Which country insures you? And in which country do you live?

You are insured in the country where you work. If you work regularly in more than one EU member state, you are insured in the country where you live. (A short-term posting of less than one year to another country is ignored.) Retired people who have only worked in one EU member state will remain 'attached' to that country for pension benefits and other purposes for the rest of their lives. People who have worked in several states will have built up pension entitlements in each member state in which they worked for more than one year. Otherwise, some benefits stem from your presence in a country. Each potential benefit, both in Britain and in France, has restrictions stipulating which categories of people are entitled to it.

French Benefits

If you need to claim *sécurité sociale* benefits in France, your entitlement will be determined by the contributions you have made in France as well as any relevant contributions made in the UK. Social security contributions are only paid by people who are tax-resident in France (*see* pp.144–5).

• **Health benefits**: See the healthcare section above.

• **Accidents at work, occupational sickness and invalidity and disability benefits**: These are only available, logically, to those working in France. You should continue receiving British benefits if you're entitled to them.

• **Pensions**: Unless you have worked in France most of your life, you are not likely to receive a French pension, but you will continue to receive your British pension. Pensions in EU countries are paid on the basis of 'totalisation' – this means if you've lived in various countries, all your contributions in any EU country will be added together to calculate your entitlement. For example, if France pays a minimum pension after 20 years of contributions and a full pension after 40 years, and if you have paid enough contributions to qualify anywhere in the EU, you get the pension. If you have worked for five years out of 40 in France and the balance elsewhere, the French government will pay 5/40ths of your pension at the rates applicable in France. If you had worked for 15 years in the UK, the British government would pay 15/40ths, and so on.

- **Unemployment benefits**: If you lose your job, the French unemployment benefit authority must take into account any periods of employment or NI contributions paid in other EU countries when calculating your entitlement to benefits in France. You must, however, have paid at least some *sécurité sociale* payments in France prior to claiming unemployment benefits there, which means you cannot go to France for the purpose of claiming benefit. You should obtain form E301 from the British benefit authorities. If you travel to France to seek employment, there are restrictions on your entitlement to benefit and you must comply with all French procedural requirements. (You must have been unemployed and available for work in your home country for at least four weeks before going to France. You must contact your home unemployment benefit authority and obtain a form E303 before leaving. You must register for work in France within seven days of arrival. You will be entitled to benefit for a maximum of three months. If you cannot find a job during that period you will only be entitled to continued unemployment benefit in your home country if you return within the three-month period; if you do not, you can lose all entitlement to benefits. You are only entitled to one three-month payment between two periods of employment.)

- **Family benefits**: If the members of your family live in France with you and you pay *sécurité sociale*, they are entitled to the same benefits as a French national. If your family does not live in France, and if you are entitled to benefits under the rules of more than one country, they will receive the highest amount to which they would have been entitled in any of the relevant states. Pensioners normally receive family benefits from the EU state that pays their pension.

Retirement, Pensions and Death

If you are already retired and you only ever paid national insurance contributions in the UK, you will receive your British retirement pension in France. You will be paid without deduction (except remittance charges), and your pension will be updated whenever the pensions in the UK are updated.

If you have not yet retired and you move to France to start a business, your entitlement to your British pension will be frozen and the pension to which you are entitled will be paid to you at British retirement age. The official French retirement age is currently 60 for men and women, but there are political attempts to raise it to 65.

Deaths must be registered within 24 hours at the town hall (mairie), and also recorded at the British consulate. Burial is much more common in France than cremation. Funerals are as exceedingly expensive as they are in the UK, and taking a body home is also costly.

French inheritance law is much more restrictive than British law and does apply to people who own property in France (yes, you!). Certain groups of people have almost automatic rights to inherit all or a part of your property, such as spouses and offspring. French inheritance law does not apply to the property you own outside France. (For more information, see 'Finding a Home', pp.192–4.) It's always best to make a French will to supplement an English one. If you do not, the English will should be treated as valid in France and will be used to distribute your estate. The cost of implementing the English will is much higher than the cost of implementing the French one. Always use a lawyer to advise you on the contents of your will. If you fail to draft a will of any kind, your heirs will be left with a complex and costly liability. Untangling which assets are covered by which country is done on a case-by-case basis and requires many hours of debate among expensive lawyers.

Education

The French School System

If you are moving to France with children, you will need to understand the French schooling system before you decide whether to enrol them in a private foreign-language school or a public French school. There are pros and cons to both, and your decision ultimately depends on your priorities for your child and your child's inclinations. Most importantly, you'll need to factor in your child's ability to integrate and make friends. Perhaps s/he would feel more comfortable with other English-speaking youngsters (see 'English-language schools', p.236). But if your child is outgoing, curious and responsive to a new language and culture, s/he will gain a lot more from a French school. Before long, your offspring will be more fluent in French than you.

The general rule of thumb is, the younger the child, the easier it will be for him or her to integrate into the French schooling system. You'll also find that the French system has built-in flexibilities that differ from what you and your child are accustomed to. At the end of the 1980s, a package of wide-reaching educational reforms established schooling stages (*cycles pédagogiques*) that allow each student to progress at his or her own speed. Instead of repeating or 'failing' an academic year, a student completes each cycle at his or her own pace with counselling by a joint teachers' committee (*conseil des maîtres de*

> ### Educating and Raising Children in France
> One of France's most admired virtues is the importance its society gives to the family nucleus. Foreigners find France to be, by and large, a fantastic place to raise offspring. Tight and generous communities are formed around local schools and, in general, the society proudly lends a hand to help raise its youngest citizens. If you are coming with the children, you and your little ones will fit in famously. There are very few places in France – most of them hoity toity bars and restaurants – where children aren't welcome. Most restaurants offer a low-cost *menu-enfant* with kid-pleasing dishes, invariably including *frites*, and more and more places have highchairs. Under-fours travel for free on trains and most buses, and 4–11-year-olds go for half price. Long-distance trains often have a special play area.

cycles). The objective is to rid the pupil of the pressures associated with peers and keeping pace. It also allows students who are faster learners to move forward individually.

If you have a toddler, you may want to consider the national system of **nursery schools** (*écoles maternelles*), which is subsidised by the state. These teach pre-school children basic social skills, movement and self-awareness, and provide the foundations for future instruction in reading and writing. The local town hall (*mairie*) can provide information on the *écoles maternelles* closest to where you live. Pupils usually start between the ages of two and four (one-third of French students start at age two). If you are two working parents or a single parent, there are **nurseries** and **daycare centres** (*jardins d'enfants* or *crèches*) that will prepare a child before he or she is of age to attend an *école maternelle*. French nursery schools are regarded as some of the best in Europe.

School hours in the *école maternelles* are usually 8.30am–12pm and 1.30–4pm. Lunch at the school cafeteria (*cantine*) and a nap period separate the two. In general, there is no school on Wednesday (despite the problems this causes working parents), and many *départements* have a morning session on Saturday. The *école maternelle* is divided into three stages: the lower section (*petite*) for ages two to four; a middle section (*moyenne*) for ages four to five; and an upper section (*grande*) for ages five to six.

Children start **primary school** (*école primaire*) at the age of six and continue until the age of 11. It sounds confusing, but students start *école primaire* at the *onzième* level (also called CP) and finish at the *septième* (CM2) before moving on to secondary school. There is no exam at the end of *école primaire*, and schooling options are both public and private.

Primary schools, which provide 26 hours of instruction per week, are the basic building block of the French schooling system. By the end of it, each child can read and write in French and will have formed a solid background in other academic disciplines, such as history, geography, civic studies, mathematics, science, computers, sports, music, and arts and crafts. A foreign language is also included in the curriculum, and more than 80% of students choose to study English. The programme is also heavily focused on field trips (*classe de découverte*), in which students might spend a week in the mountains, by the sea or in a foreign country.

Secondary school starts at the age of 11, when a child enters a *collège*, and is compulsory until the age of 16. At the age of 15, the top students are selected following an exam to attend a *lycée* (which lasts until the age of 18 and ends with the gruelling *baccalauréat* exam). Students who move on to a *lycée* are completing the *cycle long*. Those who opt for the short cycle (*cycle court*) usually finish their education at a vocational school. Some schools are a *collège* and a *lycée* in one, and admission to higher education is all but guaranteed. This depends on where you live.

Collège education is divided into two two-year stages that range from the *sixième* to the *troisième* (which a child completes at the age of 15). The first or *cycle d'observation* (*6ème* and *5ème*) includes a common curriculum for all students, covering all subjects ranging from science and maths to history and language instruction. New subjects such as economics, technology, physics, geology and chemistry are also introduced. Lessons total 24 hours per week. In the last two years, or *cycle d'orientation* (*4ème* and *3ème*), each student is allowed increased flexibility to pursue his or her individual interests. For example, s/he can opt to take a second foreign language or a classic language such as Greek or Latin, or can choose more technology-related courses. Classes generally total 25 hours per week. At the end of the last year of *collège*, a student takes a written exam in French, mathematics, history and geography that earns him or her the *brevet des collèges*. Passing that exam guarantees admission to the *lycée*.

The ***lycée*** covers three years of specialised education. In chronological order, they are the *seconde* (*2ème*), the *première* (*1er*) and, lastly, the *terminale*. The whole focus, now, of the student is deciding which *baccalauréat* exam to take and, of course, passing it. The '*bac*' is taken at the age of 18 or 19 and only 50% of students pass it. Those who do are guaranteed admission to a French university. There are seven *baccalauréat* categories, which are divided into two principal groups (although there are some 30 individual *baccalauréat* exams to choose from). The first is the general *baccalauréat* in literature, economics, science or social science. The second is the technical *baccalauréat* in science and tertiary technology, industrial technology, or laboratory technologies. The examinations are taken in stages at the end of the *première* and the *terminale* years of *lycée*. The science-based *baccalauréat* is the most prestigious. Sometimes the *bacs* are referred to by letters. Bac S is for *scientifique*, while *bacs* ES (*économique et sociale*) and L (*littéraire*) are for students who are interested in the economy, French, philosophy and languages. All those who pass the exam are known as *bacheliers*.

English-language Schools

The most authoritative source on educational facilities in France for English-speaking children (*établissements d'enseignement anglophone ou bilingue en France*) is the Education Information Service of the British Council in Paris. Its list was created in collaboration with the American Embassy in Paris and is divided into three categories:

- schools with tuition entirely in the English language.
- international sections in French *lycées*.
- international/bilingual schools.

For the full list, together with the websites of the establishments concerned, see **www.britishcouncil.fr**.

Universities

There are two types of university in France: traditional universities and the *grandes écoles*. Admission to one of the country's 72 **universities** (a large proportion of which are located in Paris, including the world-famous Sorbonne) is granted to any pupil who passes the French *baccalauréat* exam (*see* above). More than a million students attend them – representing one-third of *bac*-holders – and the student body is mixed with international students. They are funded by the state and run by the Education Ministry. They do not charge admission, although other student fees may apply.

A large percentage of the students who start university in France end up dropping out: the bureaucratic procedures are stifling, and overcrowding is a problem. The average age of a university graduate is 29, and many of those who do graduate become frustrated when they realise their degree will not guarantee them a job.

On the other side of the academic spectrum are the lavishly funded **grandes écoles**, which were first founded by Napoleon and focus on specialised subjects such as civil engineering, agriculture or political science. France has about 200 *grandes écoles*, some of which are private, and some run by the individual ministries that oversee their specialisation, meaning that more attention is given to programmes and facilities than is the case with universities. Fewer than 100,000 students attend these schools and the admission criteria are rigorous; hey are also very expensive to attend.

France is also home to a growing collection of excellent **international business schools** that provide top-level executive education. Among these are INSEAD Management School, which offers an American-style MBA degree, EDHEC Business School France, ESCP–EAP Graduate School of Management and CERAM in Sophia-Antipolis.

References

France at a Glance 238
Useful Contacts 239
British Consular Services in France 242
French Telephone Codes 243
Regional Climate 243
Départements 244
Largest Cities 245
National and Local Holidays 246
Further Reading 247
Dictionary of Useful and Technical Terms 249
Internet Vocabulary 258

France at a Glance

Official name: République Française
Capital city: Paris
Type of government: Republic
Head of government: prime minister
Chief of State: president
Area: 547,965 sq km
Coastline: 3,427km
Climate: Generally cool winters and mild summers, but mild winters and hot summers along the Med, with occasional strong, cold, dry, north-to-northwesterly wind (*mistral*).
Terrain: Mostly flat plains or gently rolling hills in north and west; remainder is mountainous, especially Pyrenees in south, Alps in east
Border countries: Andorra 56.6km, Belgium 620km, Germany 451km, Italy 488km, Luxembourg 73km, Monaco 4.4km, Spain 623km, Switzerland 573km
Languages and dialects: French 100%, rapidly declining regional dialects and languages (Provençal, Breton, Alsatian, Corsican, Catalan, Basque, Flemish)
Ethnic groups: Celtic and Latin with Teutonic, Slavic, North African, Indochinese, Basque minorities
Population: 59,765,983 (July 2002)
Religion: Roman Catholic 83–88%, Protestant 2%, Jewish 1%, Muslim 5–10%, unaffiliated 4%
Administrative divisions (22 regions): Alsace, Aquitaine, Auvergne, Basse-Normandie, Bourgogne, Bretagne, Centre, Champagne-Ardenne, Corse, Franche-Comté, Haute-Normandie, Ile-de-France, Languedoc-Roussillon, Limousin, Lorraine, Midi-Pyrénées, Nord-Pas-de-Calais, Pays de la Loire, Picardie, Poitou-Charentes, Provence-Alpes-Côte d'Azur, Rhône-Alpes
France is subdivided into 95 *départements* (see 'Départements', pp.244–5)
Overseas departments: French Guyana, Guadeloupe, Martinique, Réunion. Overseas territorial collectivities: Mayotte, Saint Pierre and Miquelon
Dependent areas: Bassas da India, Clipperton Island, Europa Island, French Polynesia, French Southern and Antarctic Lands, Glorioso Islands, Juan de Nova Island, New Caledonia, Tromelin Island, Wallis and Futuna
Constitution: 28 September 1958; amended concerning election of president in 1962; amended to comply with provisions of EC Maastricht Treaty in 1992; Amsterdam Treaty in 1996, Treaty of Nice in 2000; amended to tighten immigration laws in 1993
Legal system: Civil law system with indigenous concepts; review of administrative but not legislative acts
Elections: President elected by popular vote for a five-year term (changed from seven-year term in 2001); prime minister nominated by the National Assembly majority and appointed by the president
Cabinet: Council of Ministers appointed by president on suggestion of prime minister
Legislative branch: Bicameral Parliament, or Parlement, consists of the Senate (Sénat) and the National Assembly or Assemblée Nationale.

Source: CIA World Fact Book 2002

Useful Contacts

Accountants

Bentley Jennison Accountants
Suite 3, Bishton Court, Telford TF3 4JE
t (0195) 220 0808
www.bentley-jennison.co.uk

Cabinet Henderson
Nastringues, 24230 Vélines
t 05 53 23 44 52

Conseil et Expertise
21/23 bd Richard Lenoir, 75011 Paris
t 01 49 29 55 10

Dixon Wilson
19 av de l'Opéra, 75001 Paris
t 01 47 03 12 90

Jeffreys Henry
5–7 Cranwood St, London EC1V 9EE
t (020) 7670 9010
(plus offices in Paris, Lille and Nice)

Business Agencies

Agence Nationale pour la Création d'Entreprises (APCE)
14 rue Délambre, 75014 Paris
t 01 42 18 58 58
www.apce.com

Axxis France
www.axxis.fr
(a 'one stop shop' for business acquisitions)

Centre National pour l'Aménagement des Structures des Exploitations Agricoles (CNASEAS)
2 rue Maupas, 87040 Limoges
t 05 55 12 00 00
www.cnasea.fr

Confederation of British Industry
t (020) 7395 7400
www.cbi.org.uk

Department of Trade & Industry (DTI)
Kingsgate House, 66–74 Victoria St
London SW1A 6SW
t (020) 7215 5000
www.dti.gov.uk

Entente des Générations pour l'Emploi et l'Entreprise (EGEE)
15/17 av de Ségur, 75007 Paris
t 01 47 05 57 71
www.egee.asso.fr

European Commission in the UK
8 Storeys Gate, London SW1P 3AT
t (020) 7973 1992
www.ced.org.uk

Invest in France
28 rue du Dr Finlay, 75015 Paris
t 01 44 37 05 80
www.investinfrance.org

Réseau des Boutiques de Gestion
t 01 43 20 54 87
www.boutiques-de-gestion.com
(independent management shops that assist with business start-ups)

Trade Partners UK Information Centre
Kingsgate House, 66–74 Victoria Street
London Sw1E 6SW
t (020) 7215 8000
www.tradepartners.gov.uk

Sale of Existing French Businesses

Demain
www.demain.fr

Chambers of Commerce and Industry

Franco-British Chamber of Commerce and Industry
31 rue Boissy d'Anglas, 75008 Paris
t 01 53 30 81 32
www.francobritishchamber.com

References

French Chamber of Commerce in Great Britain
21 Dartmouth St
London SW1H 9BP
t (020) 7304 4040
www.ccfgb.co.uk

American Chamber of Commerce in Paris
156 bd Haussmann
75008 Paris
t 01 56 43 45 67
www.amchamfrance.org

Assemblée des Chambres Françaises de Commerce et d'Industrie (ACFIE)
45 av d'Iéna
75116 Paris
t 01 40 46 37 00
www.lille.cci.fr/ccis.index.html

Chambres de Métiers

Assemblée Permanente des Chambres de Métiers (APCM)
12 av Marceau
75008 Paris
t 01 44 43 10 00
www.apcm.fr

Department of Work

Direction Départementale du Travail, de l'Emploi et de la Formation Professionnelle de Paris
109 rue Montmartre
75084 Paris
t 01 44 76 69 30
(call for local departments)

Grant Aid

Délégation à l'Aménagement de Territoire et à l'Action Régionale (DATAR)
1 av Charles Floquet
75007 Paris
t 01 40 65 12 34
and

21–24 Grosvenor Place,
London SW1X 7HU
t (020) 7823 1895
www.datar.gouv.fr
www.investinfrance.org

Insurance

Centre de Documentation et d'Information de l'Assurance (CDIA)
26 bd Haussmann
75009 Paris
t 01 42 46 13 13
www.ffra.com

Commission de Contrôle des Assurances
54 rue de Châteaudun
75009 Paris
t 01 55 07 41 41

Fédération Françaises des Sociétés d'Assurance (FFSA)
26 bd Haussmann
75009 Paris
t 01 42 47 90 00

Lawyers

John Howell & Co (author of this book)
Solicitors & International Lawyers
22 Endell St
London WC2H 9AD
t (020) 7420 0400
www.europelaw.com

French Lawyer
22 Cassland Rd
London E9 7AN
t (0)845 644 3061
www.french-lawyer.com

Holman Fenwick and Willan
Marlow House
Lloyds Ave
London EC3N 3AL
t (020) 7488 2300

International Property Law Centre
Unit 2 Waterside Park
Livingstone Rd
Hessle
Yorkshire HU13 0EG
t 01482 350850
www.maxgold.com

Lefèvre Pelletier et Associés
136 av des Champs-Elysées
75008 Paris
t 01 53 93 30 00
www.lpalaw.com.fr

Prettys Solicitors
Elm House
25 Elm St
Ipswich
Suffolk IP1 2AD
t (01473) 232121
www.prettys.co.ik

Stephenson Harwood
1 St Paul's Churchyard
London EC7M 8SH
t (020) 7329 4422

Loans

France Initiative Réseau
14 rue Délambre
75014 Paris
t 01 40 64 10 20
www.fir.asso.fr
(advice on where to look for loans)

Micro Credits
www.adie.org
(an EU-backed loan scheme for very small businesses)

Subsidies in France
www.subsidies-in-france.com
(helps businesses get subsidies and loans)

Templeton Associates
t (01225) 422282 (UK)
t 05 58 41 74 33 (France)
www.templeton-france.com

Professional/Industrial Organisations

Conseil National des Professions de l'Automobile (CNPA)
50 rue Rouget de L'Isle
92158 Suresnes
t 01 40 99 55 00

Union des Métiers des Industries de l'Hôtellerie (UMIH)
22 rue Anjou
75008 Paris
t 01 44 94 19 94
www.umih.fr

Rural

Centre National des Jeunes Argiculteurs (CNJA)
14 rue do la Boétie
75008 Paris
t 01 42 65 17 51
www.cnja.com

Fédération Nationale des Sociétés d'Aménagement Foncier et d'Establissement Rural (FNSAFER)
91 rue de Faubourg St-Honoré
75008 Paris
t 01 44 69 86 00
www.frenchland.com/www.safer.fr

Terres d'Europe
3 rue de Turin
75008 Paris
t 01 44 69 86 10
www.safer-fr.com

SMEs (PMEs)

Confédération Générale des Petites et Moyennes Entreprises (CGPME)
10 terrasse Bellini
92806 Puteaux
t 01 47 62 73 73

British Consular Services in France

The five British Consulates General in France are in Paris, Bordeaux, Lille, Lyon and Marseille. The one in Paris provides full consular services, including passport and visa services. The others provide general consular assistance to British nationals, as well as legalisation and notarial services and voter registration information. All of them also provide a range of commercial services.

For more information and emergency contact numbers go to **www.britishembassy.gov.uk** or **www.britishinfrance.com**.

British Consulate-General in Paris
18bis rue d'Anjou, 75008 Paris
t 01 44 51 31 00
Open Mon, Wed, Thurs and Fri 9.30–12.30 and 2.30–5; Tues 9.30–4.30

Covers Aube, Calvados, Cher, Côtes-du-Nord, Essonne Eure, Eure-et-Loir, Finistère, Ille-et-Vilaine, Indre, Indre-et-Loire, Loir-et-Cher, Loire, Loire-Atlantique, Loiret, Maine-et-Loire, Manche (St-Lô), Marne, Haute-Marne, Mayenne, Meurthe-et-Moselle, Meuse, Morbihan, Moselle, Nievre, Oise, Orne, Bas-Rhin, Haut-Rhin, Sarthe, Paris (Seine), Hauts-de-Seine, Seine-St-Denis, Seine-Maritime, Seine-et-Marne, Val de Marne, Val d'Oise, Vendée, Vosges, Yonne, Yvelins, French Guiana, Guadeloupe, Martinique, New Caledonia and Tahiti.

British Consulate-General in Bordeaux
353 bd du président Wilson, 33073 Bordeaux
t 05 57 22 21 10
Open Mon–Fri 9am–noon and 2–5

Covers Ariège, Aveyron, Charente, Charente-Maritime, Corrèze, Creuse, Dordogne, Haute-Garonne, Gers, Gironde, Landes, Lot, Lot-et-Garonne, Pyrénées-Atlantiques, Hautes-Pyrénées, Deux-Sèvres, Tarn, Tarn-et-Garonne, Vienne and Haute-Vienne.

British Consulate-General in Lille
11 square Dutilleul, 59800 Lille
t 03 20 12 82 72
Open Mon–Fri 9.30–12.30 and 2–5

Covers Nord, Pas-de-Calais, Somme, Aisne and Ardennes.

British Consulate-General in Lyon
24 rue Childebert, 69002 Lyon
t 04 72 77 81 70
Open Mon–Fri 9–12.30 and 2–5.30

Covers Auvergne, Bourgogne, Franche-Comté and Rhône-Alpes.

British Consulate-General in Marseille
24 av du Prado, 13006 Marseille
t 04 91 15 72 10
Open Mon–Fri 9–noon and 2–5

Covers Alpes-de-Haute-Provence, Alpes-Maritimes, Aude, Bouches du Rhône, Corsica, Gard, Hautes-Alpes, Hérault, Lozère, Monaco, Pyrénées-Orientales, Var and Vaucluse.

French Telephone Codes

The French have eliminated area codes, giving everyone a 10-digit telephone number; even if you are within the same region as the number you are calling, you must dial all 10 digits. The regional prefixes are: Paris and Ile de France 01; Northwest 02; Northeast 03; Southeast and Corsica 04; Southwest 05.

Regional Climate

Average Temperatures, °Centigrade (daily maximum and minimum), and Rainfall (monthly mm)

	Jan	Feb	Mar	Apr	May	June	July	Aug	Sept	Oct	Nov	Dec
Le Havre												
max	6	6	8	10	13	16	18	19	17	14	9	7
min	4	3	6	7	11	13	16	16	14	11	7	5
rainfall	14	10	12	11	11	9	9	9	11	12	12	13
Carcassonne												
Max	9	11	14	16	19	24	28	28	24	18	13	10
Min	2	3	4	6	10	13	15	15	12	9	5	3
rainfall	76	64	66	66	71	66	53	58	71	86	89	86
Lyon												
max	6	8	12	14	19	23	27	26	22	16	10	7
min	1	1	3	6	10	14	16	16	12	8	4	2
rainfall	43	41	51	61	76	79	66	79	76	86	69	51
Corsica												
max	13	13	14	17	21	24	27	28	26	22	17	14
min	4	4	6	7	11	14	17	17	15	12	8	5
rainfall	74	64	61	53	41	23	8	15	43	91	102	84
Nice												
max	13	13	14	16	19	23	26	27	24	20	16	13
min	6	6	8	9	13	17	19	20	17	13	9	6
rainfall	76	74	74	64	48	38	18	30	66	112	117	89

	Jan	Feb	Mar	Apr	May	June	July	Aug	Sept	Oct	Nov	Dec
Paris												
max	6	7	11	14	18	21	24	24	21	15	9	7
min	1	1	3	6	9	12	14	14	11	8	4	2
rainfall	20	16	18	17	16	14	13	12	14	17	17	19
Strasbourg												
max	4	6	11	14	19	22	24	24	21	14	8	5
min	-1	-1	2	4	9	12	14	13	11	7	2	0
rainfall	36	33	36	46	66	74	76	71	61	51	48	3

Source: USA Today/US Met Office

Départements

France is divided into 22 regions (see p.238) and 95 départements.
Départements 91–95 are part of the Ile-de-France region, which also includes metropolitan Paris (75), Seine-et-Marne (77) and Yvelines (78).

01	Ain	25	Doubs	50	Manche
02	Aisne	26	Drôme	51	Marne
03	Allier	27	Eure	52	Haute-Marne
04	Alpes-de-Haute-Provence	28	Eure-et-Loir	53	Mayenne
		29	Finistère	54	Meurthe-et-Moselle
05	Hautes-Alpes	30	Gard		
06	Alpes-Maritimes	31	Haute-Garonne	55	Meuse
07	Ardèche	32	Gers	56	Morbihan
08	Ardennes	33	Gironde	57	Moselle
09	Ariège	34	Hérault	58	Nièvre
10	Aube	35	Ille-et-Vilaine	59	Nord
11	Aude	36	Indre	60	Oise
12	Aveyron	37	Indre-et-Loire	61	Orne
13	Bouches-du-Rhône	38	Isère	62	Pas-de-Calais
14	Calvados	39	Jura	63	Puy-de-Dôme
15	Cantal	40	Landes	64	Pyrénées-Atlantiques
16	Charente	41	Loir-et-Cher		
17	Charente-Maritime	42	Loire	65	Hautes-Pyrénées
18	Cher	43	Haute-Loire	66	Pyrénées-Orientales
19	Corrèze	44	Loire-Atlantique	67	Bas-Rhin
20	Corse	45	Loiret	68	Haut-Rhin
21	Côte-d'Or	46	Lot	69	Rhône
22	Côtes-d'Armor	47	Lot-et-Garonne	70	Haute-Saône
23	Creuse	48	Lozère	71	Saône-et-Loire
23	Dordogne	49	Maine-et-Loire	72	Sarthe

73	Savoie	81	Tarn	89	Yonne
74	Haute-Savoie	82	Tarn-et-Garonne	90	Territoire de Belfort
75	Paris	83	Var	91	Essonne
76	Seine-Maritime	84	Vaucluse	92	Hauts-de-Seine
77	Seine-et-Marne	85	Vendée	93	Seine-Saint-Denis
78	Yvelines	86	Vienne	94	Val-de-Marne
79	Deux-Sèvres	87	Haute-Vienne	95	Val-d'Oise
80	Somme	88	Vosges		

Largest Cities

Paris, home to more than 2 million people and some of the most visited and recognised monuments on the planet, is at the centre stage of western civilisation. Like the world's two other truly cosmopolitan corners (London and New York), this is not merely a place where you make your home – it becomes part of the description of who you are. The inhabitants who are not artists are the bankers, entrepreneurs and specialists charged with powering the nation's economy. The average Parisian seems to exhibit higher doses of snobbery and chauvinism than most of us are accustomed to (or are willing to accommodate), yet he or she makes a stimulating and informed conversationalist.

Paris is a healthily competitive environment. You wouldn't want to be caught in a public place without adequate grooming, and you wouldn't want to enter a debate without having first shaped your opinions on current events and history. Like it or not, Paris pushes you to be better – or, as some might phrase it, 'to be more Parisian'.

It may have a reputation as a dangerous and rather seedy port, but **Marseille** – France's second biggest city, with more than 800,000 inhabitants – is experiencing a renaissance. The former Greek colony flourished during the Crusades and its Mediterranean port eventually marked the entrance point for countless foreign immigrants – Algerians, Jews, Turks and Italians – who have since become part of the country's ethnic mix. But after the 18th century it fell on hard times. An ambitious public works campaign has kicked off to restore hundreds of historic buildings and give the city a much-needed facelift.

Besides the sheer drama of the setting of **Lyon**, located in the Rhône Valley and boasting about 445,000 inhabitants, the city is prized as a – if not *the* – gastronomic capital of France. Meanwhile, thanks to an excellent university and its energetic 20-something population, **Toulouse** to the southwest – home to just over 400,000 people – is one of the most exciting places to live in France. This distinctive city is a business and commercial centre and an important crossroads for the south.

On the Côte d'Azur, **Nice** – with about 335,000 people – was part of Italy until 1860 and its Italian heart still beats strong. The Promenade des Anglais, the beachfront walk, is named after the many English visitors who took time off in Nice. There are very few places where you can swim in clear blue water just a few steps away from a bustling metropolis – Nice is one of them.

Only 50km from the Atlantic Ocean, vibrant, inspiring **Nantes** has a population of 280,000 who may well be the friendliest folk in France, including many students. After growing rich on the slave trade, it fell back on the sugar refinery business and is still home to many famous biscuit factories, although these days it's also attracting many hi-tech industries.

Strasbourg, the gorgeous regional capital of Alsace in eastern France, is an important EU headquarters with a historic centre that is remarkably well preserved given that most of France's troubles poured in from the east over the Rhine riverbanks. Now this city hosts thousands of students and EU workers among its population of 270,000, and bustles with restaurants and museums. Many foreigners live in the corridor of trellised countryside that extends south of Strasbourg to Colmar along the Vosges.

National and Local Holidays

1 Jan	*Nouvel An* or *Jour de l'An*. Late-night revelling on 31 Dec (*St-Sylvestre*) is usually followed by family dinners on New Year's Day. Relatives and friends call and small gifts may be exchanged. If you have a doorman (*concierge*) this is a good time to give him a tip (*étrennes*).
Easter Monday	*Lundi de Pâques*. Good Friday is not a national holiday but Easter Monday is. This is another excuse for family reunions and the consumption of huge amounts of food.
1 May	*Fête du Travail*. International Labour Day in France is associated with the traditional exchange of lily of the valley (*muguet*), sold in bunches or small terracotta pots and exchanged as a symbol of good luck and friendship.
8 May	*Fête de la Libération* or *Victoire* (French Liberation Day 1945). Elaborate street parades are staged throughout France.
Ascension Day	*L'Ascension*. Christian holiday.
Whitsun	*La Pentecôte*. Christian holiday.
14 July	*Le Quatorze Juillet* (Bastille Day). The mother of all French holidays, ending with a spectacular firework display. Parties and parades start the night before to build momentum.
15 Aug	*L'Assomption* (Assumption). This Christian holiday is otherwise known as the beginning of the end of summer. Offices close and people head to the beaches or the mountains to escape the heat – working is considered criminal.

1 Nov	*La Toussaint* (All Saints' Day). A holiday now overshadowed by Halloween, celebrated the night before; French kids dress up in scary costumes and carve pumpkins into jack-o'-lanterns. On 2 Nov (All Souls' Day) it is customary to visit the graves of deceased relatives.
11 Nov	*Fête de l'Armistice* (Armistice Day). The equivalent of Veterans' Day.
25 Dec	*Noël* (Christmas). *Le Réveillon* on 24th is the traditional Christmas dinner.

In addition to these 11 national holidays, most cities and towns celebrate their own saint day, when local banks, schools and public offices are closed. When a holiday falls on a Tuesday or Thursday, it is tagged onto a weekend by taking off the Monday or Friday too; the four-day block is known as *le pont* ('bridge').

Further Reading

Reference

Applefield, David, *Paris Inside Out*
Barbour, Philippe, Dana Facaros and Michael Pauls, *France*
Hampshire, David, *Living and Working in France*
Igoe, Mark, and John Howell, *Buying a Property: France*
Link, Terry, *Adapter Kit France*
Platt, Polly, *French or Foe?*
Pybus, Victoria, *Live & Work in France*
Reilly, Saskia, and Lorin David Kalisky, *Living, Studying, and Working in France*
Steele, Ross, *The French Way*
Welty Rochefort, Harriet, *French Toast*

History

Ardagh, John, *France in the New Century*
Ardagh, John, *Cultural Atlas of France*
Barzini, Luigi, *The Europeans*
Braudel, Fernand, *The Identity of France*
Briggs, Robin, *Early Modern France: 1560–1715*
Buisseret, D. J., *Henry IV*
Cézanne, Paul, *Letters*
Cobb, Richard, *The French and their Revolution*
Cronin, Vincent, *Louis XIV*
Cronin, Vincent, *Napoleon*
Gilot, Françoise, *Life with Picasso*
Gramont, Sanche de, *The French: Portrait of a People*

Gregory of Tours, *The History of the Franks*
Hibbert, Christopher, *The French Revolution*
Keegan, John, *The First World War* and *The Second World War*
Knecht, R. J., *Catherine de' Medici*
Knecht, R. J., *The Rise and Fall of Renaissance France*
Mitford, Nancy, *The Sun King*
Pope Hennessy, James, *Aspects of Provence*
Price, Roger, *A Concise History of France*
Schama, Simon, *Citizens*
Madame de Sévigné, *Selected Letters*
Seward, Desmond, *The Hundred Years War*
Tapié, V. L., *France in the Age of Louis XIII and Richelieu*
Todd, Emmanuel, *The Making of Modern France*
Van Gogh, Vincent, *Collected Letters of Vincent Van Gogh*
Warner, Marina, *Joan of Arc: The Image of Female Heroism*
Weber, Eugene, *Paris 1900*
Weir, Alison, *Eleanor of Aquitaine*
Whitfield, Sarah, *Fauvism*
Wright, Gordon, *France in Modern Times*
Zeldin, Theodore, *France 1845–1945*
Zeldin, Theodore, *The French*

Literature and Travel

Atkinson, Patricia, *The Ripening Sun*
Balzac, Honoré de, *Lost Illusions*
Barnes, Julian, *Cross-Channel*
Camus, Albert, *L'Etranger*
Camus, Albert, *La Peste*
Daudet, Alphonse, *Letters from my Windmill*
Dickens, Charles, *A Tale of Two Cities*
Dumas, Alexandre, *The Count of Monte-Cristo*
Dumas, Alexandre, *The Man in the Iron Mask*
Dumas, Alexandre, *The Three Musketeers*
Faulks, Sebastian, *Birdsong*
Fitzgerald, F. Scott, *Tender is the Night*
Flaubert, Gustave, *Madame Bovary*
Giono, Jean, *To the Slaughterhouse, Two Riders of the Storm*
Hemingway, Ernest, *A Moveable Feast*
Hugo, Victor, *The Hunchback of Notre-Dame*
Hugo, Victor, *Les Misérables*
Ionesco, Eugène, *La Leçon*
James, Henry, *Collected Travel Writings*
Lamorisse, Albert, *The Red Balloon*

Leroux, Gaston, *The Phantom of the Opera*
Maupassant, Guy de, *Selected Short Stories*
Mayle, Peter, *Hotel Pastis*
Mayle, Peter, *Toujours Provence*
Mayle, Peter, *A Year in Provence*
Pagnol, Marcel, *Jean de Florette* and *Manon of the Springs*
Proust, Marcel, *Remembrance of Things Past*
Rosenblum, Mort, *The Secret Life of the Seine*
Rostand, Edmond, *Cyrano de Bergerac*
Royle, Nicholas (editor), *The Time Out Book of Paris Short Stories*
Saint-Exupéry, Antoine de, *Le Petit Prince*
Sartre, Jean-Paul, *Essays in Existentialism*
Sartre, Jean-Paul, *Truth and Existence*
Smollett, Tobias, *Travels through France and Italy*
Turnbull, Sarah, *Almost French*
Verne, Jules, *Around the World in 80 Days*
Verne, Jules, *Paris in the 20th Century*
Wharton, Edith, *A Motor-Flight Through France*
Wylie, Laurence, *Village in the Vaucluse*
Zola, Émile, *Germinal*

Dictionary of Useful and Technical Terms

abonnement	standing charge, or magazine subscription
accueil	reception, welcome
acompte	deposit
acquérir	to buy, acquire
acte authentique	legal paper drawn up (with all due formalities), by a public officer empowered by law (e.g. a *notaire*) in the place where s/he officiates
acte de commerce	commercial act
acte de vente	a conveyance or transfer of land (sometimes referred to as *acte d'achat*)
acte sous seing privé	private agreement in writing with no witnesses (the pre-sale agreement)
actuellement	currently
affaire	bargain/business
agence immobilière	estate agent
Agence Nationale Pour l'Emploi (ANPE)	National Employment Office
agence	agency
agrandissement	extension, enlargement
agréé	registered
alimentation	supply (water, electricity, etc.), food

aménagé	converted
ancien	old
antenne	aerial, antenna
antenne parabolique	satellite dish
arrhes	deposit, sum paid in advance by the purchaser, forfeited if purchaser withdraws or double the amount refunded if the vendor withdraws
artisan maçon	expert builder, mason
assurance complémentaire maladie	independent health insurance
atelier	workshop, studio
attestation	certificate
attestation d'acquisition	a notarial certificate that the property purchase has been completed
avocat	solicitor
bail	lease to tenant
balcon	balcony
banque	bank
bâtiment	building
béton	concrete
bois	wood
bon état	good condition
bord de mer/rivière	beside the sea/river
bureau	office
cabinet	small room
cadastre	local town planning register, or legal description of property deed
caisse des dépôts et consignations	deposits and consignment office
Caisse d'Epargne	savings bank
Caisse des Allocations Familiales	child benefit office
Caisse Nationale d'Assurance Vieillesse ou de Retraite	pensions office
Caisse Primaire d'Assurance Maladie	medical expenses office
campagne	country
carreleur	tiler
carte de paiement	payment card
carte de résident	resident's card
carte de santé	medical record book
carte de séjour	government permit to reside in France (also called *permis de séjour*)
carte grise	car registration
carte professionnelle	granted by the *préfecture* to estate agents to carry out business
carte verte	car insurance

Dictionary of Useful and Technical Terms

carte vitale	health card
cause réelle et sérieuse	legitimate cause
caution solidaire	guarantor
cave	cellar
centre commercial	shopping centre
centre des impôts	tax office
certificat d'urbanisme	zoning certificate (equivalent to a local authority search)
cession	sale
chambre	bedroom
chambre de métiers	chamber of trades
charges	maintenance charges on a property
charges comprises	service charges included
charges sociales	social charges
charpentier	carpenter
chaudière	water heater/boiler
chauffage	heating
chauffe-eau	hot water heater
chaumière	thatched cottage
chèque de banque	banker's draft
chiffre d'affaire	turnover
clause d'accroissement	(also see *tontine*) agreement that purchase is made for the benefit of the last surviving purchaser
clause pénale	penalty clause governing performance of an agreement
climatisation	air-conditioning
cloison	partition
code du travail	labour code
commerçant	commercial trader
commissariat de police	police station
comptabilité	accounting, book-keeping
compensable	the clearing of a cheque
comprenant	including
compromis de vente	contract for sale and purchase of land
compte à terme	deposit account
compte courant	current account
Compte d'Epargne Logement	home-buyers saving scheme
compte titre	shares account
concessionnaire	distributor
concours	selective entrance exam
condition suspensive	conditional terms stated in the pre-sale agreement (e.g. the acquiring of a loan, the gaining of a positive zoning certificate)
Conseil de Prud'homme	labour court
conservation des hypothèques	mortgage/land registry
constat à l'amiable	accident report form
constructible	land which is designated for building under local planning scheme

contrat à durée déterminée	fixed-term contract
contrat à durée indéterminée	permanent contract
contrat de réservation	the purchase contract used for purchase 'on plan' (sometimes called contract *préliminaire*)
contrat multirisques habitation	all risks household policy
contrôle technique	MOT
conventionné (médecin)	(doctor) working in the health service
conventions collectives	collective bargaining agreements
copie exécutoire	enforceable copy
copropriété	co-ownership
courtier	broker
cuisine	kitchen
dallage	paving
déclaration de sincérité	compulsory formula providing that the purchase price has not been increased by a counter-deed
dépendance	outbuilding
dépôt de vente	sale room
devis	estimate
distributeur automatique de billets	cash machine, ATM
domicile fiscal	tax address
droit au bail	right to a lease
droit de préemption	pre-emptive right to acquire the property instead of purchaser
droit de succession/donation	inheritance/gift tax
ébéniste	cabinet maker
échafaudage	scaffolding
échelle	ladder
éclairage	lighting
écurie	stable
EDF/GDF	the state utilities: *Electricité/Gaz de France*
émoluments	the scale of charges of the notaire
emplacement	site
emprunt	loan
encadrement	framing
enregistrement (droits d')	registration of the title of ownership (following which are the payment of transfer duties)
entreprise individuelle	one-person business
entreprise unipersonnelle	one-person limited company
entretien	maintenance
épaisseur	thickness
équipé	equipped
escalier	stair
espace	space
espèces	cash
établi	work bench

Dictionary of Useful and Technical Terms

étage	storey, floor
étagère	shelf
étanche	watertight
état des lieux	schedule of condition or schedule of dilapidation depending on whether it applies to the beginning or end of a lease
expédition	the certified copy of a notarial document showing the date of its registration and the registration duty paid, or act of sending something
expert comptable	chartered accountant
expert foncier	professional to check on the state and value of the property (usually an architect)
expertiser	to value a property, to appraise by expert
facture	invoice/bill
faillite	bankruptcy
faute grave	serious fault
ferme	farm
finitions	finishings
FNAIM – Fédération Nationale des Agents Immobiliers	national association of estate agents, providing a compensation fund for defaulting agents
Fonds Commun de Placement	unit trusts
fonds de commerce	business plus goodwill
fonds de roulement	capital supplied by all flat-owners, in an apartment block, on top of service charges to meet unexpected liabilities
forfait	fixed amount
fosse septique	septic tank
frais de dossier	arrangement fee
frais de notaire	notary's fee
franchisé	franchisee
franchiseur	franchisor
garantie d'achèvement	guarantee of completion
gardien	caretaker
Gendarmerie Nationale	state police
géomètre	surveyor appointed by the *notaire* to certify the dimensions of the property according to the *cadastre*
gérant	legal manager
grange	barn
Greffe du Tribunal de Commerce	clerk of the commercial court
grenier	attic
guichet	counter, ticket office
honoraires libres	any amount above the recommended social security fee

HT – hors-taxe	not including sales tax
huissier	has many official duties, including bailiff and process server; is used to record evidence (for example on the state of property) where legal proceedings are considered
hypothèque	mortgage – where the property is used as security for the loan
impôt foncier	land tax
indemnité d'éviction	compensation for eviction
indivision	joint ownership
isolation	insulation
jardin	garden
jouissance	right of possession which must occur simultaneously with the transfer of ownership
lavabo	washbasin
lettre de change	bill of exchange
lettre de non-gage	letter showing there are no outstanding debts attached
livraison	delivery
livret A, B jeune or CODEVI	savings accounts
location	renting (tenancy)
logement	accommodation
loi Carrez	law by which property measurements are certified
loi Scrivener	the law protecting borrowers from French lenders and sellers on French property purchases in all cases other than a purchase on plan
longueur	length
lotissement	housing estate
lots	land registry plots applied in apartment blocks
maçon	builder, mason
mairie	town hall
maison de campagne	country house
maison de maître	gentleman's house
maison mère	parent company
mandat	power of attorney, proxy
mandat de recherche	private agreement giving power to estate agent to look for property
manoir	manor house
marchand de biens	property dealer
mas	farmhouse (south of France)
mazout	heating oil (domestic use)
médecines douces	alternative medicine
médecin généraliste	GP (general practitioner)

médecin spécialiste	specialist
menuiserie	woodwork factory, shop
meubles	furniture
monuments historiques	listed buildings
mur	wall
mutuelle (complémentaire santé)	top-up health cover
niveau	level
notaire	notary
notaire public	notary public
nue-propriété	reversionary interest where the purchaser has no occupational rights over the property until the death or prior surrender of the live tenant
occupation	occupant of the premises (either tenant or occupant without good title)
offre d'achat/de vente	an offer to buy or sell property which is not itself a binding contract
ordonnance	prescription
Organismes de Placement de Capital en Valeurs Mobilières	unit trusts
pacte civil de solidarité (PACS)	formalisation of non-marital (including same-sex) relationships
paiement comptant	cash payment
paiement de notes de frais	benefit in kind
participation aux résultants	profit sharing
parties communes	common parts of buildings
parties privatives	parts of the building restricted to the private use of the owner
peinture	paint
pépinière	garden centre, nursery
perceuse	drill
permis de construire	planning permission, building permit
pharmacie de garde	chemist on duty
pièce	room
pierre	stone
piscine	swimming pool
placard	cupboard
plain pied	single storey
plan de financement	financing scheme
plan d'occupation des sols	zoning document
plomberie	plumbing
plus-value	capital gain realised on the sale of the property
Préfecture de Police	police headquarters
prélèvement	direct debit
prime à l'aménagement du territoire	regional selective assistance

prime de frais d'installation	settling in funds
prise	electric socket, plug
prise de terre	earth socket, plug with ground
privilège de prêteur de deniers	mortgage
promesse de vente	agreement to sell
promoteur immobilier	property developer
propriétaire	owner
propriété	property
quincaillerie	hardware shop
quotient familial	family quota (insurance)
rangements	storage space
redevance TV	TV licence
refait	restored
registre du commerce et des sociétés	registrar of companies
règlement national d'urbanisme	national town planning rules
rejeter	to bounce a cheque
relevé d'identité bancaire (RIB)	bank account details
rénové	renovated
répertoire des métiers	register of trade
réservation	the deposit paid in a *contrat de réservation*
réservation (contrat de)	type of contract for the purchase of property *état d'achèvement futur*
réservoir	cistern
résiliation	cancellation of a contract
responsabilité civile	public liability cover
restauré	renovated
retraite	retirement
revenu minimum d'insertion	income support
revêtement	surface, covering
rez-de-chaussée	ground floor
robinet	tap
SAFER	local government organisation to ensure the proper use of agricultural land; sometimes they hold pre-emptive rights to buy land
salle de bains	bathroom
salle de séjour	living room
salon	drawing room
SAMU (Service d'Aide Médicale d'Urgence)	emergency medical service
Sapeurs-Pompiers	fire brigade
sécurité sociale	social security
séjour (salle de)	living room
Service Mobile d'Urgence et de Réanimation	emergency medical unit

Dictionary of Useful and Technical Terms

société	legally registered company
société à responsabilité limitée (SARL)	limited liability company
société anonyme (SA)	company with limited shares
société civile (SC)	non-trading company
société civile immobilière	non-trading property company
société commerciale	commercial company
société d'investissement à capital variable	unit trust
société de fait	de facto company
société en commandite (SEC)	joint stock company
société en nom collectif (SNC)	general partnership company
sol	ground
sous seing privé	non registered deed
sous-sol	underground, basement
surface commerciale	commercial premises
syndicat de copropriétaires	assembly of co-owners
tacite reconduction	automatic renewal (of a contract or insurance policy)
tantième	proportion of the common parts of a *copropriété* owned jointly with other apartment owners
taxe d'habitation	rate levied on the occupation of property
taxe foncière	local tax on the ownership of property
taxe nationale	state tax
taxe professionnelle	business licence fee
terrain	grounds
testament	will
timbre fiscal	revenue stamp
titre de propriété	title deeds
toit	roof
toiture	roofing
tontine	joint ownership
tournevis	screwdriver
tout à l'égout	main drainage system
tribunal administratif	civil service court
tribunal de commerce	commercial court
troisième âge	senior citizens (old age pensioners)
TTC – toutes taxes comprises	including all tax and VAT
tuile	roof tile
TVA – taxe sur la valeur ajoutée	value added tax (VAT)
urgences	emergency units
usufruit	usufruct (right to use an asset)
vente en l'état futur d'achèvement	purchase of an un-built property
vestibule	entrance hall

vignette	fiscal stamp
virement bancaire	credit transfer
vue	view

Internet Vocabulary

You'll see a variety of terms for **e-mail address**; the official one is *courriel*, but you will also see *adresse électronique, email, e-mail, emél, mél* and *mail*. The e-mail system is *messagerie/courrier électronique*.

arobas	at sign (@)
barre/oblique	slash /
deux points	colon (:)
groupe de discussion	newsgroup, chat group
imprimer	to print
lien/hyperlien	link/hyperlink
mot de passe	password
moteur de recherche	search engine
navigateur/explorateur	browser
naviguer	browse, navigate
page d'accueil	home page
page web	web page
pièce jointe	attachment
point (point-com)	dot (dotcom)
rafraîchir	refresh, reload
redémarrer	reboot
se loguer	to log on
signet	bookmark
site web/site Internet	website
télécharger	download
tiret	hyphen
tout attaché/en un seul mot	all one word
tout en minuscules	all in lower case
www (trois double-vé)	World Wide Web

France touring atlas

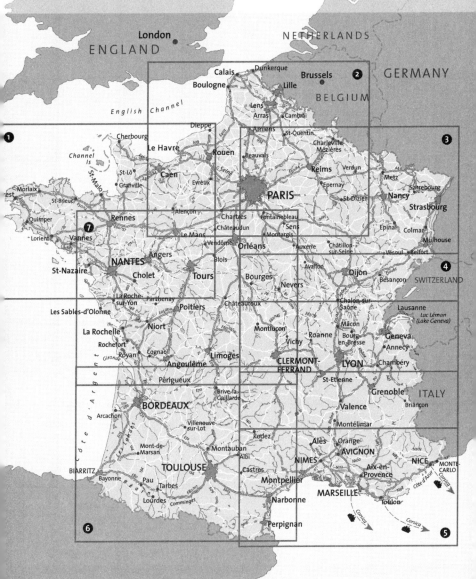

20 km
10 miles
N
Alderney
Guernsey
Sark
Channel Islands
Jersey
Trégastel
Ploumanach
Perros-Guirec
Ile de Bréhat
Pointe de l'Arcouest
Brignogan-Plages
Roscoff
Trébeurden
Pleumeur-Bodou
Lézardrieux
St-Pol-de-Léon
Lannion
Tréguier
Paimpol
l'Aber-Wrach
Plouescat
Locquirec
Carantec
St-Michel-en-G
Pontrieux
Plouha
Ile d'Ouessant
Lesneven
Morlaix
St-Quay-Portrieux
Sables-d'Or
Cap Fréhel
St-Briac
Dinard
Le Folgoët
Lampoul
Binic
Le Val-André
Erquy
St-Cast
Lancieux
E50
St-Thégonnec
Guingamp
Brest
Landerneau
Guimiliau
Les Rosaires
Pléneuf
St-Jacut
Châtelaudren
St-Laurent-de-la-Mer
Plancoët
Le Conquet
Elorn
785
Monts d'Arrée
St-Brieuc
Lamballe
Plougastel-Daoulas
Callac
Bulat-Pestivien
Pointe de St-Mathieu
764
Huelgoat
Quintin
Dinan
E60/165
E50/12
Camaret
Le Faou
Brennilis
St-Herbot
E401/176
Pointe de Penhir
Landévennec
Lannédern
Carhaix-Plouguer
CÔTES-D'ARMOR
Léhon
Morgat
Crozon
Ménez-Hom
FINISTÈRE
Moncontour
Cap de la Chèvre
Pleyben
164
T66
Rance
Châteaulin
Châteauneuf-du-Faou
Douarnenez
Mur-de-Bretagne
Montagnes Noires
Ile de Sein
Locronan
St-Aignan
Tréboul
Pointe du Raz
Audierne
Loudéac
Quimper
Le Faouët
Canal de Nantes
Comper
Penhors
Kernascléden
Pontivy
Forêt de Paimpont
Plonéour-Lanvern
Fouesnant
Tréhorenteuc
Paimpont
Pont-l'Abbé
E60/165
Blavet
Concarneau
Quimperlé
Bénodet
Quistinic
Josselin
Plélan-le-Grand
St-Guénolé
Loctudy
Pont-Aven
Riec
Scorff
24
Ploërmel
Pointe de Penmarch
Guilvinec
Moëlan
MORBIHAN
776
Pipriac
Hennebont
Lorient
166
Ste-Anne-d'Auray
Rochefort-en-Terre
Port-Louis
Groix
Etel
Ile de Groix
Erdeven
Auray
775
Redon
Vannes
Carnac
Locmariaquer
Vilaine
St-Pierre
Quiberon
La Roche-Bernard
Pénestin
Pontchâteau
Houat
Brière
St-Joachim
774
Bréca
Marsh
Ile-de-Fédrun
Guérande
St-André-des-Eaux
Hœdic
Le Croisic
Belle-Ile
Batz-sur-Mer
St-Nazaire
La Baule
St-Brévin
St-Michel-Chef-Chef
E60/213
Pornic
Noirmoutier
Ile de Noirmoutier
38
Fromentine
La Barre-de-Monts
Notre-Dame-de-Mont
Challans
St-Jean-de-Monts
Soullans
Port-Joinville
Ile d'Yeu
St-Hilaire-de-Riez
St-Gilles-Croix-de-Vie

2
20 km
10 miles
N
BELGIUM
Bray-Dunes
Leffrinckoucke
Bergues
Wormhout
Cassel
Hazebrouck
Tourcoing
Roubaix
Armentières
Lille
Bethune
Carvin
Hénin-Beaumont
St-Amand-les-Eaux
NORD
Notre-Dame-de-Lorette
Lens
Aubigny
Vimy
Douai
Denain
Valenciennes
Arras
Bavay
Maubeuge
Hautmont
Le Quesnoy
Cambrai
Caudry
Le Cateau
Ors
Avesnes
Givet
Meuse
Haybes
Fumay
Revin
Monthermé
Bapaume
Albert
Le Catelet
Bony
Bohain-en-V
St-Michel
Rocroi
Peronne
Corbie
St-Quentin
Guise
Vervins
Charleville-Mézières
A203/E44
Sedan
Crécy
Roye
Tergnier
Poix-Terron
Montdidier
Noyon
Chauny
Sissonne
ARDENNES
Mouzon
Avioth
Montmédy
AISNE
Laon
Maignelay-Montigny
Blérancourt
Coucy-le-Château
Rethel
Stenay
Filain
Craonne
Compiègne
Vendresse
Vouziers
Buzancy
Forêt de Compiègne
Pierrefonds
Soissons
Creil
Crépy-en-Valois
Villers-Cotterêts
Reims
Montfaucon d'Argonne
Senlis
Chantilly
Parc-Astérix
Nanteuil
Ermenonville
La Ferté-Milon
Marfaux
Pourcy
Verzenay
Verzy
Verdun
Hautvillers
Ay
Marne
Epernay
Château-Thierry
Ste-Menehould
MEUSE
Roissy
Tremblay
Meaux
La Ferté-s/s-Jouarre
MARNE
Châlons-en-Champagne
Vertus
N35 (Voie Sacrée)
Torcy
Disneyland Paris
Coulommiers
PARIS
Mondement-Montgivroux
Fère-Champenoise
Revigny
Bar-le-Duc
Ornain
Sézanne
Vitry-le-François
St-Dizier
SEINE-ET-MARNE
Corbeil-Essonnes
Provins
Lac de Der Chantecoq
Melun
Romilly
Aube
Wassy
Joinville
Forêt de Fontainebleau
Fontainebleau
AUBE
Lac du Temple
Brienne-le-Château
Cirey-sur-Blaise
Troyes
Lac d'Orient
Vignory
Nemours
Sens
Bar-sur-Aube
Clairvaux
Colombey-les-Deux-Eglises
Andelot
HAUTE-MARNE
Villeneuve-sur-Yonne
Bar-sur-Seine
Essoyes
Chaumont
Courtenay
Chaource
Montargis
Joigny
Les Riceys
Flogny
Arc-en-Barrois
3
3

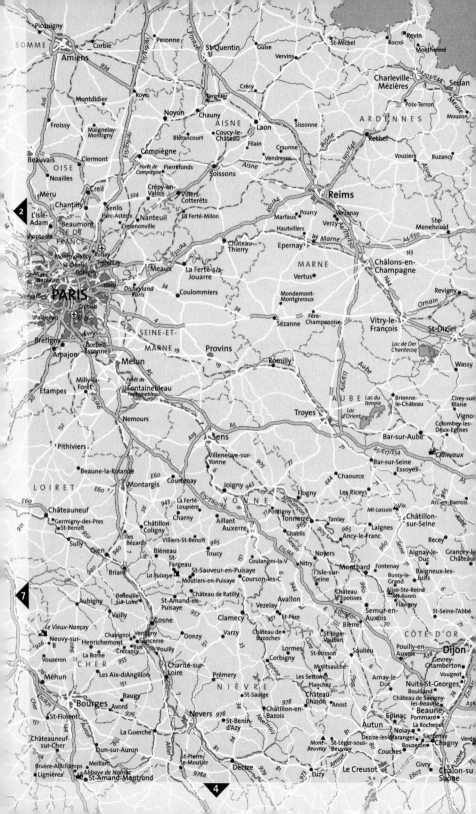

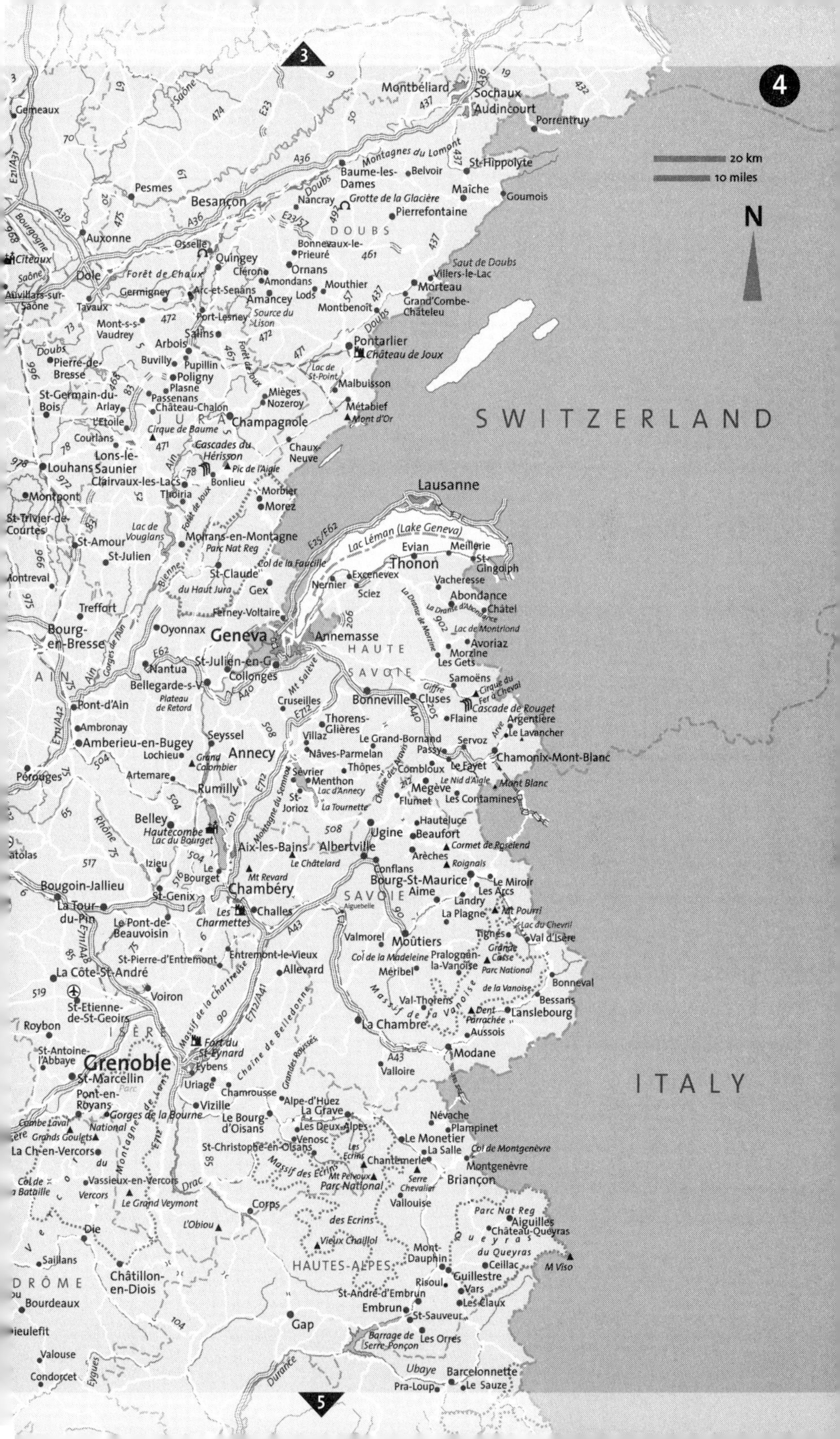
3
4
20 km
10 miles
N
SWITZERLAND
ITALY
Montbéliard
Sochaux
Audincourt
Porrentruy
St-Hippolyte
Maîche
Goumois
Belvoir
Baume-les-Dames
Montagnes du Lomont
Gemeaux
Pesmes
Besançon
Nancray
Grotte de la Glacière
Pierrefontaine
DOUBS
Auxonne
Osselle
Quingey
Bonnevaux-le-Prieuré
Cîteaux
Dole
Forêt de Chaux
Cléron
Ornans
Amondans
Mouthier
Saut de Doubs
Villers-le-Lac
Morteau
Grand'Combe-Châteleu
Aumont
Germigney
Arc-et-Senans
Amancey
Lods
Montbenoît
Auvillars-sur-Saône
Tavaux
Port-Lesney
Source du Lison
Mont-s-s-Vaudrey
Salins
Arbois
Pontarlier
Château de Joux
Pierre-de-Bresse
Buvilly
Pupillin
Poligny
Lac de St-Point
Malbuisson
St-Germain-du-Bois
Plasne
Passenans
Arlay
Château-Chalon
Mièges
Nozeroy
Métabief
Mont d'Or
L'Etoile
JURA
Champagnole
Cirque de Baume
Courlans
Lons-le-Saunier
Cascades du Hérisson
Pic de l'Aigle
Chaux-Neuve
Louhans
Clairvaux-les-Lacs
Bonlieu
Montpont
Thoiria
Morbier
Morez
Lausanne
St-Trivier-de-Courtes
Lac de Vouglans
Forêt de Joux
St-Amour
Moirans-en-Montagne
Parc Nat Reg
St-Julien
Lac Léman (Lake Geneva)
Evian
Meillerie
St-Gingolph
Thonon
Col de la Faucille
St-Claude
Excenevex
Nernier
Sciez
Vacheresse
Gex
du Haut Jura
Abondance
Châtel
Treffort
Ferney-Voltaire
La Dranse d'Abondance
Lac de Montriond
Oyonnax
Geneva
Annemasse
HAUTE
Avoriaz
Morzine
Les Gets
Bourg-en-Bresse
Nantua
St-Julien-en-G
Collonges
SAVOIE
Samoëns
AIN
Bellegarde-s-V
Mt Salève
Cirque du Fer à Cheval
Plateau de Retord
Cruseilles
Bonneville
Cluses
Cascade de Rouget
Pont-d'Ain
Thorens-Glières
Flaine
Argentière
Le Lavancher
Ambronay
Seyssel
Villaz
Le Grand-Bornand
Amberieu-en-Bugey
Annecy
Nâves-Parmelan
Passy
Servoz
Chamonix-Mont-Blanc
Lochieu
Grand Colombier
Pérouges
Sèvrier
Thônes
Combloux
Le Fayet
Artemare
Menthon
Lac d'Annecy
Chaîne des Aravis
Le Nid d'Aigle
Mont Blanc
Rumilly
Megève
St-Jorioz
La Tournette
Flumet
Les Contamines
Belley
Hautecombe
Lac du Bourget
Montagne du Semnoz
Hauteluce
Ugine
Beaufort
Rhône
Cormet de Roselend
Aix-les-Bains
Albertville
Le Châtelard
Arèches
Roignais
Izieu
Conflans
Le Bourget
Mt Revard
Bourg-St-Maurice
Le Miroir
Bougoin-Jallieu
Chambéry
Aime
Les Arcs
St-Genix
SAVOIE
Landry
La Tour-du-Pin
Les Charmettes
Challes
Aiguebelle
Mt Pourri
La Plagne
Le Pont-de-Beauvoisin
Lac du Chevril
Valmorel
Moûtiers
Tignes
Val d'Isère
St-Pierre-d'Entremont
Entremont-le-Vieux
Col de la Madeleine
Pralognan-la-Vanoise
Grande Casse
La Côte-St-André
Allevard
Méribel
Parc National de la Vanoise
Bonneval
Voiron
Massif de la Chartreuse
St-Etienne-de-St-Geoirs
Val-Thorens
Massif de la Vanoise
Bessans
Dent Parrachée
Lanslebourg
Roybon
ISÈRE
La Chambre
Aussois
Fort du St-Eynard
St-Antoine-l'Abbaye
Grenoble
Eybens
Chaîne de Belledonne
Modane
St-Marcellin
Uriage
Valloire
Pont-en-Royans
Chamrousse
Grandes Rousses
Alpe-d'Huez
Vizille
La Grave
Gorges de la Bourne
Névache
Combe Laval
Grands Goulets
National
Le Bourg-d'Oisans
Les Deux-Alpes
Plampinet
Venosc
Le Monetier
La Ch-en-Vercors
du
Montagne de Lans
St-Christophe-en-Oisans
Les Ecrins
La Salle
Col de Montgenèvre
Chantemerle
Montgenèvre
Col de la Bataille
Vassieux-en-Vercors
Massif des Ecrins
Mt Pelvoux
Serre Chevalier
Briançon
Vercors
Le Grand Veymont
Drac
Parc National
Vallouise
Corps
Parc Nat Reg
Aiguilles
L'Obiou
des Ecrins
Château-Queyras
Die
Queyras
Vieux Chaillol
Mont-Dauphin
du Queyras
Saillans
HAUTES-ALPES
Ceillac
M Viso
Châtillon-en-Diois
Guillestre
DRÔME
Risoul
Vars
St-André-d'Embrun
Bourdeaux
Les Claux
Embrun
St-Sauveur
Gap
Dieulefit
Barrage de Serre-Ponçon
Les Orres
Valouse
Durance
Ubaye
Barcelonnette
Condorcet
Eygues
Pra-Loup
Le Sauze
5

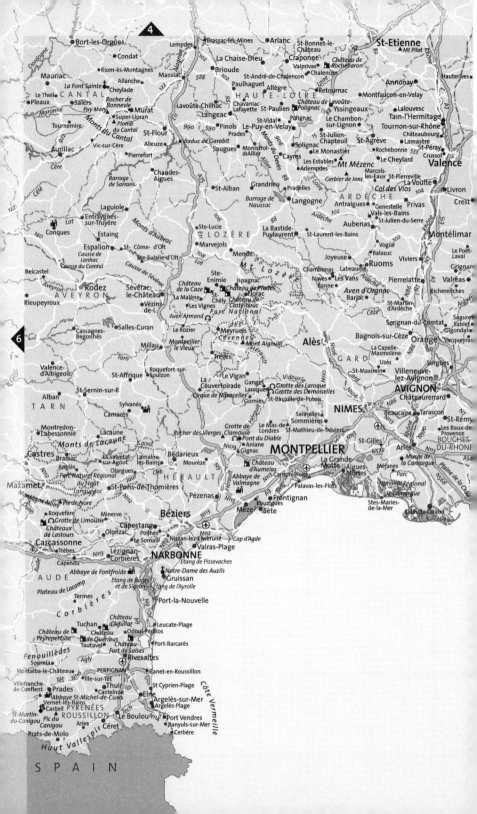

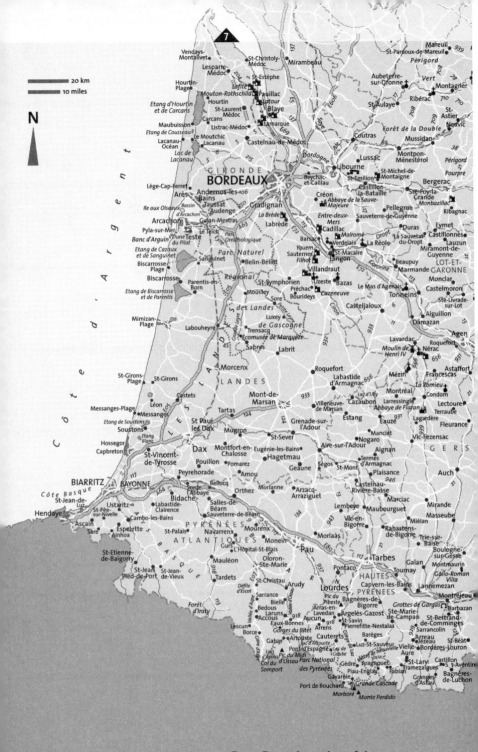

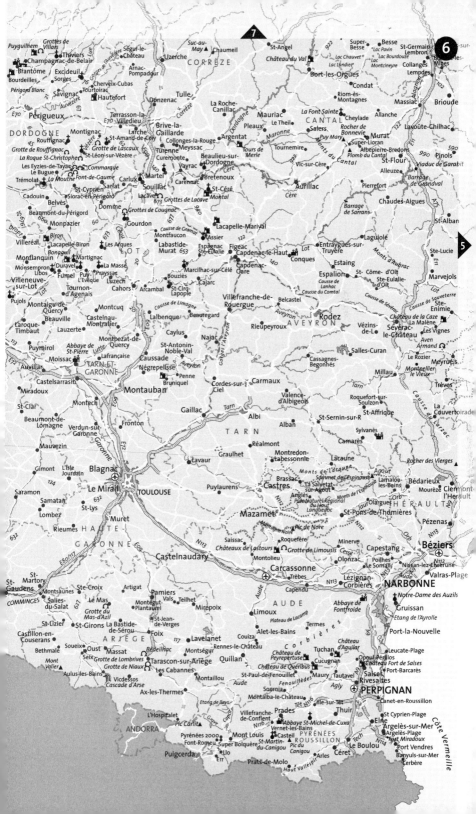

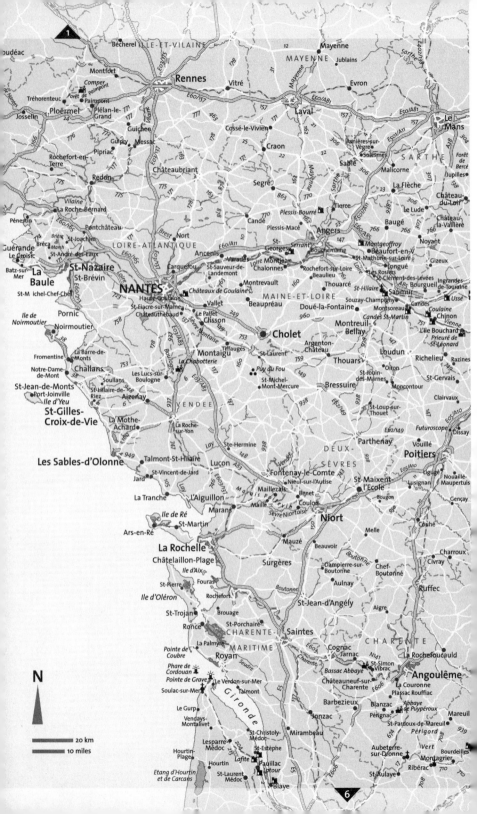

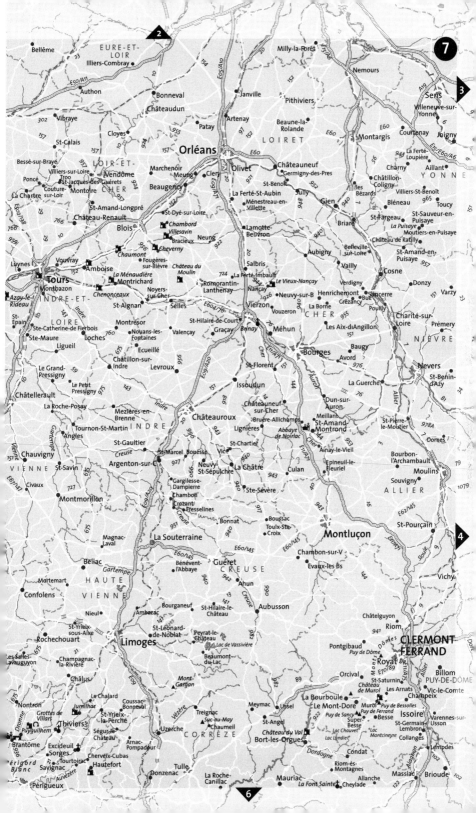

Appendices

Sample CV in French Format 276
Sample Job Application Letter 277
Helpful Words and Phrases 278

Sample CV in French Format

Lucy Evans
31 avenue du Général de Gaulle
73100 Aix-les-Bains
04 78 89 60 23

Née le 21 Novembre 1974
Célibataire

EXPERIENCE PROFESSIONNELLE

2003 to date	Responsable du marketing chez *European Communication*, Aix-les-Bains, centre de formation continue pour la communication et le marketing au sein des pays européens
2001–2003	Chargée du développement d'un nouveau site Internet, service des ventes et du marketing, *Communication & Marketing Publications* Ltd, Basingstoke, Grande-Bretagne
1999–2000	Assistante de marketing, *Smith Banking Services*, Londres, Grande-Bretagne
1998	Stage de formation: deux semaines au sein du service marketing de *Colgate Palmolive UK Ltd*, Guilford, Grande-Bretagne

ETUDES ET FORMATION

1993–1998	B.Sc. (≈ Licence) en Sciences Économiques, London School of Economics
1992	A Levels (≈ deuxième partie du Baccalauréat): Mathématiques, Physique, Économie, Histoire
1990	GCSEs (≈ première partie du Baccalauréat): Mathématiques, Physique, Biologie, Chimie, Commerce, Anglais, Français, Espagnol, Histoire, Géographie

COMPETENCES LINGUISTIQUES

Français courant (lu, parlé et écrit)
Bon niveau en Espagnol (lu et écrit)

COMPETENCES INFORMATIQUES

Très bonne maîtrise de l'outil informatique (Mac et PC): MS Office, Adobe Creative Suite, Dreamweaver.

DIVERS

Permis de conduire
Intérêt pour le cinéma et les voyages

Sample Job Application Letter

Lucy Evans
31 avenue du Général de Gaulle
73100 Aix-les-Bains

        M. Jean-Pierre Durand
        Responsable des ressources humaines
        International Communication Centre
        25 rue Diderot
        69002 Lyon

        Aix-les-Bains, le 3 Décembre 2005

Monsieur,

Suite à votre annonce, parue dans *Le Monde* du mercredi 24 novembre, je souhaite poser ma candidature au poste de responsable du marketing pour lequel vous recrutez actuellement.

Installée en France depuis 2003, je suis responsable du marketing chez European Communication, un centre de formation continue spécialisé dans les stages de communication et de marketing pour les entreprises françaises qui travaillent en étroite collaboration avec d'autres pays européens, essentiellement la Grande-Bretagne et l'Allemagne. Après plus de deux ans au sein de European Communication, je suis prête pour un nouveau défi et, connaissant l'excellente réputation de votre entreprise dans la region, je trouverais la possibilité de faire partie de votre équipe particulièrement motivante.

Je pense posséder les qualifications et les compétences requises pour le poste, comme vous pourrez le constater au vu de mon curriculum vitae. Je me tiens bien entendu à votre entière disposition si vous souhaitez me rencontrer.

Vous remerciant d'avance de l'attention que vous voudrez bien porter à ma candidature, je vous adresse, monsieur, mes salutations distinguées.

Avec mes remerciements anticipés pour l'attention que vous voudrez bien porter à ma candidature, veuillez agréer, Monsieur, l'expression de mes salutations distinguées.

Lucy Evans

p.j.: curriculum vitae

Helpful Words and Phrases

Words to Help You to Prepare Your CV

Situation personnelle et état civil (personal information), **nom de famille** (last name), **prénom** (first name), **adresse** (address), **numéro de téléphone** (telephone number), **bureau** (office telephone), **domicile** (home telephone), **portable** (mobile), **adresse électronique** (e-mail), **nationalité** (nationality), **âge** (age), **situation de famille** (marital status and number of children), **célibataire** (single), **marié(e)** (married), **divorcé(e)** (divorced), **veuf/veuve** (widowed), **projets professionnels** or **objectifs** (objectives), **expérience professionnelle** (professional experience), **formation** (education), **langues** (languages), **bonnes connaissances** (conversant), **lu, écrit, parlé** (proficient), **courant** (fluent), **bilingue** (bilingual), **langue maternelle** (mother tongue), **connaissances linguistiques et informatiques** (language and computer skills), **informatique** (IT), **divers** (miscellaneous), **passe-temps** (interests), **loisirs** (leisure activities), **activités personnelles/extra-professionnelles** (hobbies).

Basic Phrases for Covering Letters

Je me réfère à votre annonce With reference to your advertisement
Je me permets de poser ma candidature au poste de... I wish to apply for the post of...
J'aimerais changer de situation I would like to change jobs
J'aimerais pratiquer davantage... I would like to make better use of...
Ma formation de... My training as...
Mon expérience de... My experience in...
Je vous prie de bien vouloir me faire savoir Please let me know
Je vous serais très reconnaissant e) I would be very grateful
Je vous prie de bien vouloir m'envoyer des renseignements plus complets sur le poste de... Please send more information regarding the position of...
Je vous prie de bien vouloir me faire savoir s'il me serait possible d'obtenir un emploi dans votre entreprise Please let me know if there is work available in your company
Je vous prie d'avoir l'obligeance de... Please be so kind as to...
Je suis au regret de vous faire savoir que... I'm sorry to inform you that...
J'ai bien reçu votre lettre du... I received your letter of...
Je vous remercie pour votre lettre du... Thank you for your letter of....
Dans votre lettre, vous me demandiez... In your letter, you asked me...
En réponse à votre lettre... In response to your letter...
Je suis désireux/euse de travailler en France afin de perfectionner/d'acquérir... I'm interested in working in France in order to perfect/to acquire...

Index

accidents at work 174, 231
accountants 75, 130–2, 239
accounts and book-keeping 104, 132–3
acte de vente 205–7
advisers 78–9
   grants for advice 112–13, 114
agency contracts 101
agency offices 97–8
agriculture *see* farming
aid *see* grants and aid
air-conditioning 43
airlines 221–2
alcohol licences 61
applying for a job 169–70, 276–8
apprentice tax 142
architects 187
art galleries 76
art restoration 76
artisans 81–2, 124
artists 66
attitudes to business 16–17
auctions 182–4
auditors 130
avocat 25

bailiffs 25
balance of payments 22
banker's drafts 204–5
banks 217–18
   bill payments 211
   business loans 116
   cheques 217, 218
   offshore accounts 218
   opening an account 217
   opening hours 217
   transferring money 204–5
bars 60–1
bed and breakfast 41, 55, 56–7
benefit payments 120, 172–4, 230–2
bill payments 211
birth rate 20
bonds and securities 152
bonus payments 172–3
book-keeping 132–3

branch offices 98–100, 110–1
branding 91
broadband services 215
budget 21–2
builders' surveys 187
building a home 185–6
building trades 38
bureaucracy 5–6, 17
buses 220
business agencies 239
business culture 16–17
business ideas 30–76
   accountants 75
   art galleries 76
   art restoration 76
   artists 66
   buying an existing business 33, 102, 103–6
   catering 60–3
   computer technology 75, 76
   continuing previous occupations 74–5
   e-commerce 4–5
   and experience 9, 30–1
   farming 66–9
   gardening 66
   income requirements 35
   jewellers 34–5
   joint ventures 34–5, 106
   medicine 70–3
   pretending to be a French business 33–4
   property businesses 36–56
   and qualifications 9, 30–1, 35–6, 38, 124, 157–9
   relocation services 76
   research 31
   restaurants 33
   secretarial work 64
   solicitors 75
   surveyors 32
   target markets 31–2
   teaching 76, 168
   tourism 13, 22, 56–60
   translators 63–4
   TV services 76
   wedding services 76

business plans (British-style) 87–95
   appendices 93
   cashflow forecasts 92
   competitors 91
   cost projections 91
   executive summary 89–90
   funding 91–2
   legislation 91
   management 92–3
   marketing plan 90
   milestones 93
   performance of an existing business 90
   pricing 91
   product/service description 90
   promotion and branding 91
   risk assessment 93
   sales projections 91
   software 95
   staffing 92–3
business plans (French-style) 93–5
business practices 162–4
   corporate hierarchies 164
   introductions 162–3
   meetings 163–4
business schools 236
business structure 79–87
   foreign companies 86
   limited companies 84–6
   partnerships 82–4
   sole traders 79–82
business tax 53, 141
   see also corporate taxes
buying an existing business 33, 102, 103–6
   accounts 104
   due diligence 103
   franchises 105–6
   profit margins 104
   purchasing procedure 105
   SIREN numbers 103, 124
   valuations 103–4
buying a car 225
buying premises 117–18

buying a property 179–209
　auctions 182–4
　building from scratch 185–6
　civil state 197–8
　community of owners 198–9
　completion dates 205
　contracts 199–203
　　subject to survey 188
　costs 207–8
　deed of sale 205–7
　deposits 185, 199, 200, 201
　enquiries 197
　estate agents 180–2, 208
　lawyers 184, 195–6, 240–1
　legal process 194
　location 179
　mortgages 184–5, 189–92
　ownership structure 184, 192–4, 198–9
　payment procedures 196
　power of attorney 204
　price negotiations 196
　renovations 36–8, 185–6, 191
　research 180
　stage payments 202
　surveys 186–8
　under-declaration of purchase price 196

campsites 57–60
capital gains tax 148, 151–2
capital growth 53–4
caravan sites 57–60
cars 222–6
　buying a car 225
　car tax 142
　driving licences 223–4
　importing a car 224–5
　insurance 225–6
　road network 222–3
　rules of the road 222
carte de séjour 154–6
cash payments 205
cashflow forecasts 92
catering businesses 60–3
CFE (Centre de Formalités des Entreprises) 122
chambers of commerce 78, 239–40
Chambres de Métiers 240
chambres d'hôtes see bed and breakfast
cheques 217, 218
children as property owners 193
children on property title 193

chiropractors 72
citizenship 156
Civil Code 24
civil state 197–8
clerk to the court 25
climate 14–15, 41
　rainfall 243–4
　temperature chart 243–4
collège 235
commerçants 81
commune 24
community of owners 198–9
company directors 151
competitors 91
complementary medicine 73
completion dates 205
computer technology 75, 76
constitution 24
consulates 242–3
consumption patterns 21
contracts of employment 119, 170–1
contracts for house purchase 199–203
　on finished property 199–201
　full contract 201
　offers to buy 199
　preliminary contracts 199
　promise to sell 199–200
　reservation contract 202
　sales agreement 200–1
　subject to survey 188
　on unfinished property 201–3
co-operatives 109–10
corporate hierarchies 164
corporate taxes 127–42
　apprentice tax 142
　business tax 53, 141
　car tax 142
　cinema credit 137
　customs duties 140–1
　deductible expenses 135–8
　depreciation rules 135–6
　depressed regions credit 136
　on foreign company owned real estate 139
　groups of companies 136
　holding companies 140
　home construction tax 142
　innovative company exemption 138
　losses 140
　one-man venture capital exemption 138

contracts for house purchase (cont'd)
　payroll tax 141–2
　professional training tax 142
　on repatriated profits 139
　research credit 136–7
　tax rates 134–5
　training credit 136–7, 138
　work-life balance credit 137
　write-offs 136
costs
　of building/restoring properties 185–6
　of buying a property 207–8
　of mortgages 191–2, 208
country properties 179
courts 27–8
Couveuse schemes 108–9
covering letters 169, 277–8
credit cards 217–18, 219
crime 226–7
culture 15–17
　business culture 16–17
　national culture 15–16
customs duties 140–1
CVs 169, 276, 278

daycare centres 234
death registration 233
debit cards 217–18, 219
deed of sale 205–7
dental technicians 74
dentists 71
départements 23, 244–5
Department of Work 240
departmental grants 112
deposits
　and buying at auction 183
　on purchased property 185, 199, 200, 201
　on rental property 209
depreciation rules 135–6
depressed regions credit 136
dialling codes 243
directors of companies 151
disability benefits 173–4
dismissal 120–1, 172
distance selling directive 65
doctors 70–1
domicile 144
double taxation treaties 145
driving licences 223–4

e-commerce 4–5, 65
economy 18–22
　employment statistics 16

Index: ECO–INT

economy (cont'd)
  regional breakdown 7
  statistics 19
  types of business start-ups 7
  unemployment 6, 21
education 233–6
  job opportunities in 76, 168
electricity 38, 211–12
electronic money transfer 204
emergencies 227, 230
employer-employee relations 16–17
employing building workers 37
employing staff 92–3, 118–21
  benefits 120, 172–4
  budgeting for 118
  contracts 119, 170–1
  dismissal 120–1, 172
  holiday entitlements 5, 120, 172
  permits 119
  redundancy 120–1, 172
  training and education 120
  working hours 5, 119–20, 171
employment agencies 167
employment contracts 119, 170–1
employment creation grants 114
employment statistics 164
English-teaching 76, 168
English-language schools 236
enquiries 197
enterprise creation grants 114
entrepreneurship 5–7, 16
entreprises agricoles 82
equipment for rental properties 44
estate agents 180–2, 208
  fees 208
  job opportunities 39–40, 76
  valuations and surveys 186
EU grants 111
EURL (*Entreprise Unipersonnelle à Responsabilité Limitée*) 85
European Development Fund 111
European Social Fund 111
exchange controls 205
exchange rate risk 192
executive summary 89–90
expenses deductible for tax 135–8
experience 9, 30–1
export aid 113, 115

family benefits 232
farming 20–1, 66–9
  agricultural income tax 151
  entreprises agricoles 82
  grants 69
finance 91–2, 106–16
  co-operatives 109–10
  delaying full financial commitment 106–7
  from banks 116
  grants and aid 110–15
  importing/exporting funds 101, 139
  salaried self-employment 107–8
  shelter schemes 108–9
  see also loans; mortgages
finding a job 164–9
fixed-term contracts 170
foreign companies 86
  real estate 139
foreign trade 22
franchises 105–6
freelancers 130–1
full contracts 201
furnished lettings 50, 52

gaps in the market 7–10
gardening 66
gas 212
geography 14
gift taxes 152–3
gîtes 54–6
government 23–4
grandes écoles 236
grants and aid 5, 110–15, 240
  for advice 112–13, 114–15
  departmental grants 112
  employment creation 114
  enterprise creation 114
  EU grants 111
  export aid 113, 115
  for farmers 69
  for innovation 113
  launch grants 112
  national grants 111–12
  for premises 115
  reduced rate loans 114
  regional development funds 115
  regional export aid 115
  regional grants 113–15
  for regional improvement 115
  to the unemployed 112
  for young people 112

grape harvest 165
groups of companies 136

health 228–30
  insurance 173
  see also medical jobs
holding companies 140
holiday entitlements 5, 120, 172
home construction tax 142
home insurance 208
home working 96, 118
hotels 57
hotline consultancy 75
hours of work 5, 119–20, 171

ideas for a business *see* business ideas
illegal working 166
immigration system 153–6
  citizenship 156
  EU citizens 153–4
  non-EU citizens 154–6
importing a car 224–5
importing/exporting funds 101, 139
income requirements 35
income tax
  non-residents 148
  residents 149–51
indemnity insurance 39
independent agents 134
inheritance law 233
inheritance tax 148–9, 152
innovation grants 113
innovative company tax exemption 138
inspecting a property *see* surveys
insurance 240
  health 173
  home 208
  indemnity 39
  motor 225–6
  and rental properties 49
Internet
  access providers 215–16
  banking 217
  bill payments 211
  broadband services 215
  job websites 166–7
  marketing a rental property 47
  property websites 180
  search engines 216
  useful terms 258
  useful websites 8, 12–13

interviews 169–70
introductions 162–3
investment income tax 151

jewellers 34–5
joint ownership 192–3
joint ventures 34–5, 106
judges 26
judicial auctions 182

land registry 207
language 4, 18
  job application phrases 278
  learning French 176–8
  teaching English 168
  useful terms 249–58
launch grants 112
lawyers 24–7, 75, 184, 195–6, 240–1
learning French 176–8
leases 209
legal aid 28
legal system 24–8
  civil code 24
  constitution 24
  courts 27–8
  lawyers 24–7
letting agreements 49–50
letting a property 40–56
  access 41–2
  capital growth 53–4
  and climate 41
  equipment 44
  facilities and attractions 42, 43
  furnished lettings 50, 52
  gîtes 54–6
  insurance 49
  letting agreements 49–50
  location 40–2
  management agents 48–9
  marketing 46–7
  pre-visit packs 44–5
  rental yields 45–6
  restrictions 40–1
  squatters' rights 50
  swimming pools 42, 43–4
  target clientele 41
  taxation 50–3, 150
  type of property 42–5
  unfurnished lettings 50, 52–3
  welcome packs 44
liaison offices 96–7

licences 86–7
  alcohol 61
  driving 223–4
life plan 95–6
limited companies 84–6, 194
loans 116, 192, 241
  reduced rate 114
  see also finance; mortgages
local representative offices 96–7
local taxes 146–7
  business tax 53, 141
  property tax 141
location 32, 40–2
Loi Dutreil 5, 6, 80
Loi PME 5
Loi Raffarin 42
Loi Scrivener 189–90
losses and corporate tax 140
lycée 235
Lyon 245

magazines see newspapers and magazines
maintenance and repair work 38–9
management agents 48–9
marketing a business 90
marketing a rental property 46–7
Marseille 245
masseurs 72
maternity leave 120, 173
matrimonial regime 197–8
medical jobs 70–3
  chiropractors 72
  complementary medicine 73
  dental technicians 74
  dentists 71
  doctors 70–1
  masseurs 72
  nurses 71
  osteopaths 72
  qualifications 73
meetings 163–4
métro 220
Micro BIC scheme 52, 151
micro businesses 80
migration rate 20
milestones 93
minority languages 18
mobile phones 214–15
money transfers 204–5
mortgages 184–5, 189–92
  applications for 190–1
  costs 191–2, 208

mortgages (cont'd)
  exchange rate risk 192
  lender's surveys 187
  Loi Scrivener 189–90
  maximum loans 190
  on new properties 191
  for restoration projects 191
  on UK properties 189
  see also loans
motor insurance 225–6

NAF codes 124
Nantes 246
National Assembly 23
national culture 15–16
national grants 111–12
national holidays 246–7
newspapers and magazines 8
  advertising a rental property 47
  job adverts 165
Nice 245–6
notary (notaire) 26–7, 195–6
  fees 207
number of small businesses 6
nursery schools 234
nurses 71

offers to buy 199
offshore bank accounts 218
offshore companies 194
one-man venture capital exemption 138
opening a bank account 217
opening hours
  banks 217
  national holidays 246–7
  shops 219
opening a shop 62–3, 81
opportunities 7–10
osteopaths 72
ownership of property 184, 192–4, 198–9
  children as owners 193
  children on the title 193
  community of owners 198–9
  joint ownership 192–3
  limited companies 194
  offshore companies 194
  sole ownership 192
  UK companies 194

parent business relationships 96–101
Paris 245
Parliament 23

partnerships 34–5, 82–4
    taxation 127–8
  paternity leave 173
  payroll tax 141–2
  pays 23–4
  pensions 174, 231–2, 232–3
    taxation 151
  performance of an existing
    business 90
  permanent establishment 133
  personal taxes 127–8, 142–53
    agricultural income 151
    on bonds and securities 152
    capital gains tax 148, 151–2
    company directors 151
    credits system 143
    and domicile 144
    gift taxes 152–3
    income tax
      non-residents 148
      residents 149–51
    inheritance tax 148–9, 152
    investment income 151
    local taxes 146–7
    non-taxable income 153
    payment dates 143
    pension income 151
    planning 143
    property income 50–3, 150
    residency rules 144–5
    on shareholdings 152
    submitting tax returns 143
    UK taxes 145–6
    wealth tax 147
  pets 227–8
  planning
    attitudes to 17
    business plans (British-style) 87–95
    business plans (French-style) 93–5
    life plan 95–6
    software 95
    for tax 143
  planning permission 58
  police 226–7
  population 13
  portage salarial 107–8
  postal services 216–17
  power of attorney 204
  preliminary contracts 199
  premises 32, 116–18, 121
    buying 117–18
    grants 115
    renting 117
    working from home 96, 118

presidential elections 23
pretending to be a French
  business 33–4
pricing 91
primary schools 234–5
prime minister 23
product/service description 90
professional training tax 142
professions 9, 30, 81
profit margins 104
promise to sell 199–200
promotion and branding 91
property businesses 36–56
  building trades 38
  development 36
  employing building workers 37
  estate agencies 39–40, 76
  letting a property 40–56
  maintenance and repair 38–9
  restoration 36–8, 185–6, 191
  SCI (*Société Civile Immobilière*) 83–4
property taxes 141
  income tax 50–3, 150
public holidays 246–7
public spending 21–2
public transport *see* transport

qualifications 9, 30–1, 35–6, 38, 73, 124, 157–9

railways 221
rainfall 243–4
redundancy 120–1, 172
regional breakdown of
  businesses 7
regional development funds 115
regional export aid 115
regional grants 113–15
régions 23
registering a business 37, 86–7, 124
regulated professions 9, 30, 81
regulation 17
relocation services 76
removal companies 178
renovations 36–8, 185–6, 191
rental yields 45–6
  see also letting a property
renting a home 209
renting premises 117
repatriated profits 101, 139
representative offices 96–7

representatives 97–8
research and information 8–9, 31, 180
research tax credit 136–7
reservation contracts 202
residence permits 154–6
residency rules 144–5
restaurants 33, 61
restoration projects 36–8, 185–6, 191
retirement 232–3
  see also pensions
risk assessment 93
road network 222–3

SA (*Société Anonyme*) 85
salaried representatives 97–8
salaried self-employment 107–8
salaries *see* wages
sales agreement 200–1
sales projections 91
SARL (*Société à Responsabilité Limitée*) 85
SAS (*Société par Actions Simplifiées*) 86
satellite television 216
savings rate 5
SCA (*Société en Commandité par Actions*) 84
schools *see* education
SCI (*Société Civile Immobilière*) 83–4
SCOP (*Société Coopérative Ouvrière de Production*) 86
search engines 216
secondary schools 235
secretarial work 64
Senate 23
septic tanks 213
service sector 22
service/product description 90
shareholdings 152
shelter schemes 108–9
shopping 179, 218–19
  opening hours 219
  opening a shop 62–3, 81
sickness leave 173–4
SIREN numbers 103, 124
SIRET numbers 37, 124
size of business 80
SME (small or medium-sized
  enterprises) 80, 241
SNC (*Société en Nom Collectif*) 83

social security contributions 125–6
social services *see* benefit payments
Société Civile 84
Société d'Exercice Libérale 84
Société de Fait 84
software for business plans 95
sole ownership 192
sole traders 79–82
　taxation 127–8
solicitors *see* lawyers
special enquiries 197
speed limits 223
squatters' rights 50
staff *see* employing staff
stage payments 202
statement of sincerity 206
Strasbourg 246
strikes 17
structure of a business *see* business structure
subsidiary companies 100–1
surveys 186–8
　working as a surveyor 32
SWIFT money transfers 204
swimming pools 42, 43–4, 213

target markets 31–2, 41
tax credits system 143
taxation 5, 21–2, 127–53
　double taxation treaties 145
　of e-commerce businesses 65
　evasion 129
　and freelancers 130–1
　French taxes
　　liability 133–4
　　local taxes 53, 141, 146–7
　　see also corporate taxes; personal taxes
　Micro BIC scheme 52, 151
　of partnerships 127–8
　and rental property 50–3, 150
　of sole traders 127–8
　television tax 216
　UK taxes 145–6
　VAT (TVA) 53, 65, 124, 127, 186, 208
　withholding tax 139–40

teaching jobs 76, 168
telephones 163, 213–14
　dialling codes 243
　emergencies 227, 230
　mobile phones 214–15
television 216
　offering TV services 76
temperature chart 243–4
temporary work 165, 170
Toulouse 245
tourism 13, 22, 56–60
　bed and breakfast 41, 55, 56–7
　campsites 57–60
　caravan sites 57–60
　hotels 57
town properties 179
tradespeople *see* artisans
training and education 120
　tax credit 136–7, 138
trains 221
transfer pricing 101
transferring money 204–5
translators 63–4
transport 220–6
　airlines 221–2
　buses 220
　cars 222–6
　métro 220
　trains 221
TVA *see* VAT (TVA)
types of business start-ups 7

under-declaration of house purchase price 196
unemployment 6, 21
　benefit payments 232
　grants 112
unfurnished lettings 50, 52–3
universities 236
utilities 210–15
　bill payments 211
　electricity 211–12
　gas 212
　mobile phones 214–15
　telephones 163, 213–14
　water 212–13

valuation of businesses 103–4
VAT (TVA) 53, 65, 124, 127, 186
　on new property 208

vineyards 67
visas 154
voluntary auctions 182
volunteer work 167
VRP (travelling salesperson) 98

wages 171
　bonus payments 172–3
　disposable income 5
water supplies 212–13
wealth tax 147
weather *see* climate
websites *see* internet
wedding services 76
welcome packs 44
welfare benefits 120, 172–4, 230–2
wells 213
wine
　grape harvest 165
　running a vineyard 67
withholding tax 139–40
work-life balance tax credit 137
working in France 162–74
　applying for a job 169–70, 276–8
　attitudes to work 16
　benefit payments 120, 172–4, 230–2
　business practices 162–4
　CVs (*Curriculum Vitae*) 169, 276, 278
　dismissal 120–1, 172
　employment agencies 167
　employment contracts 119, 170–1
　EU citizens 162
　finding a job 164–9
　first impressions 163
　illegal working 166
　interviews 169–70
　non-EU citizens 162, 170–1
　redundancy 120–1, 172
　temporary work 165, 170
　volunteer work 167
working from home 96, 118
working hours 5, 119–20, 171
write-offs 136

young people grants 112